Eine Arbeitsgemeinschaft der Verlage

Böhlau Verlag · Köln · Weimar · Wien
Verlag Barbara Budrich · Opladen · Farmington Hills
facultas.wuv · Wien
Wilhelm Fink · München
A. Francke Verlag · Tübingen und Basel
Haupt Verlag · Bern · Stuttgart · Wien
Julius Klinkhardt Verlagsbuchhandlung · Bad Heilbrunn
Lucius & Lucius Verlagsgesellschaft · Stuttgart
Mohr Siebeck · Tübingen
Orell Füssli Verlag · Zürich
Ernst Reinhardt Verlag · München · Basel
Ferdinand Schöningh · Paderborn · München · Wien · Zürich
Eugen Ulmer Verlag · Stuttgart
UVK Verlagsgesellschaft · Konstanz
Vandenhoeck & Ruprecht · Göttingen
vdf Hochschulverlag AG an der ETH Zürich

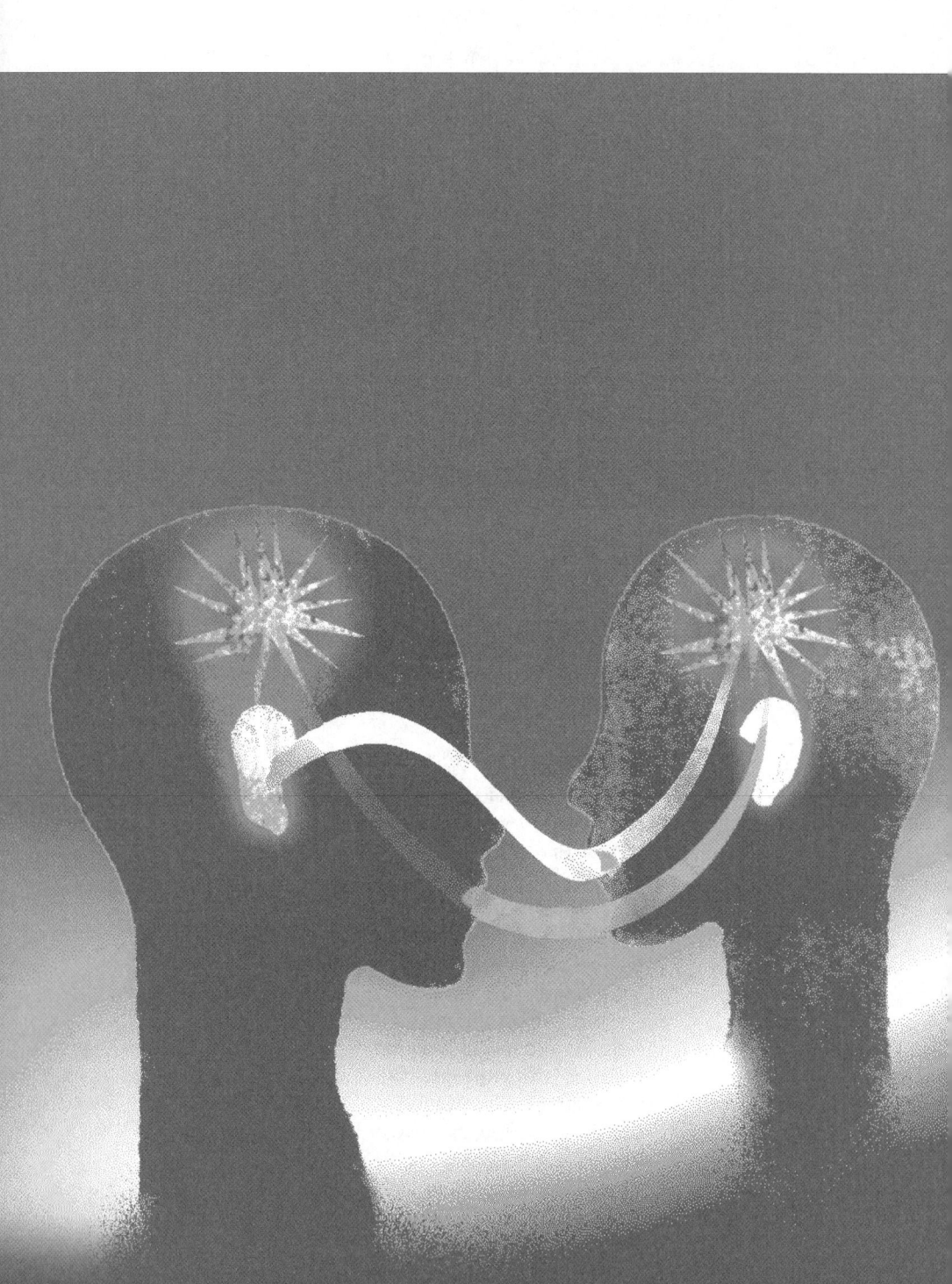

MARKUS BIESWANGER | ANNETTE BECKER

Introduction to English Linguistics

3., überarbeitete und aktualisierte
Auflage
140 Abbildungen und Tabellen

UTB basics

A. Francke Verlag Tübingen und Basel

Markus Bieswanger ist Juniorprofessor für Anglistische Linguistik an der Universität Flensburg, **Annette Becker** lehrt am Englischen Seminar der Ruhr-Universität Bochum.

Bibliografische Information der Deutschen Nationalbibliothek

Die Deutsche Nationalbibliothek verzeichnet diese Publikation in der Deutschen Nationalbibliografie; detaillierte bibliografische Daten sind im Internet über http://dnb.d-nb.de abrufbar

3., überarbeitete und aktualisierte Auflage 2010
2., aktualisierte Auflage 2008
1. Auflage 2006

© 2010 · Narr Francke Attempto Verlag GmbH + Co. KG
Dischingerweg 5 · D-72070 Tübingen
ISBN 978-3-7720-8372-3

Internet: http://www.francke.de
E-Mail: info@francke.de

Layout und Einbandgestaltung: Atelier Reichert, Stuttgart
Satz: Informationsdesign D. Fratzke, Kirchentellinsfurt
Druck und Bindung: CPI – Ebner & Spiegel, Ulm
Printed in Germany

ISBN 978-3-8252-2752-4 (UTB-Bestellnummer)

Contents

Preface

This textbook is intended for beginning students of English linguistics, and for their instructors. It is specifically designed to accompany introductory classes to linguistics and does not require any previous knowledge. The text is easily accessible, as it is written in user-friendly English. Moreover, it contains numerous examples and around 140 figures. It goes without saying that a brief introductory textbook cannot and thus should not even attempt to cover all details of a growing and increasingly fragmented discipline like linguistics. This book is meant as a starting point that introduces beginners to the core branches and central concepts of the field, addressing

▶ what linguists are interested in,
▶ how the English language has been evolving,
▶ how we produce and use speech sounds,
▶ how we may form words,
▶ how we may form sentences,
▶ what sounds, words and sentences have to do with meaning,
▶ how language is used in context,
▶ and what language has to do with social factors.

Key terms are highlighted in **bold letters**, whereas examples are given in *italics*. The index lists all key terms and the names of the most important authors mentioned in the text. At the end of each chapter, you will find exercises (complete with answers in the appendix) and an annotated bibliography directing you to sources of more detailed information and further reading. The selection of the material is based on our teaching experience. Individual chapters may, for the most part, be read independently of each other, although we suggest that readers follow the order as presented in the book.

We are indebted to our students, colleagues and friends for many inspiring questions, discussions and suggestions. Our special thanks go to Werner Bauer, Anita Fetzer, James Fisk, Marlis Hellinger, Jan Hoffmeister, Gerda Lauerbach, Ursula Lenker, Sylvia Mieszkowski, Carolina Plaza-Pust, Gregory Poarch, Nicola Prendergast, Michael Schiffmann, Britta Schneider, Jule Türke and Christine Vogt-William for their valuable comments on earlier versions of the individual chapters. We would also like to thank our editor Jürgen Freudl for his amazing patience and professional support, and Sibylle Klöcker for her help with compiling the index. All remaining shortcomings of the book are, of course, entirely our own responsibility.

If you have any questions, comments or suggestions for future editions, please feel free to contact us at Annette.Becker@ruhr-uni-bochum.de and markus.bieswanger@uni-flensburg.de.

Annette Becker & Markus Bieswanger

Preface to the Second Edition

For the second edition of this textbook, we have updated the annotated bibliographies at the end of each chapter and revised some explanations and figures. However, to ensure compatibility with the first edition, changes have been kept to a necessary minimum. We would like to thank colleagues and students from a number of different universities — too numerous to name them all individually — who used our book in introductory classes and gave generously of their time to supply us with valuable feedback. Your effort is very much appreciated, even though we have been unable to accommodate everything that has been suggested to us. Questions, comments and suggestions for future editions are still more than welcome and may be sent to the email addresses given at the end of the original preface.

Markus Bieswanger & Annette Becker

Preface to the Third Edition

This third edition continues to follow the overall plan of the previous editions. All chapters of the second edition as well as the bibliographies at the end of each chapter have been updated and several exercises have been revised. The chapter on syntax has been substantially rewritten and now focuses more on traditional approaches to syntactic analysis and their application. We are indebted to those who assisted in the preparation of this edition. In addition to the individuals we thanked in the prefaces to the previous editions, we would like to specifically thank Carina Farrero, Guido Isekenmeier, Verena Minow, Jonathan Mole and Julia Salzinger for their helpful comments on earlier drafts of the new chapter on syntax. We would like to invite you to continue to send comments and suggestions for future editions to the email addresses given at the end of the original preface.

Markus Bieswanger & Annette Becker

Introduction | 1

Contents

Abstract

This chapter defines the scope of linguistics and gives a brief overview of the branches and central concepts of the discipline.

1.1 | What is Linguistics?

Linguistics is all about human **language**, that means it is primarily concerned with the uniquely human capacity to express ideas and feelings by voluntarily produced speech sounds or their equivalents, such as gestures in sign languages used by deaf persons. Linguistics can be broadly defined as **the scientific study of language** or **of particular languages**. Scholars who systematically study language usually refer to themselves as **linguists**. Compare the following definitions from the *Oxford Advanced Learner's Dictionary of Current English*:

> lin·guist /ˈlɪŋgwɪst/ *noun*
> 1 a person who knows several foreign languages well: *She's an excellent linguist.* ◊ *I'm afraid I'm no linguist* (= I find foreign languages difficult).
> 2 a person who studies languages or linguistics

In this book, we will use the term *linguist* as defined by the second of the above dictionary entries. From the point of view of linguistics, a linguist does thus not necessarily have to speak many different languages fluently, just as a professional geographer does not have to know the location of all the rivers, towns and cities in the world by heart.

Humans in all parts of the world have been interested in language for thousands of years and have developed a wide variety of perspectives in language studies. As a result, linguists today approach language from a vast and growing number of different angles or specialise in certain aspects of language.

1.2 | Branches of Linguistics

Traditional Core
Branches

The field of linguistics encompasses a wide range of "ways" to study language, which are reflected in the subdivision of linguistics into **branches** (or **subfields**). Traditionally, linguists identify five **core branches** of linguistics, **phonetics** (namely the study of speech sounds in general), **phonology** (the study of the sound systems of individual languages), **morphology** (the study of the creation, structure and form of words), **syntax** (the study of structural units larger than one word, i.e. phrases and sentences), and **semantics** (the study of word and sentence meaning). This is also the order in which these fields appear in Chapter 3 to 6 in this book. We will thus pursue a bottom-up approach, starting with speech sounds, i.e. the smallest units of language, and working our way up towards larger structures of language:

					Fig. 1.1
branch	**phonetics**	**phonology**	**morphology**	**syntax**	**semantics**
concerned with	speech sounds in general	sound systems of languages	words and their components	phrases and sentences	word and sentence meaning

Traditional core branches of linguistics (simplified)

These core areas of linguistic study, however, are not the only branches that are subsumed under the umbrella term *linguistics*. A number of branches of linguistics have appeared in recent years and decades, of which **pragmatics** (the study of meaning in context) and **sociolinguistics** (the study of the relationship between language and society) have been selected for this book, as they are among the most dynamic and widely studied subfields of linguistics today. Many linguists now include both pragmatics and sociolinguistics when they speak about the core branches of linguistics.

Expanding the Core

Similarly to sociolinguistics, which has developed as a result of overlapping interests of linguistics and sociology, many other branches of linguistics have been set up to describe **interdisciplinary approaches**: for example, anthropological linguistics (anthropology and linguistics), biolinguistics (biology and linguistics), clinical linguistics (medicine and linguistics), computational linguistics (computer science and linguistics), ethnolinguistics (ethnology and linguistics), philosophical linguistics (philosophy and linguistics) and psycholinguistics (psychology and linguistics), to name only a few.

More Branches

The branches of linguistics we have mentioned so far belong for the most part to the traditional core or have developed from the collaboration of linguistics and a neighbouring field of study. We

Different Kinds of Branches

will now briefly turn to two examples of branches that are distinguished for other reasons, namely **applied linguistics** and **corpus linguistics**.

Applied linguistics can be broadly defined as the branch of linguistics that seeks to solve language-related problems in the real world. Originally, applied linguistics essentially focussed on the relevance of linguistic study for language teaching, particularly foreign language teaching, but has since much expanded its scope. Other fields of application now include, for example, the linguistic analysis of language disorders and the planning of national language policies. Today, the label "applied" in the broader sense is occasionally even used in combination with other branches of linguistics, as in applied psycholinguistics or applied sociolinguistics.

Corpus linguistics, on the other hand, is not defined by the possible application of the results of linguistic study, but by the methodology used. A corpus is a collection of authentic language material, now frequently in the form of machine-readable databases. Corpus linguists are interested in actual language use. For example, linguists can search these corpora for all occurrences of a certain linguistic feature and interpret both the number of occurrences as well as the context in which such a feature occurs.

The variety of approaches and specialisations frequently shows in differences in terminology. In this book, we will, wherever possible, use widely accepted terminology that can be found in most international textbooks of linguistics. However, it has to be kept in mind that there is some variation in the use of linguistic terminology, even among linguists. We will point out some of the most important cases of terminological variation as we go along.

1.3 | Central Concepts of Linguistics

Ferdinand de Saussure

Linguistics at the beginning of the 21st century is still to a large extent based on the ideas of the Swiss linguist **Ferdinand de Saussure** (1857-1913), which were responsible for a fundamental change of direction of linguistic study in the early 20th century. This holds particularly true for linguistics as viewed from a European perspective. Saussure's ideas were only published after his death, when some of his students compiled the *Cours de linguistique* *générale* (or *Course in General Linguistics*) from his lecture materials in 1916. Many linguists have since considered Saussure the founder of modern linguistics.

Ferdinand de Saussure (1857-1913) | **Fig. 1.2**

One of the major changes brought about by Saussure's ideas is the distinction between the study of languages at a certain point in time called **synchrony** (or **synchronic linguistics**), and the study of language change over time termed **diachrony** (or **diachronic linguistics**, or **historical linguistics**). Saussure's call for the primacy of synchrony led to a paradigm shift from a predominantly historical orientation of linguistics in the 19th century to a predominantly synchronic orientation of linguistics in the 20th and 21st century. Historical linguistics has not completely ceased to exist, but it is now rather based on systematic synchronic descriptions at different points in time during the history of a language.

Synchrony versus Diachrony

> **"The object of study in linguistics is not a combination of the written and the spoken word. The spoken word alone constitutes that object."**
> (Saussure 1916:24-25)

Another major change was caused by Saussure's call for the **primacy of the spoken word**. Most linguistic study in the 19th century had been concerned with the written form of language, but Saussure (1983:24) insisted that "[t]he sole reason for the existence of the latter [i.e. the written form] is to represent the former [i.e. the spoken form]". This notion is of fundamental importance to Saussure's model of the linguistic sign (cf. Fig. 1.3).

Spoken versus Written Language

A further fundamental change of direction in linguistic study that is connected with Saussure's ideas, and the last we would like to mention here, is the transition from a **prescriptive** (or normative) period of linguistics to a **descriptive** approach. Descriptive linguistics aims to describe the facts of linguistic usage as they are

Prescriptivism versus Descriptivism

in practice, whereas prescriptive linguistics attempts to prescribe rules of "correctness", i.e. to lay down normative rules as to how language should be used. Since the beginning of the 20th century, linguistics has been increasingly critical of **prescriptivism** and has been favouring the approach of **descriptivism**.

Structuralism

At the heart of Saussure's ideas is the focus of linguistics on the **structure** of the language system shared by members of a certain speech community. This is why the Saussurean type of linguistics is also referred to as **structural linguistics** (or **structuralist linguistics**). The centre of study is the **language system** (or *langue*) and not the concrete **language use** by the individual (or *parole*). Structural linguistics aims at the description and analysis of all elements of the language system and the relationships that exist between them. These elements and their interrelationships are investigated at all structural levels of linguistics, such as sounds, words and sentences.

The Linguistic Sign

Related to Saussure's call for the primacy of the spoken word is another one of his groundbreaking contributions to modern linguistics, namely his model of the **linguistic sign**. According to Saussure, the linguistic sign is made up of two inseparably connected parts, like two sides of a coin. The linguistic sign consists of a sound or usually a **sound sequence** (or **sound pattern**), the so-called *signifiant* (or **signifier**), at the level of expression, and a **concept**, the so-called *signifié* (or **signified**), at the level of meaning:

Fig. 1.3	

Saussure's model of the linguistic sign (adapted from Saussure 1983:67)

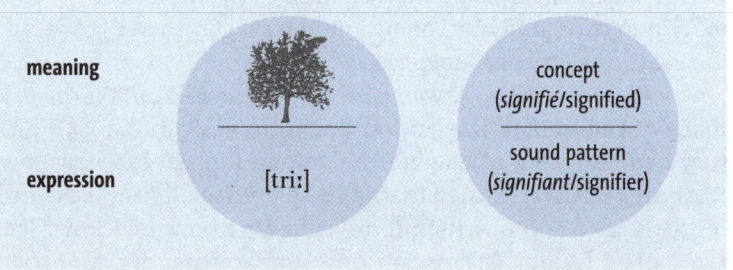

meaning   concept
(*signifié*/signified)

expression   [triː]   sound pattern
(*signifiant*/signifier)

Arbitrariness

Saussure emphasises that there is no internal natural link between the sound shape and the meaning of the linguistic sign. Neither does the form of a word dictate its meaning, nor is the meaning predictable from the form. This is illustrated by the fact that the same concept can be referred to by completely different sound patterns in different languages. For example, the same animal that can be represented by [dɒg] in English, is usually referred to as [hunt] in German and [ʃjɛ̃] in French. The relationship between the sound pattern and the concept is thus said to be **arbitrary**. The principle of **arbitrariness** of the linguistic sign states that the connection between the sound pattern and the concept of a sign is by **convention** only.

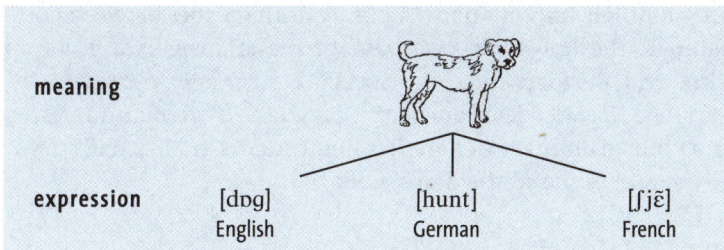

| **Fig. 1.4**

Arbitrariness of the linguistic sign

There are, however, a small number of expressions for which the principle of arbitrariness does not hold completely true. Words such as *boom* [buːm] or *bang* [bæŋ] show at least a partial correspondence of sound pattern and meaning. Such expressions which include sounds that are similar to the noises they describe are called **onomatopoeic**. **Onomatopoeia** is thus frequently cited as an exception to the principle of arbitrariness.

Onomatopoeia

The important influence of Saussure's ideas and structuralist linguistic thinking on modern linguistics is essentially undisputed. However, at least two other influential linguistic schools of thought have to be mentioned when we speak about the discipline of linguistics since the beginning of the 20th century.

Post-Saussurean Developments

One of the other important schools of thought started to develop around 1930 and is commonly referred to as **functionalism** (or **Prague School of functionalism**). Functionalism partly continues structuralist ideas but focuses on the function or functions of language and individual linguistic features. For example, the so-called organon model of languages as suggested by Karl Bühler distinguishes between three main functions of language: an expressive function that allows the addressers to express their own beliefs and feelings, a representative function that allows us to talk about the world, and an appellative function that allows the addresser to make a request or issue a command.

Functionalism

Generative Linguistics

Since the 1950s, a linguistic school of thought called **generative linguistics** (or **formalism**) has become increasingly influential, particularly in American linguistics. The term generative was introduced by Noam Chomsky in his book *Syntactic Structures* in 1957. Extremely simplified, we can say that the generative approach reflects the fact that all speakers of a language can produce, or generate, a theoretically unlimited number of grammatical sentences from a limited number of means, i.e. words and the rules for their combination. Chomsky distinguishes between **competence**, the knowledge we have of the language we grow up with, and **performance**, the speech we actually produce. Our complete knowledge of our native language is often also referred to as our **grammar**. Generative linguistics is traditionally most influential in the subfield of syntax.

Fig. 1.5

Structuralism, functionalism and formalism (adapted from Kortmann 2005:32)

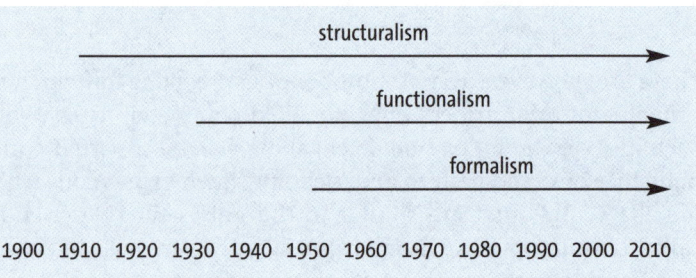

Today, structuralism, functionalism and formalism exist side by side in modern linguistics, as indicated in Fig. 1.5. Additionally, the interest in historical linguistics has been on the rise since the early 1990s. Historical linguistics now incorporates findings and methods developed in different branches of synchronic linguistics, making use of language corpora and forming new subfields such as historical semantics, historical pragmatics and historical sociolinguistics.

Bibliography

Aronoff, Mark & **Janie Rees-Miller**. 2001. *The Handbook of Linguistics*. Malden, MA: Blackwell. *(An overview of linguistics and its subdisciplines)*

Bauer, Laurie. 2007. *The Linguistics Student's Handbook*. Edinburgh: Edinburgh University Press. *(An ideal supplement to introductory textbooks)*

Bergmann, Anouschka et al., eds. 2007. *Language Files: Materials for an Introduction to Language & Linguistics*. 10th edition. Ohio: Ohio State University Press. *(A hands-on introduction to general linguistics with many useful exercises)*

Brown, Keith, ed. 2006. *Encyclopedia of Language and Linguistics*. 2nd edition. Oxford: Elsevier. *(The most comprehensive reference work in the field of linguistics)*

Bühler, Karl. 1990 (1934). *Theory of Language: The Representational Function of Language*. Translation by Donald Fraser Goodwin. Amsterdam: Benjamins. *(A classic work in the field of functionalism)*

Chomsky, Noam. 1957. *Syntactic Structures*. The Hague: Mouton. *(The foundation of generative linguistics)*

Chomsky, Noam. 2004. *The Generative Enterprise Revisited*. Berlin: Mouton de Gruyter. *(Two interviews with Noam Chomsky)*

Crystal, David. 2008. *A Dictionary of Linguistics & Phonetics*. 6th edition. Malden, MA: Blackwell. *(Alphabetic dictionary of linguistic terms)*

Crystal, David. 2010. *The Cambridge Encyclopedia of Language*. 3rd edition. Cambridge: Cambridge University Press. *(An accessible guide to a wide range of language-related issues)*

Finch, Geoffrey. 2005. *Key Concepts in Language and Linguistics*. 2nd edition. Basingstoke: Palgrave Macmillan. *(An introduction to the terminology of the core areas of linguistics)*

Fromkin, Victoria A., ed. 2001. *Linguistics: An Introduction to Linguistic Theory*. Malden, MA: Blackwell. *(A detailed introduction to the traditional core areas of linguistics from a generative perspective)*

Fromkin, Victoria A. et al. 2010. *An Introduction to Language*. 9th edition. Boston: Wadsworth. *(A fairly comprehensive introduction to linguistics)*

Harris, Roy. 2003. *Saussure and His Interpreters*. 2nd edition. Edinburgh: Edinburgh University Press. *(A reassessment of Saussure's ideas)*

Kortmann, Bernd. 2005. *English Linguistics: Essentials*. Berlin: Cornelsen. *(Rich in information, based on a class for advanced undergraduates)*

Mair, Christian. 2008. *English Linguistics: An Introduction*. Tübingen: Narr. *(A compact introduction to the linguistics of English)*

Matthews, Peter H. 2007. *The Concise Oxford Dictionary of Linguistics*. 2nd edition. Oxford: Oxford University Press. *(A concise dictionary of linguistics; since 2003 also available online to subscribers at www.oxfordreference.com)*

Matthews, Peter H. 2003. *Linguistics: A Very Short Introduction*. Oxford: Oxford University Press. *(An extremely short and lighthearted introduction for linguistic novices)*

Meyer, Paul Georg et al. 2005. *Synchronic English Linguistics*. 3rd edition. Tübingen: Narr. *(A detailed introduction to the linguistics of contemporary English)*

O'Grady, William et al., eds. 2004. *Contemporary Linguistics: An Introduction*. 5th edition. Boston: St. Martin's. *(Another fairly comprehensive introduction to linguistics)*

Robins, Robert H. 1997. *A Short History of Linguistics*. 4th edition. Harlow: Addison Wesley Longman. *(Covers thousands of years of language study in different parts of the world)*

Saussure, Ferdinand de. 1983 (1916). *Course in General Linguistics*. Originally published as *Cours de linguistique générale*. Translation by Roy Harris, edited by Charles Bally and Albert Sechehaye. London: Duckworth. *(The basis of structural linguistics)*

A Brief History of English |2

Abstract

This chapter provides a brief overview of the history of the English language from its very beginnings to the present day. We will travel through the different periods of the English language and take a look at the status of the English language around the world today.

2.1 | The Linguistic History of English

Why Study the History
of English?

Why include the history of the English language in an introductory work on English linguistics? Why should we bother to deal with the state of the English language many centuries ago, as if modern English was not complicated enough already? The answer is that the history of the English language can provide explanations for many features and irregularities of contemporary English, e.g. the origins of the common plural marker -s or many of the irregular verbs in contemporary English. Taking a look at the history of English also reminds us that English has only been around for a comparatively short time and is historically related to a number of other languages.

> "Time changes all things: there is no reason why language should escape this universal law."
> (Ferdinand de Saussure)

Language Change

We have seen in the previous chapter that, following Saussure, linguistics is now commonly divided into **synchronic linguistics** and **diachronic linguistics**. Diachronic linguistics, or historical linguistics, is the study of **language change**. It is concerned with both the description and explanation of such change. Linguists generally agree that **all living languages are constantly changing** as the needs of the people who use them change as well.

The mechanisms and motivations of linguistic change are still under discussion and by no means completely understood. Traditionally, historical linguistics distinguishes between two main types of change: change due to **internal factors**, which refers to language change that occurs in isolation, and change that results from **external factors**, which is largely caused by contact with other languages and, among other things, can result in the **borrowing** of linguistic features, e.g. in the adoption of foreign vocabulary. Language change affects all linguistic levels of a language.

Periods

Reflecting the changes the English language has undergone during its roughly 1500 years of existence, the history of English is commonly divided into **four main periods**, namely **Old English** (**OE**), also referred to as **Anglo-Saxon**, **Middle English** (**ME**), **Early Modern English** (**EModE**) and **Modern English** (**ModE**), which includes so-called **Present Day English** (**PDE**). The periods are distinguished on the basis of historical events as well as characteristic linguistic developments. The dividing lines, however, are somewhat fuzzy as languages change rather gradually than abruptly.

| Fig. 2.1

period	historical landmarks	key linguistic features
Pre-English (before c450 AD)	Celts	► Celtic language spoken
		► some Celtic traces, esp. in place names
	Romans (43-410)	► Latin becomes the official language
		► a few Latin traces from this period through Celtic transmission
Old English (c450-c1150)	Germanic tribes arrive (Angles, Saxons, Jutes and Frisians) from the middle of the fifth century	► mostly Germanic word-stock
		► fully inflected
		► inflections begin to be levelled
Middle English (c1150-c1500)	Norman Conquest in 1066	► enormous influx of French vocabulary
		► levelled inflections
		► Great Vowel Shift starts
Early Modern English (c1500-c1700)	introduction of printing into England by William Caxton in 1476	► Great Vowel Shift
		► standardisation and regularisation
		► large-scale borrowing from Latin, Greek, French and other European languages
	spread of English around the world starts (colonisation)	
Modern English (c1700-present)		► almost no inflections
Present Day English (c1900-present)	English as a global language	► borrowing from many languages world-wide

The periods of the English language

Old English (c450-c1150)

| 2.1.1

Archaeological evidence shows that humans had lived in what we now refer to as the British Isles long before the Germanic tribes that later became the English people arrived. Unfortunately, we do not know much about the languages spoken in England before English. This is mainly due to the lack of written records. The only groups about whose languages we have some definite knowledge are the Celts and the Romans.

Pre-English

The Celts

The spread of the Celts across the British Isles and thus the spread of Celtic customs and the languages they spoke took place several centuries BC. These customs and languages survived Roman rule in Britain from 43-410 AD at least partly, probably owing to a certain degree of social as well as geographical separation from the Romans. The Celtic influence on the English language, however, is very small, as the Celts were defeated and/or pushed back into the northern and western parts of Great Britain when the Germanic tribes invaded England in the fifth century AD (cf. 2.1.2).

Traces of Celtic influence due to language contact with English survive almost exclusively in place names. Such place names are more common in the North and the West than in the East and Southeast. Some names of settlements such as *London* and *Leeds* most likely go back to Celtic designations, but the majority of place names that can be traced back to Celtic origins are names connected with hills and rivers. Celtic words referring to hills can be found in place names like *Bredon* in Worcestershire (cf. Welsh *bre* 'hill') or *Pendle* in Lancashire (cf. Welsh *pen* 'top'). The name *Thames* goes back to a Celtic river name, and one of the various Celtic words for 'water' survives in the name of the river *Usk* (cf. Scottish Gaelic *uisge* and Irish *uisce* 'water' as in *uisge/uisce beatha* 'water of life', i.e. the first element *uisge/uisce* is the origin of ModE *whisk(e)y*).

The Romans

The Romans first arrived in Britain in 55 BC under Julius Caesar, but permanent settlement did not take place until nearly a hundred years later. The full-scale Roman invasion of the island started in 43 AD and resulted in Roman occupation. Latin became the official language during the time of Roman rule but was not used extensively by the native population and did not replace the Celtic language in Britain. Roman occupation of Britain ended with the withdrawal of the last of the Roman legions in the year 410 AD, quite some time before the Germanic tribes arrived on the island, i.e. there was no direct contact at this time. Latin influence on English from this period is thus very slight as it had to be transmitted through Celtic and was limited by the same factors as Celtic influence itself. One of the few Latin elements that have come into English in this way is OE *ceaster*, which represents Latin *castra* 'camp' and is a common designation in Old English for a settlement. The English town of *Chester* thus owes its name to Roman influence.

There were, however, two periods of more extensive influence of Latin on Old English: firstly, the transmission of elements from

Latin into the Germanic dialects before the Germanic tribes left the Continent for Britain, and secondly, an enormous influence due to the systematic Christianisation of Britain by Roman missionaries starting in the year 597.

The history of English started in the area now called England in the middle of the fifth century, when a number of Germanic tribes, namely the Jutes, Saxons, Angles and at least a part of the Frisians, invaded Britain, settled in the South and the East and brought their Germanic dialects with them. They gradually expanded their settlement, and by doing so the English-speaking territory, until by about 800 they occupied all but the Scottish highlands in the north, the Welsh highlands in the west and the western tip of Cornwall, which all remained Celtic-speaking. The Venerable Bede (c672-735), priest and scholar, describes the events in his *Historia ecclesiastica gentis Anglorum* ('Ecclesiastical History of the English People', written in Latin and completed in 731) as follows:

Origins of English

> In the year of our Lord 449 [...] the nation of the Angles, or Saxons, being invited by the aforesaid king [Vortigern] arrived in Britain with three long ships [...] they engaged with the enemy, who were come from the north to give battle, and obtained the victory; [...] a more considerable fleet was quickly sent over, bringing a still greater number of men, which, being added to the former, made up an invincible army [...] Those who came over were of the three most powerful nations of Germany – Saxons, Angles and Jutes. From the Jutes are descended the people of Kent, and of the Isle of Wight, and those also in the province of the West-Saxons who are to this day called Jutes, seated opposite to the Isle of Wight. From the Saxons [...] came the East-Saxons, the South-Saxons, and the West Saxons. From the Angles [...] are descended the East-Angles, the Midland-Angles, Mercians, all the race of the Northumbrians, that is, of those nations that dwell on the north side of the river Humber, and the other nations of English.
>
> Excerpt from Bede's *Ecclesiastical History of the English People* (shortened from Crystal 2002:164)

Resulting from the dialect divisions of the invading tribes and the different languages they came in contact with, there was linguistic variation in English right from the very beginning. Three main dialect areas can thus be distinguished for Old English: *West Saxon* (southern and southwestern England), *Kentish* (southeastern England) and *Anglian*, which is commonly subdivided into *Mercian*

Dialects of Old English

(central England south of the river Humber) and *Northumbrian* (England north of the river Humber and southeastern Scotland). The Old English texts which have survived come from all of the above dialect areas. However, most of the preserved Old English material is written in the West Saxon dialect, reflecting the rise of the West Saxon kingdom and the resulting position of the dialect as a kind of literary standard after 900.

Fig. 2.2

The origins and distribution of the main dialects of Old English (Crystal 2002:174)

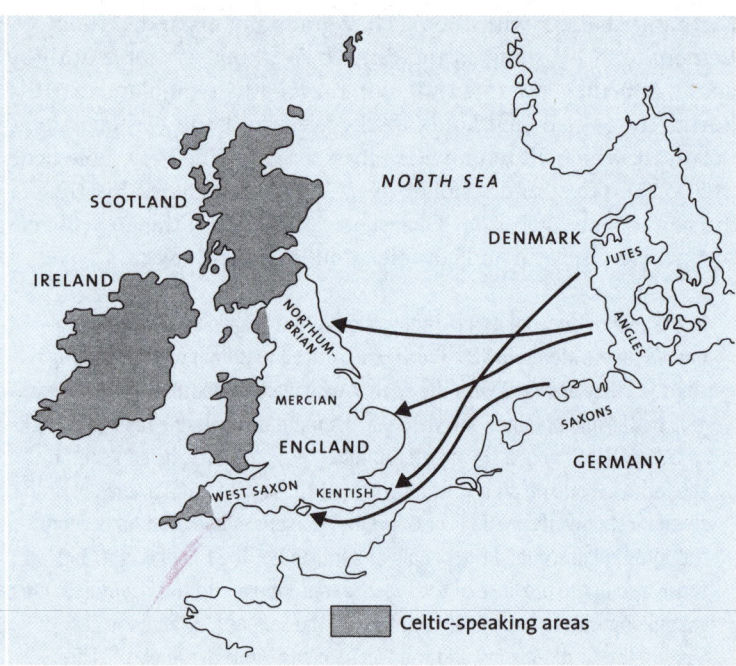

The Names *English* and *England*

The Germanic invaders called the Celtic inhabitants *wealas* 'foreigners', from which the name *Welsh* is derived. In turn the Celts referred to their Germanic conquerors as *Saxons*, a practice followed by the early Latin writers calling them *Saxones* and *Saxonia*. Soon, however, *Angli* (for the people) and *Anglia* (for the country) were also in use to refer to the West Germanic tribes generally. OE *Engle* 'Angles' derives from this usage and the Old English writers called their language *Englisc* (the spelling <sc> represents the sound /ʃ/, represented by <sh> in ModE *English*) from the beginning. The name *Engla lond* 'land of the Angles' (*Engla* is genitive plural of *Engle*) for the country does not appear until around 1000 AD.

Genetically, English is thus a Germanic language that is a member of the Indo-European family of languages and related to other Germanic languages on the Continent. Close relatives are other members of the West Germanic branch of the Germanic languages, e.g. Frisian, Dutch and German, as we can see in the traditional branch diagram (or tree diagram):

English, a Germanic Language

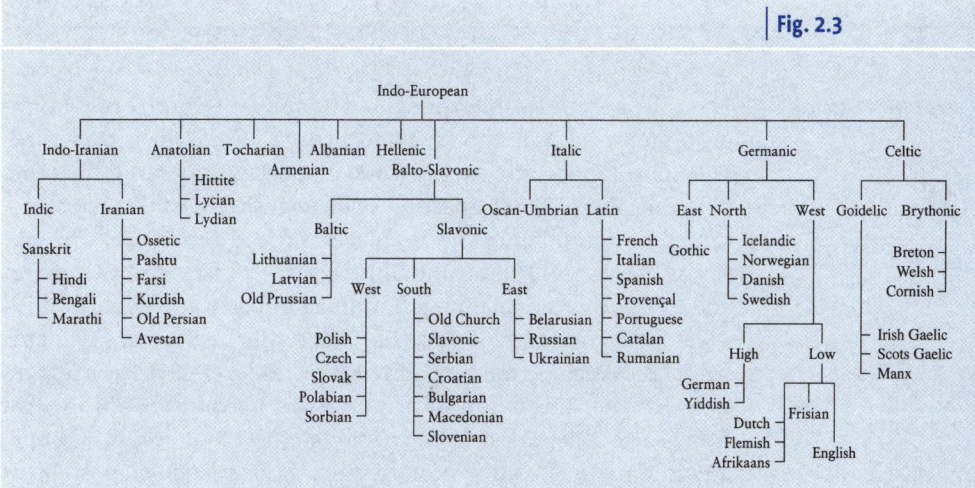

Fig. 2.3

The Indo-European language family (adapted from Fennell 2001:22)

The first attestations of Old English, written in alphabetic script using the letters of the Roman alphabet, date from around the year 700. Some older Old English runic inscriptions were written in the **futhorc** (or futharc) alphabet, named after the first elements of the names of its first six letters. The Latin alphabet was not designed to represent certain sounds used in Old English and had to be supplemented by a number of runes from the futhorc, namely the runes *thorn* <þ>, *wynn* <ƿ>, *ash* <æ>, *eth* <ð> and *yogh* <ȝ>. It is due to these characters and other major changes the language has undergone in the course of its history that an Old English text is not immediately accessible to speakers of Modern English without additional knowledge.

First Written Records

Fig. 2.4

The futhorc runic alphabet (Moessner 2003:4)

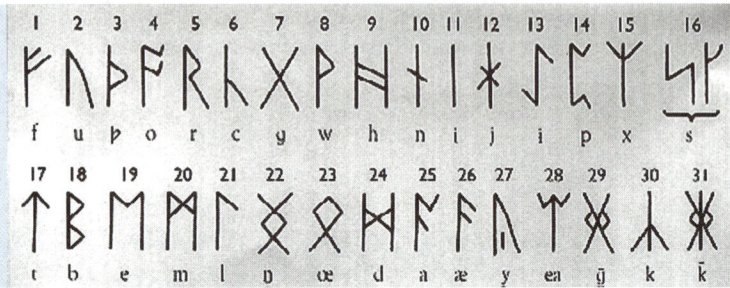

Old English Literature

There is a considerable though not abundant corpus of Old English literature in both **verse and prose** that has been preserved. The most important single work of poetry is *Beowulf*, a heroic poem of about 3,000 lines, but Old English poetry is also represented by a number of shorter pieces, such as *The Seafarer*, the war poem *The Battle of Maldon* and Christian poetry written by Cædmon and Cynewulf to name but a few. In addition to verse, Old English developed a tradition of prose literature rather early, mostly on behalf of the Anglo-Saxon King Alfred the Great (871-899). He is responsible for the translation of a number of books into Old English from Latin, including Bede's *Historia ecclesiastica gentis Anglorum*, and initiated the compilation of the *Anglo-Saxon Chronicle* (or *Anglo-Saxon Chronicles*), a record of the most important events of English history that was continued for more than two centuries after his death. Other rather well-preserved examples of Old English prose are texts written in the context of the Benedictine Reform, particularly the works of an abbot called Aelfric (c955-c1010).

Some Linguistic Characteristics of Old English

Despite the dialect distinctions of Old English mentioned above, there are a number of characteristic linguistic features shared by all major varieties of Old English.

Vocabulary

From a modern perspective, one of the most striking features of Old English is the very limited number of words derived from Latin and the absence of borrowings from French, the latter of which make up a large part of the vocabulary of Modern English. The **vocabulary of Old English is almost exclusively of West Germanic origin** — with the exception of a few borrowings from Celtic and Latin, and **some Scandinavian influence** on vocabulary and place names from 787 AD onwards — but more than 80 per cent of those words have since disappeared from the language. The surviving West Germanic words, however, form the core of the Modern English vocabulary and occur frequently in everyday speech. They express basic concepts, such as *child* (OE *cild*) or *to drink* (OE *drincan*), and constitute a large part of Modern English function words, i.e. auxiliaries, conjunctions, determiners, prepositions, pronouns and the like (cf. 4.1).

Old English was an **inflected language** like Latin or Modern German, which means that the grammatical function of words in a sentence was indicated largely by means of **inflection**, most commonly in the form of endings. As a result, the word order in Old English is rather free. Fully inflected languages like this are called **synthetic**, as opposed to **analytic** languages (cf. 2.1.2).

Morphology and Syntax

Nouns in Old English not only employed inflection to indicate **number** (singular/plural) but also **case** and **gender**. As in Modern German, **four cases** are distinguished: **nominative, genitive, dative** and **accusative**. According to the regular pattern of endings used to indicate these distinctions, the Old English nouns can be grouped together in **declensions**, which can be traced back to an earlier form of Germanic. Over one-third of the Old English nouns belonged to the so-called declension of masculine *a*-stems while about a quarter each were feminine *o*-stems and neuter *a*-stems (cf. table below). Old English distinguishes **masculine, feminine** and **neuter** and has so-called **grammatical gender**, which means that the gender of Old English nouns does not correspond to biological sex. For example, inanimate objects can thus be feminine (e.g. OE *giefu* 'gift') and masculine (e.g. OE *stān* 'stone', the so-called macron above the *a* indicating a long vowel), whereas the designations for female persons can be neuter (e.g. OE *wīf* 'wife' and *mægden* 'girl'). This system can still be found in contemporary German, where *das Mädchen* 'girl' is neuter and *der Stein* 'stone' is masculine.

| Fig. 2.5 |

Old English masc. *a*-stem *stān* 'stone', neut. *a*-stem *scip* 'ship' and fem. *o*-stem *giefu* 'gift'

	Singular	Plural	Singular	Plural	Singular	Plural
Nominative	stān	stān-*as*	scip	scip-*u*	gief-*u*	gief-*a*
Genitive	stān-*es*	stān-*a*	scip-*es*	scip-*a*	gief-*e*	gief-*a*
Dative	stān-*e*	stān-*um*	scip-*e*	scip-*um*	gief-*e*	gief-*um*
Accusative	stān	stān-*as*	scip	scip-*u*	gief-*e*	gief-*a*

Examples illustrating selected Old English nominal declensions

The Old English **adjective** had even more distinctions than the noun, partly preserving a fifth case (*instrumental*) and distinguishing two separate types of declension referred to as *weak* and *strong*. The Old English **personal pronoun** and the **demonstrative pronoun**, among other things the precursor of the definite article *the*, were fully inflected as well.

The Old English **verbal system** formally distinguished only two simple tenses, the **present** and the **preterite** (or past). The system was divided into **strong and weak verbs**, on the basis of the formation of the preterite. Strong verbs were characterized by alterations of their root vowel, known as **ablaut** (or apophony, or (vowel) gradation, or vowel alternation). They are divided into seven classes, for the most part according to the typical sequence of root vowels that appear in the infinitive, the first and third person preterite singular, the preterite plural and the past participle: e.g. *drīfan* 'to drive', *drāf*, *drifon*, *(ge)drifen* (strong verbs class I). Many Modern English "irregular" verbs still show an alternation of their root vowel, e.g. drive, drove, driven. Weak verbs are subdivided into three different classes but all have in common that they form their preterite and past participle by adding an ending called a dental suffix (cf. 3.1.2), e.g. *hīeran* 'to hear' has a preterite *hīerde* and a past participle *(ge)hīered* (weak verbs class 1). The dental suffix is the origin of the Modern English "regular" past tense marker *-ed*.

Pronunciation

The **consonants** of Old English were similar to the consonants of Modern English as the consonant system has not undergone any major structural changes in the history of English. As far as **vowels** are concerned, the situation is completely different. Particularly the long vowels have undergone considerable change from Old English to Modern English, e.g. OE *mōna* > ModE *moon* and OE *stān* > ModE *stone* (cf. Fig. 2.11).

2.1.2 │ Middle English (c1150-c1500)

The Norman Conquest

In the year **1066**, the troops of William the Conqueror, Duke of Normandy, invaded Britain. This invasion is known as the **Norman Conquest**. King Harold and almost the entire British nobility were killed at the Battle of Hastings, and William was crowned King of England in the same year. His reign not only brought about fundamental changes in society, religion and politics, it also had the greatest effect on the English language of all events in the course of its history. The Normans became the ruling class in England. Accordingly, French, strictly speaking the Norman French dialect, became the preferred language of the upper class and at the so-called Anglo-Norman Court. More and more speakers of English descent gradually acquired at least some knowledge of French resulting in a **strong influence of French on the English language**, despite the fact that the everyday language of the masses remained English at all times. These influences were clearly visible by about 1150, which is why this date is often given as the approximate dividing line between Old English and Middle English.

Written sources from the early Middle English period are scarce, as English had low prestige and most administrative and religious material was written in French or Latin. On the whole, however, a relatively large corpus of Middle English literature from a variety of different dialects survives, especially from after 1250. A large proportion of the surviving literature was composed in verse. The most important single author of the period was **Geoffrey Chaucer** (c1342-1400), poet and composer of a collection of 24 stories called the *Canterbury Tales*, probably the most influential and most widely read Middle English text.

Middle English Literature

Fig. 2.6

The Canterbury Tales

Some Characteristic Linguistic Features of Middle English

French influence and other developments towards the end of the Old English period led to some marked differences between Old English and Middle English.

Vocabulary

One of the most striking features of Middle English is the easily observable **immense influence of French on the English vocabulary**. Several centuries of intimate language contact led to the transference of an enormous number of words of French origin to English until the end of the Middle English period. Many thousands of words from all spheres of life were adopted, including *government, religion, art, justice, fashion, army, navy, literature* and *poet*. Estimates claim that between 30 and 40 per cent of the Modern English vocabulary is of French origin. But whatever the exact figure, there can be no doubt that the majority of these words entered the English language during Middle English times, replacing many inherited Germanic words.

Fig. 2.7

Comparison of Modern English terms for animals and the corresponding types of meat (source: OED)

| **animal** | cow, ox | sheep | deer | swine, sow |
| **meat** | beef | mutton | venison | pork |

The above table shows designations for some animals in Modern English that are continuations of the inherited Old English terms, whereas the names for the corresponding types of meat are all of French origin. This reflects the structure of the English society in Middle English times, during which the English-speaking lower classes were responsible for hunting and taking care of domesticated animals as opposed to the French-speaking upper classes that were able to afford and thus consume the produced meat. The names of a number of more affordable commodities accessible to the lower classes, such as *milk* or *cheese*, again continue the Old English terms.

Morphology and Syntax

The extensive changes of the Middle English period, however, show not only in the vocabulary but also the grammar of English. A widespread **loss of inflections** took place and changed English into a more **analytic language** (cf. 2.1.1 and 2.1.4). This means that the English language increasingly depended on a relatively

fixed word order to express the relation of words in a sentence. Middle English is thus traditionally called the **period of levelled inflections**. The decay of inflections already started towards the end of the Old English period and was probably largely due to the fact that the inherited Germanic words had the stress on the first syllable, which means that the vowels in the unstressed endings tended to lose their full quality.

Inflectional endings of the **noun** and the **adjective** were so much reduced that they could no longer express all the distinctions of case, number and gender. The adjective lost all distinctions between weak and strong declensions and finally all traces of inflectional markers altogether. In the nominal system, the originally distinctive endings *-a, -u, -e, -an, -um* were first reduced to *-e*, pronounced as the so-called *indeterminate vowel schwa* [ə] (cf. 3.1.2), and finally lost. Different case forms fell together in only one form, a process known as **syncretism**. Only one form remained for the plural and the only inflectional relic in the singular was the genitive in *-(e)s*; this means that the nominal inflection had already essentially reached its modern state.

	general singular	genitive singular	general plural	
				Fig. 2.8
ME	*ston(e)*	*ston-es*	*ston-es*	*Forms of*
ModE	*stone*	*stone's*	*stones*	*ME ston(e) and*
				ModE stone

The reduction of endings of nouns and adjectives, and the establishment of the invariable article *the* were among the causes responsible for the **loss of grammatical gender** in Middle English. **Natural gender**, sometimes also referred to as logical gender, recognises the sex of animate beings, while all inanimate objects are generally neuter. There are only very few exceptions such as countries and ships.

The **verb** also exhibited the general tendency towards weakening of endings and levelling of inflections, but showed lesser degrees of structural change. The main changes of the verbal system during the Middle English period were the **loss of many strong verbs** and the gradual process of **conversion from the strong to the weak conjugation** found in a number of formerly strong verbs. The weak class of verbs was further strengthened by the **adoption of many verbs from foreign languages**, particularly from French at the time, which were for the most part included into the weak system. These processes contributed to the reduction of the number of so-called irregular verbs in Modern English.

Pronunciation

We have already mentioned above that the **consonants** of English have not changed much since Old English times and thus only a few rather minor changes took place from Old English to Middle English, such as the loss of initial *h-* before *l*, *n* and *r* in words like OE *hring* > ME *ring*. The **vowel system**, on the other hand, underwent some fundamental changes, such as some instances of lengthening and shortening in certain environments and the reduction of /a/, /e/, /o/ and /u/ to /ə/ in unstressed position, which is at least to a large extent responsible for the loss of inflections in English (see above).

2.1.3 | Early Modern English (c1500-c1700)

The Introduction of Printing

The beginning of the Early Modern English period is connected with the effects brought about by the **introduction of printing** into England in the second half of the fifteenth century. Printing from moveable type was invented in Germany in the middle of the fifteenth century and brought to England by **William Caxton** (c1422-1491), who set up his printing press in Westminster in 1476. Books no longer had to be copied by hand and for the first time in the history of English a great number of identical books could be produced. Printing gave written works a much wider circulation, contributed to the **standardisation** of the English language and fostered **norms of spelling and punctuation**.

> **"What's in a name? That which we call a rose by any other word would smell as sweet."**
> (William Shakespeare. *Romeo and Juliet* II, ii, 1-2)

Early Modern English Literature

Mainly as a result of the efficiency of printing, more people from different layers of society got access to then more affordable written material. Over 20,000 titles in English had appeared in England by 1640 and an enormous corpus of Early Modern English texts has survived until today. Among the most important influences on the development of the English language in the Early Modern English period were the works of **William Shakespeare** (1564-1616) and the **King James Bible of 1611**, also referred to as the **Authorised Version**.

Fig. 2.9

A page from Shakespeare's First Folio (published 1623)

152

THE TRAGEDIE OF
HAMLET, Prince of Denmarke.

Actus Primus. Scœna Prima.

Enter Barnardo and Francisco two Centinels.

Barnardo.
Who's there?
Fran. Nay answer me: Stand & vnfold your selfe.
Bar. Long liue the King.
Fran. Barnardo?
Bar. He.
Fran. You come most carefully vpon your houre.
Bar. 'Tis now strook twelue, get thee to bed *Francisco.*
Fran. For this releefe much thankes: 'Tis bitter cold, And I am sicke at heart.
Barn. Haue you had quiet Guard?
Fran. Not a Mouse stirring.
Barn. Well, goodnight. If you do meet *Horatio* and *Marcellus*, the Riuals of my Watch, bid them make hast.
Enter Horatio and Marcellus.
Fran. I thinke I heare them. Stand: who's there?
Hor. Friends to this ground.
Mar. And Leige-men to the Dane.
Fran. Giue you good night.
Mar. O farwel honest Soldier, who hath relieu'd you?
Fra. Barnardo ha's my place: giue you goodnight.
Exit Fran.
Mar. Holla *Barnardo.*
Bar. Say, what is *Horatio* there?
Hor. A peece of him.
Bar. Welcome *Horatio*, welcome good *Marcellus.*
Mar. What, ha's this thing appear'd againe to night.
Bar. I haue seene nothing.
Mar. *Horatio* saies, 'tis but our Fantasie,
And will not let beleefe take hold of him
Touching this dreaded sight, twice seene of vs,
Therefore I haue intreated him along
With vs, to watch the minutes of this Night,
That if againe this Apparition come,
He may approue our eyes, and speake to it.
Hor. Tush, tush, 'twill not appeare.
Bar. Sit downe a-while,
And let vs once againe assaile your eares,
That are so fortified against our Story,
What we two Nights haue seene.
Hor. Well, sit we downe,
And let vs heare *Barnardo* speake of this.
Barn. Last night of all,
When yond same Starre that's Westward from the Pole
Had made his course t'illume that part of Heauen

Where now it burnes, *Marcellus* and my selfe,
The Bell then beating one.
Mar. Peace, breake thee of: *Enter the Ghost.*
Looke where it comes againe.
Barn. In the same figure, like the King that's dead.
Mar. Thou art a Scholler; speake to it *Horatio.*
Barn. Lookes it not like the King? Marke it *Horatio.*
Hora. Most like: It harrowes me with fear & wonder
Barn. It would be spoke too.
Mar. Question it *Horatio.*
Hor. What art thou that vsurp'st this time of night,
Together with that Faire and Warlike forme
In which the Maiesty of buried Denmarke
Did sometimes march: By Heauen I charge thee speake.
Mar. It is offended.
Barn. See, it stalkes away.
Hor. Stay: speake; speake: I Charge thee, speake.
Exit the Ghost.
Mar. 'Tis gone, and will not answer.
Barn. How now *Horatio?* You tremble & look pale:
Is not this something more then Fantasie?
What thinke you on't?
Hor. Before my God, I might not this beleeue
Without the sensible and true auouch
Of mine owne eyes.
Mar. Is it not like the King?
Hor. As thou art to thy selfe,
Such was the very Armour he had on,
When th'Ambitious Norwey combatted:
So frown'd he once, when in an angry parle
He smot the sledded Pollax on the Ice.
'Tis strange.
Mar. Thus twice before, and iust at this dead houre,
With Martiall stalke, hath he gone by our Watch.
Hor. In what particular thought to work, I know not:
But in the grosse and scope of my Opinion,
This boades some strange eruption to our State.
Mar. Good now sit downe, & tell me he that knowes
Why this same strict and most obseruant Watch,
So nightly toyles the subiect of the Land,
And why such dayly Cast of Brazon Cannon
And Forraigne Mart for Implements of warre:
Why such impresse of Ship-wrights, whose sore Taske
Do's not diuide the Sunday from the weeke,
What might be toward, that this sweaty hast
Doth make the Night ioynt-Labourer with the day:
Who is't that can informe me?
Hor. That can I,

At

Early Modern English was a period of considerable variation, which contributed to an increasing wish for standardisation. Apart from the extensive regularisation of spelling conventions by

Some Characteristic Linguistic Features of Early Modern English

the middle of the seventeenth century — resulting from the arrival of printing and the first English-language dictionaries — Early Modern English is mainly characterised by fundamental changes in the vocabulary and the vowel system.

Vocabulary

The Early Modern English period saw another **major expansion of the English vocabulary** and a huge influx of words from other languages. The exploration of far-away places and the ensuing contact with foreign cultures and unfamiliar environments was one of the reasons for the need of new words. The spread of new concepts and inventions from the Continent and renewed interest in the classical languages during the Renaissance (1500-1650) also led to numerous borrowings from Latin, Greek, French and other languages. The following list contains just a small fraction of the words that were borrowed during the Early Modern English period:

Fig. 2.10

Some Early Modern English borrowings (shortened from Crystal 2003b:60)

From Latin and Greek
anonymous, appropriate, atmosphere, catastrophe, chaos, crisis, criterion, emphasis, encyclopedia, enthusiasm, exact, exaggerate, excursion, exist, expensive, explain, habitual, immaturity, impersonal, lexicon, lunar, monopoly, necessitate, obstruction, parasite, parenthesis, pathetic, pneumonia, relaxation, relevant, scheme, soda, species, system, tactics, temperature, thermometer, transcribe, utopian, vacuum, virus

From or via French
alloy, anatomy, bayonet, bigot, bizarre, chocolate, colonel, comrade, detail, entrance, equip, explore, grotesque, invite, moustache, muscle, naturalise, passport, pioneer, progress, shock, ticket, tomato, vase, vogue, volunteer

From or via Italian
balcony, ballot, carnival, concerto, design, giraffe, grotto, lottery, macaroni, opera, piazza, rocket, solo, sonata, soprano, stanza, trill, violin, volcano

From or via Spanish and Portuguese
alligator, anchovy, apricot, armada, banana, barricade, cannibal, canoe, cockroach, corral, desperado, embargo, guitar, hurricane, maize, mosquito, negro, potato, port (wine), sombrero, tank, tobacco

From other languages
Algonquian: *racoon, skunk*; Arabian: *harem*; Dutch: *keelhaul, knapsack, landscape, yacht*; Hindi: *guru*; Irish Gaelic: *trousers*; Malay: *bamboo, ketchup*; Norwegian: *troll*; Russian: *rouble*; Persian: *bazaar, caravan, turban*; Tamil: *curry*; Turkish: *coffee, kiosk, yogurt*; Welsh: *flannel*

Some viewed the influx of new vocabulary as enrichment, others objected strongly to the extensive borrowing of words from foreign languages. The latter claimed that the language should remain "pure" and "unmixed", not obscured by so-called **inkhorn terms** that are not understood by a large part of the population. The borrowing of so many foreign words led to the compilation of dictionaries containing **hard words**, such as the probably first-ever monolingual English dictionary published by Robert Cawdrey in 1604.

> **"Among all other lessons this should first be learned, that wee never affect any straunge ynkehorne termes, but to speake as is commonly received."**
> (Thomas Wilson. *Arte of Rhetorique* (1553), quoted in Baugh & Cable 2002:218)

The major structural changes in English grammar were completed before the Early Modern English period started and thus the syntax and morphology at the time are already very similar to Modern English.

Morphology and Syntax

The inflectional system of the **noun** was essentially the same as in Present Day English, with only two cases (common and possessive) and the plural marker -s. Shakespeare still occasionally employs the plural ending -en in words like *eyen* 'eyes'. The **verbal system** is characterised by the continuation of the tendency of strong verbs to become weak and the rare occurrence of the progressive form.

The **word order** pattern *subject–verb–object* (SVO) had already established itself before the Early Modern English period, but deviations from this general rule were still more frequent than in Modern English. One of these common deviations was the inversion of the subject and the verb after a sentence-initial adverbial as in "and then shalt thou see clearly" (King James Bible, Matthew 7.5) instead of "and then you will see clearly" (The Revised English Bible 1989).

The **consonant** system of Early Modern English is for the most part identical with Modern English. A few minor changes took place during the Early Modern English period, such as the loss of initial /k-/ and /g-/ before /n/, as in *knee*, *know* and *gnome*, or the loss of word-internal /l/ in certain environments, as in *folk* and *palm*.

Pronunciation

The **vowel system**, however, underwent a fundamental change commonly called the **Great Vowel Shift** (**GVS**). The GVS started in the fourteenth century, took several centuries to complete and **affected all long vowels of Middle English**. The long vowels of Middle English were either **raised** or **diphthongised**, i.e. they were changed into a combination of two vowel sounds pro-

The Great Vowel Shift

nounced together (cf. 3.1.2). For example, the long /oː/ in ME *fode* 'food' was raised to long /uː/ and the long /iː/ in ME *child* and *lyf* 'life' was diphthongised to /aɪ/. The change seems to have happened as a kind of **chain reaction**. It is, however, controversial whether the vowels at the bottom of the vowel chart (cf. 3.1.2) were raised first and "pushed" the others up, called a push-chain, or whether the ones at the top were diphthongised first and "pulled" the lower ones up by leaving an open space, called a pull-chain. Some linguistics even suggest a mixture of both.

Fig. 2.11

The Great Vowel Shift (adapted from Jucker 2007:54)

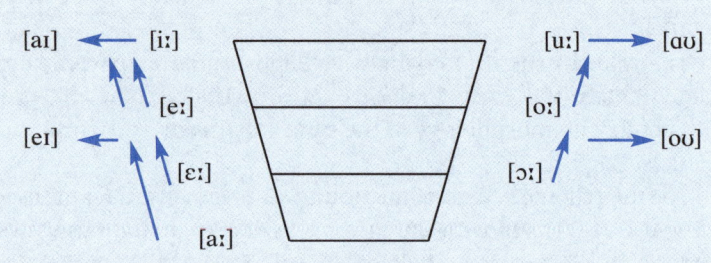

Other Changes

One of the most important changes affecting the **short vowels of Middle English** was the rounding and centralising of the high back rounded vowel /ʊ/ in the southern part of England (cf. Fig. 8.3). As a result, /ʊ/ became /ʌ/, as in ModE *but* and *cup* (see inside cover for a vowel chart).

2.1.4 | Modern English (c1700-present)

There is **no historical landmark** such as the Norman Conquest or the introduction of printing to mark the beginning of the Modern English period. The year 1700 is usually set as the beginning of the Modern English period, because the English language had by then reached its present state in most respects. It was increasingly codified and standardised in the early decades of the Modern English period. This was thanks to important works like Samuel Johnson's influential *Dictionary of the English Language* published in two volumes in 1755 and several highly popular grammar books published in the eighteenth century. (For the geographical expansion of English that started late in the Early Modern English period and reached its peak in Modern English see the following section 2.2).

Modern English is the result of over 1000 years of continuous changes.

The **lexicon** of Modern English combines words from different origins which can be assigned to **three different groups**. Firstly, the continuations of inherited Germanic words that have survived since Old English. Secondly, the vocabulary that has been adopted from Latin, Greek, French and other European languages throughout the course of the history of English. And thirdly, words that have been borrowed or made up as a result of the geographical expansion of English (cf. 2.2) as well as the social, cultural and scientific developments that have taken place since the early nineteenth century. Most recently the rapid progress in computer and communications technology has been responsible for a large number of new and frequently used words in the English language, such as *software* or *download*. The English-language domination of these technologies and other fields has led to the "export" of a large number of lexical items to many languages around the world.

As far as morphology is concerned, Modern English can be called the **period of lost inflections**. Only a very small number of regular inflectional endings has been preserved in Modern English (cf. also Fig. 2.8 in section 2.1.2):

Some Characteristic Linguistic Features of Modern English

Vocabulary

Morphology and Syntax

	Fig. 2.12
the plural -*s*	*hand ~ hands, cat ~ cats, bus ~ buses*
the possessive -'*s*	*lady ~ lady's, Peter ~ Peter's, George ~ George's*
3rd person singular present indicative -*s*	*they bring ~ she brings, they drop ~ he drops, we fish ~ she fishes*
preterite -*ed*	*play ~ played, work ~ worked, head ~ headed*
past participle -*ed*	*play ~ played, work ~ worked, head ~ headed*
the -*ing*-form	*read ~ reading*
comparative -*er*	*small ~ smaller, big ~ bigger*
superlative -*est*	*small ~ smallest, big ~ biggest*

Modern English inflections

The only traces of the Old English case system are now the possessive marker -*s* and some oblique forms of the pronoun, such as *him*, *her* and *them* in opposition to nominative *he*, *she* and *they*. The pronominal system was reduced from Early Modern English to Modern English as the opposition between the second person singular *thou/thee* and second person plural *you* was given up in favour of a generalised form *you*.

Due to the loss of inflections, English has become a highly **analytic language**, i.e. the relation of words in a sentence is now indicated by a relatively fixed **word order** that does not allow for many deviations from the basic pattern and, for example, the usage of prepositions.

Pronunciation

The **Great Vowel Shift** (cf. above) was for the most part **completed** by 1700 and, among other things, its end marks the beginning of the Modern English period. It is mostly the result of the Great Vowel Shift that pronunciation and spelling differ so much in Modern English. The explanation is clear: orthography was largely fixed in the wake of the introduction of printing in the late fifteenth century; right at that time and during the following centuries the English vowel system underwent the most fundamental change in its history.

The early twentieth century saw the rise of the prestige accent **RP** (Received Pronunciation) in England (cf. 3.1.3). RP is still widely used as a reference in foreign language teaching around the world and until recently was the exclusive accent used in British broadcasting.

2.2 | English Around the World

Up to the end of the twelfth century, the English language was geographically limited to the British Isles, excluding the Celtic-speaking parts of Cornwall, Wales, Scotland and Ireland (cf. Pre-English and Old English), but then two phases of expansion led to the global distribution of English. The **first phase** was the **spread of English in the British Isles**, which originated from England and started roughly in the twelfth century. The **second phase** of expansion, connected with the so-called **colonisation**, began during the early seventeenth century, originated in all parts of the British Isles and led to the **spread of English beyond the British Isles** and its distribution in many territories overseas.

"... our tung is of small reatch, it stretcheth no further than this lland of ours, naie not there over all ...."
(Richard Mulcaster. 1582)

The first phase of the spread of the English language that led to its distribution in the British Isles is often forgotten and rarely mentioned when talking about English around the world. It is, however, important to bear in mind that the early developments in the British Isles are largely responsible for the emergence of the subvarieties of British English (BrE), e.g. English English, Irish English, Northern Irish English, Welsh English, Scottish English, and Scots as a separate language, and also played a major role in the development of distinct overseas varieties due to the emigration of speakers of these different subvarieties.

Spread of English in the British Isles

The second main phase of the spread of English that led to its distribution beyond the British Isles is closely connected with what is usually referred to as **colonisation**. Up to the end of the sixteenth century the English language was limited to the British Isles, as Richard Mulcaster, a London schoolmaster, observed in 1582 when he wrote that "our tung is of small reatch, it stretcheth no further than this Iland of ours, naie not there over all".

Spread of English beyond the British Isles

England entered the race for colonial territory comparatively late in the early seventeenth century with the establishment of settlements in North America. Subsequently, a large number of territories throughout the world were influenced by English colonisation and the expansion of the British Empire. As a result, today, English is the **native language** (ENL, L1) of the majority of the population in a number of countries and territories including the United States of America, Canada, Australia and New Zealand. English is also used as an important **second language** (ESL, L2), i.e. English is an official or semi-official language or is used for a special purpose in over 60 countries and territories including India, Nigeria and South Africa. The following table shows estimated numbers of English speakers by territory:

Fig. 2.13

Territory	Population	L1 Speakers	L2 Speakers	Total (L1+L2)
American Samoa	67,000	2,000	65,000	67,000
Antigua & Barbuda (c)	68,000	66,000	2,000	68,000
Aruba	70,000	9,000	35,000	44,000
Australia	18,972,000	14,987,000	3,500,000	18,487,000
Bahamas (c)	298,000	260,000	28,000	288,000
Bangladesh	131,270,000	-	3,500,000	3,500,000
Barbados (c)	275,000	262,000	13,000	275,000
Belize (c)	256,000	190,000	56,000	246,000
Bermuda	63,000	63,000	-	63,000
Botswana	1,586,000	-	630,000	630,000
British Virgin Islands (c)	20,800	20,000	-	20,000
Brunei	344,000	10,000	134,000	144,000
Cameroon (c)	15,900,000	-	7,700,000	7,700,000
Canada	31,600,000	20,000,000	7,000,000	27,000,000
Cayman Islands (c)	36,000	36,000	-	36,000
Cook Islands	21,000	1,000	3,000	4,000
Dominica (c)	70,000	3,000	60,000	63,000
Fiji	850,000	6,000	170,000	176,000
Gambia (c)	1,411,000	-	40,000	40,000
Ghana (c)	19,894,000	-	1,400,000	1,400,000
Gibraltar	31,000	28,000	2,000	30,000
Grenada (c)	100,000	100,000	-	100,000
Guam	160,000	58,000	100,000	158,000
Guyana (c)	700,000	650,000	30,000	680,000
Hong Kong	7,210,000	150,000	2,200,000	2,350,000
India	1,029,991,000	350,000	200,000,000	200,350,000
Ireland	3,850,000	3,750,000	100,000	3,850,000
Jamaica (c)	2,665,000	2,600,000	50,000	2,650,000
Kenya	30,766,000	-	2,700,000	2,700,000
Kiribati	94,000	-	23,000	23,000
Lesotho	2,177,000	-	500,000	500,000
Liberia (c)	3,226,000	600,000	2,500,000	3,100,000
Malawi	10,548,000	-	540,000	540,000
Malaysia	22,230,000	380,000	7,000,000	7,380,000
Malta	395,000	13,000	95,000	108,000
Marshall Islands	70,000	-	60,000	60,000
Mauritius	1,190,000	2,000	200,000	202,000
Micronesia	135,000	4,000	60,000	64,000

Montserrat (c)	4,000	4,000	-	4,000
Namibia	1,800,000	14,000	300,000	314,000
Nauru	12,000	900	10,700	11,600
Nepal	25,300,000	-	7,000,000	7,000,000
New Zealand	3,864,000	3,700,000	150,000	3,850,000
Nigeria (c)	126,636,000	-	60,000,000	60,000,000
Northern Marianas (c)	75,000	5,000	65,000	70,000
Pakistan	145,000,000	-	17,000,000	17,000,000
Palau	19,000	500	18,000	18,500
Papua New Guinea (c)	5,000,000	150,000	3,000,000	3,150,000
Philippines	83,000,000	20,000	40,000,000	40,020,000
Puerto Rico	3,937,000	100,000	1,840,000	1,940,000
Rwanda	7,313,000	-	20,000	20,000
St Kitts & Nevis (c)	43,000	43,000	-	43,000
St Lucia (c)	158,000	31,000	40,000	71,000
St Vincent & Grenadines (c)	116,000	114,000	-	114,000
Samoa	180,000	1,000	93,000	94,000
Seychelles	80,000	3,000	30,000	33,000
Sierra Leone (c)	5,427,000	500,000	4,400,000	4,900,000
Singapore	4,300,000	350,000	2,000,000	2,350,000
Solomon Islands (c)	480,000	10,000	165,000	175,000
South Africa	43,586,000	3,700,000	11,000,000	14,700,000
Sri Lanka	19,400,000	10,000	1,900,000	1,910,000
Suriname (c)	434,000	260,000	150,000	410,000
Swaziland	1,104,000	-	50,000	50,000
Tanzania	36,232,000	-	4,000,000	4,000,000
Tonga	104,000	-	30,000	30,000
Trinidad & Tobago (c)	1,170,000	1,145,000	-	1,145,000
Tuvalu	11,000	-	800	800
Uganda	23,986,000	-	2,500,000	2,500,000
United Kingdom*	59,648,000	58,190,000	1,500,000	59,690,000
UK Islands (Channel Is, Man)	228,000	227,000	-	227,000
United States	278,059,000	215,424,000	25,600,000	241,024,000
US Virgin Islands (c)	122,000	98,000	15,000	113,000
Vanuatu (c)	193,000	60,000	120,000	180,000
Zambia	9,770,000	110,000	1,800,000	1,910,000
Zimbabwe	11,365,000	250,000	5,300,000	5,550,000
Other dependencies	35,000	20,000	15,000	35,000
Total	**2,236,800,800**	**329,140,400**	**430,608,500**	**759,748,900**

*Estimated ENL and ESL speakers in the world; (c) indicates an English-based creole (from Crystal 2003a:62-65) * Crystal's numbers for the United Kingdom do not add up.*

2.3 | English in the 21st Century

Many predictions concerning the future of the English language have been wrong, but the second president of the United States, John Adams (1735-1826) made a prophecy about the future role of English in the world on September 23, 1780, that should eventually prove true. Adams said that "English will be the most respectable language in the world and the most universally read and spoken in the next century, if not before the close of this one" and went on that it was "destined to be in the next and succeeding centuries more generally the language of the world than Latin was in the last or French is in the present age".

English as a Global Language

The emergence of an international or global language is always closely linked with political, cultural and economic power and so historically the status of English in the world today is due to two main reasons: first, as we have seen above, English spread across the world with the **expansion of British colonial power**, which reached its peak at the end of the nineteenth century. Second, the maintained international status and increasing spread of English in the twentieth century is the result of the **establishment of the United States as the leading economic and military power**. It is important to note that there is general agreement, at least among linguists, that such a development is not related to any special intrinsic linguistic qualities of the language, as has occasionally been claimed.

The present global status of English is based in part on the impressive number of English speakers and users in the world (see above), with an increasing importance being attributed to the non-native speakers of the language. Unfortunately, the terms *speaker* and *user* are not clearly defined and quantitative estimates, especially of non-native speakers, thus vary considerably. The number of native speakers seems to pose the least difficulties and is widely accepted to be somewhere between 300 and 400 million. Accurate numbers of speakers for whom English is not the mother tongue are much more difficult to establish and depend largely on the definition of the minimum level of proficiency that can be counted as "English-speaking, -using or -knowing". Estimates of non-native users of English range from several hundred million to over two billion, but whatever the exact total, English today is without doubt the most widely used language in the world. Users of English even outnumber the speakers of Chinese dialects. The vast majority of users of English today are thus non-native speakers of the language and their proportion is increasing constantly. Kachru tries to account for the different functions of English in different territories by introducing the **three circles of English**:

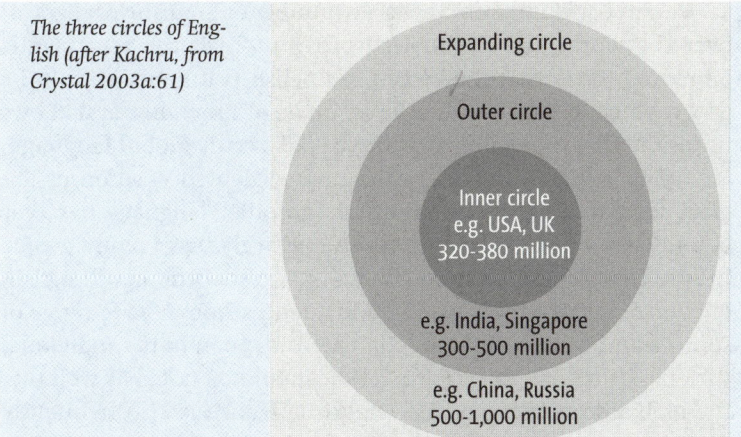

The three circles of English (after Kachru, from Crystal 2003a:61)

Expanding circle

Outer circle

Inner circle
e.g. USA, UK
320-380 million

e.g. India, Singapore
300-500 million

e.g. China, Russia
500-1,000 million

Fig. 2.14

Inseparably linked with the enormous number of speakers is another important factor that justifies the international status of English, namely its position as *the* **global lingua franca**, i.e. as a language that is used for communication by people who do not share a common native language. India is perhaps the most striking example for the use of English as a lingua franca in **intra-national** communication, where it is — together with Hindi — an essential tool for intra-Indian interaction. **Internationally** and **cross-culturally**, there are a number of activities and subjects that are carried out predominantly in English across the world. To name but a few of these **domains**, English today is the dominant global language in *international relations*, it is used as a lingua franca in most *international organisations and companies* and at nearly all *international gatherings*. English dominates the *media* and especially *academic publication and communication*, plays an important role in *international travel and transport*, including the means of controlling international

> **"... no other language has ever before been put to so many uses so massively by so many people in so many places."**
> (McArthur 1998:54)

transport on water (*Seaspeak*) and air traffic control (*Airspeak*), is currently used for *most conventional as well as electronic communication and is the main lingua franca of the Internet*. English is no longer only the language of some native English-speaking countries, it has become an **international language**, which is somewhat independent from the originally English-speaking territories.

We can conclude from the large number of English-speakers all over the world and the myriad uses in which the language is employed today that the spread of English is unique, both in its geographical reach as well as in its range of functions, and allows us for the first time in history to speak of **a truly global language**. McArthur (1999:54) sums up the unprecedented position of English succinctly when he says that "no other language has ever before been put to so many uses so massively by so many people in so many places." The spread and the diversification of English, of course, invite a multiplicity of influences from a wide range of sources and permit different changes to happen in the individual varieties of the language (cf. 8.2.1). It should be noted as well that the global dominance of the English language is also frequently perceived as a threat, particularly to small (or lesser-used) languages.

2.4 | Exercises

1. What is the main aim of diachronic linguistics?

2. Which of the following designations refer to a major dialect area of Old English:
Kentish, Anglo-Saxon, West Saxon, Anglian, Cockney

3. Decide whether the following statements are true or false.
a) *The noun system of Old English has more cases than in Modern English.* T / F
b) *The Great Vowel Shift affected all short vowels of Middle English.* T / F
c) *The arriving Germanic tribes ended the Roman occupation of England.* T / F
d) *Modern English is an analytic language.* T / F
e) *English belongs to the North Germanic branch of languages.* T / F

4. Why are the vowels /uː/ and /aɪ/ in ModE *moon* and *I* represented by the spellings <oo> and <I> respectively? Keep in mind that /ː/ indicates a long vowel.

5. As far as English is concerned, India is considered a country of the so-called outer circle (cf. Fig. 2.14). Examine and explain the function of English in India.

6. Compare the following pairs of historically related words (cf. Fig. 2.3): ModE *pepper* and ModG *Pfeffer*, ModE *post* and ModG *Pfosten*, ModE *pound* and ModG *Pfund*, ModE *path* and ModG *Pfad*, ModE *pipe* and ModG *Pfeife*. Compare the corresponding Modern English and Modern German forms and describe the obviously regular change that has happened.

Bibliography | 2.5

Bailey, Richard. 1991. *Images of English: A Cultural History of English.* Ann Arbor: University of Michigan Press. (*Focus on the cultural history of English-speaking peoples*)

Bammesberger, Alfred. 1989. *English Linguistics.* Heidelberg: Winter (*Introduction to English linguistics from a primarily historical perspective*)

Barber, Charles et al. 2009. *The English Language: A Historical Introduction.* 2nd edition. Cambridge: Cambridge University Press. (*Chronological approach; from Indo-European to Present Day English*)

Baugh, Albert C. & Thomas Cable. 2002. *A History of the English Language.* 5th edition. London: Routledge. (*One of the standard works on the history of English*)

Blake, Norman F. 1996. *A History of the English Language.* Houndmills and London: Macmillan. (*Written from a primarily British perspective; focus on Standard English*)

Bragg, Melvyn. 2003. *The Adventure of English: 500 AD to 2000 – The Biography of a Language.* London: Hodder&Stoughton. (*Entertaining overview*)

Burnley, David. 2000. *A History of the English Language: A Source Book.* 2nd edition. Harlow: Longman. (*An annotated collection of texts from all periods of English*)

Crystal David. 2002. *The English Language: A Guided Tour of the Language.* 2nd ed. London: Penguin. (*A brief survey of the many roles the English language plays today*)

Crystal, David. 2003a. *English as a Global Language.* 2nd edition. Cambridge: Cambridge University Press. (*Focus on the role of English around the world today*)

Crystal, David. 2003b. *The Cambridge Encyclopedia of the English Language.* 2nd edition. Cambridge: Cambridge University Press. (*Highly recommended overview with many illustrations*)

Crystal, David. 2005. *The Stories of English.* London: Penguin. (*A history of both Standard English as well as other varieties*)

Fennell, Barbara. 2001. *A History of English: A Sociolinguistic Approach.* Oxford: Blackwell. (*Systematic approach with focus sections on sociolinguistic topics*)

Fischer, Roswitha. 2003. *Tracing the History of English: A Textbook for Students*. Darmstadt: Wissenschaftliche Buchgesellschaft. *(Very brief but well-structured sketch of the history of English)*

Görlach, Manfred. 2002. *Einführung in die englische Sprachgeschichte*. 5th edition. Heidelberg: Winter.) (also in English translation: *The Linguistic History of English: An Introduction*, Basingstoke: Macmillan)

Graddol, David et al., eds. 1996. *English: History, Diversity and Change*. London: Routledge. *(Overview of history and variation in English today; plenty of illustrations)*

Hickey, Raymond, ed. 2004. *Legacies of Colonial English: Studies in Transported Dialects*. Cambridge: Cambridge University Press. *(Overview of colonially induced varieties of English in the world)*

Hogg, Richard M., ed. 1992/2001. *The Cambridge History of the English Language*. 6 volumes. Cambridge: Cambridge University Press. *(The standard comprehensive history of English)*

Jucker, Andreas H. 2007. *History of English and Historical Linguistics*. 2nd edition. Stuttgart: Klett. *(Short overview with text samples)*

Knowles, Gerry. 1997. *A Cultural History of the English Language*. London: Arnold. *(Short history of the English language as a product of cultural developments)*

Leith, Dick. 1997. *A Social History of English*. 2nd edition. London: Routledge. *(Highly readable, written from a sociolinguistic perspective)*

Moessner, Lilo. 2003. *Diachronic English Linguistics: An Introduction*. Tübingen: Narr. *(Overview of the methods of historical linguistics)*

Smith, Jeremy J. 2005. *Essentials of Early English*. 2nd edition. London: Routledge. *(Introduction to Old English, Middle English and Early Modern English with many illustrative texts)*

Viereck, Wolfgang et al. 2002. *dtv-Atlas Englische Sprache*. München: dtv. *(Well-illustrated survey of many aspects of English, including the history of the language)*

Phonetics and Phonology |3

Abstract

Phonetics and phonology are two separate but nevertheless intimately interconnected subdisciplines of linguistics that deal with the sounds of language. Phonetics is the scientific study of human speech sounds independent of specific languages, whereas phonology is concerned with the sound systems of individual languages and the function and patterning of certain sounds in these systems.

Phonetics vs. Phonology

3.1 | Phonetics: The Study of Speech Sounds

Phonetics is "[t]he science which studies the characteristics of human sound-making, especially those sounds used in speech, and provides methods for their description, classification and transcription." (Crystal 2003:349)

Phonetics is concerned with the wide variety of sounds used by speakers of human languages. There is a huge number of possible **speech sounds**, also called **phones** or **segments**, of which each individual language uses only a small portion. It is, however, important to note that any human, child or adult, can learn how to pronounce all of these sounds, even the ones that do not usually occur in their native languages.

There are **three types of phonetics** that reflect three different ways to approach speech sounds:

Fig. 3.1|

	type	field of study
1)	articulatory phonetics	The study of **the production of speech sounds**. It describes how the organs of speech, also called articulators, are used to produce, i.e. articulate, the individual speech sounds and classifies them according to the involved mechanism of production.
2)	acoustic phonetics	The study of **the transmission and the physical properties of speech sounds**. It is an objective approach to describing sounds, concerned with measuring and analysing the physical properties (such as duration, frequency and intensity) of the sound waves we produce when we speak.
3)	auditory phonetics	The study of **the perception of speech sounds**. It studies how sounds are perceived and processed by the listener.

The three types of phonetics

These three main phases of the speech chain can also be depicted in diagram form, as shown in Fig. 3.2, keeping in mind that the brain of the speaker controls the production of speech sounds and the brain of the listener has to analyze the sounds received by the ear.

This chapter focuses on articulatory phonetics, which has the longest history of the three subbranches of phonetics and a wide range of applications in the learning and teaching of pronunciation.

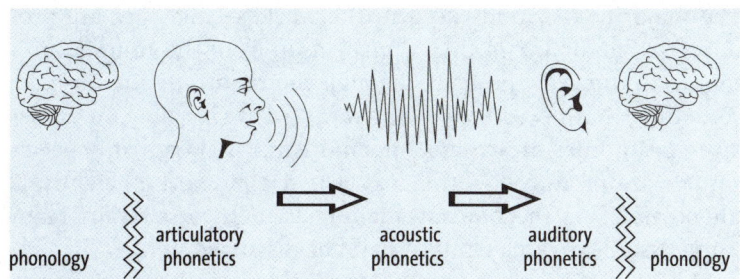

Fig. 3.2

The speech chain

Speech Sound Production

3.1.1

In order to be able to discuss the articulation of sounds, we need a basic knowledge of the **sound-producing system**. **Three basic components** are involved in the production of speech sounds: first **the lungs**, second **the larynx** (or voice box) containing the vocal folds (= folds of muscle popularly known as vocal cords) and the glottis (= the space between the vocal folds), and third **the vocal tract** above the larynx, including the oral and nasal cavities.

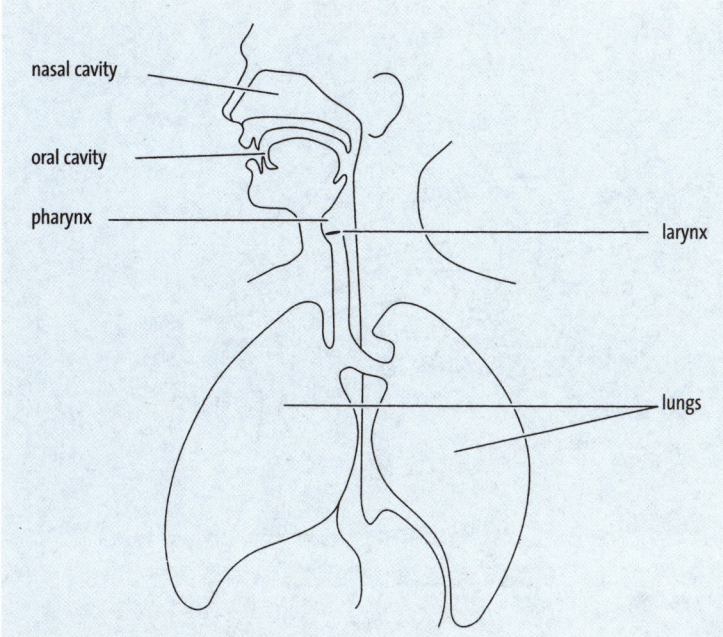

Fig. 3.3

The sound-producing system (adapted from O'Grady et al. 2004:18, cf. Bibliography of Chapter 1)

Airstream Mechanism

The majority of sounds used in the world's languages are produced by an airstream that is pushed up from the lungs (= pulmonic) and leaves the body through the mouth or the nose, or sometimes both (=egressive 'outwards'). This is called an **egressive pulmonic airstream mechanism**. All English speech sounds are produced in this way. Other airstream mechanisms are possible, e.g. mechanisms making use of ingressive airstream (=ingressive 'inwards'), but will not be discussed here.

Organs of Speech

The airstream from the lungs is modified by the so-called **organs of speech** (or **articulators**) to produce a variety of different sounds. The description and classification of sounds for the most part depends on **how and where the airstream is modified** by these articulators. We distinguish movable (or mobile) **active articulators** that can be voluntarily controlled, such as the lips or the tongue, and immovable (or non-mobile) **passive articulators** that cannot be voluntarily controlled, such as the alveolar ridge or the hard palate. Despite the name "organs of speech", however, it must be pointed out that biological functions, in particular eating and breathing rather than speech, are the primary purpose of these organs.

Fig. 3.4

The organs of speech (adapted from O'Grady et al. 2004:22, cf. Bibliography of Chapter 1)

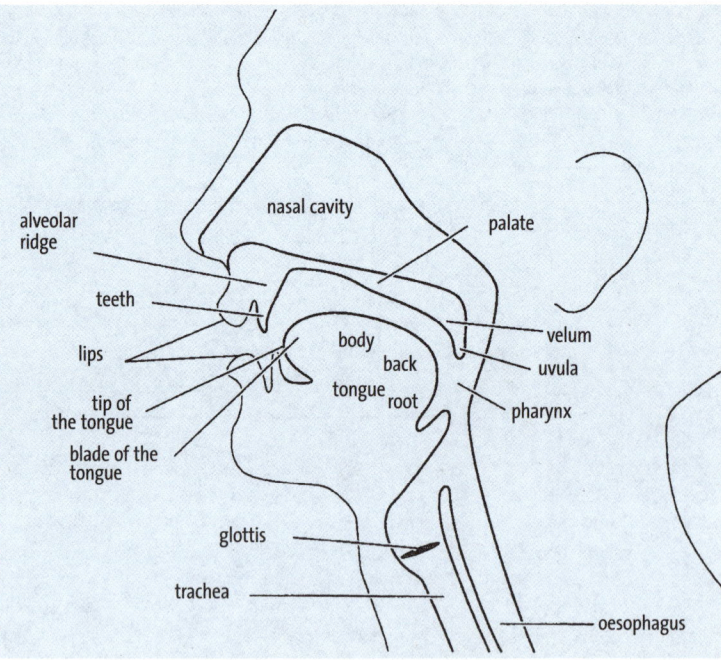

Description and Classification of Consonants and Vowels | 3.1.2

All speech sounds used by the world's many languages fall into two natural classes, namely **consonants** and **vowels**. The fundamental phonetic difference between these two types is that consonantal sounds are articulated with a narrow or complete closure in the vocal tract, whereas vowels are produced without any obstruction of the airstream.

As we have seen above, all English speech sounds are produced with a pulmonic egressive airstream mechanism. When we articulate a consonant, **the airstream is partially or fully obstructed** by some of the articulators in the vocal tract. The **description and classification of consonants** includes **three different criteria**:

Consonants

| Fig. 3.5

	criterion	possibilities
1)	**state of the glottis**	voiceless or voiced (cf. fortis and lenis below)
2)	**place of articulation**	bilabial, labiodental, (inter-)dental, alveolar, postalveolar, retroflex, palatal, velar, uvular, pharyngeal, glottal
3)	**manner of articulation**	plosive (or stop), nasal, trill, tap or flap, fricative, affricate, lateral fricative, approximant, lateral approximant

The description and classification of consonants

The air for the production of pulmonic sounds passes from the lungs through the **glottis**, which is the **opening between the vocal folds** in the larynx. When the glottis is narrow and the vocal folds are held close together, the air causes the vocal folds to vibrate; the resulting sounds are said to be **voiced**. When the glottis is open and the vocal folds are pulled apart, the airstream passes through the vocal folds without causing them to vibrate; the resulting sounds in this case are referred to as **voiceless**.

States of the Glottis

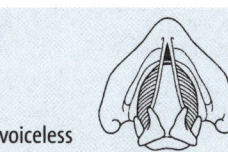
voiceless
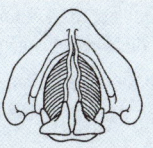
voiced

| Fig. 3.6

States of the glottis: voiced vs. voiceless (O'Grady et al. 2004:19)

There is a simple test to find out whether a sound is voiced or voiceless: touch a finger to the larynx or close your ears with your fingers while you produce a sound. You should be able to sense the difference in vibration concerning the first sounds of the words *zeal* and *seal* or *fan* and *van* respectively.

The contrast between voiceless and voiced sounds is usually accompanied by a difference in the force with which the airstream is pushed up from the lungs. Voiceless sounds are made with strong breath force and are thus called **fortis** (Latin 'hard'). Voiced sounds, on the other hand, are usually made with comparatively weak force and are referred to as **lenis** (Latin 'soft') sounds. Some linguists use the fortis versus lenis contrast instead of the voiceless versus voiced contrast for the description of consonants. We will employ the more commonly used distinction between voiceless and voiced consonants here, keeping in mind that there is in most cases a symmetrical relationship between voiceless versus voiced and fortis versus lenis.

Place of Articulation

In describing and classifying a consonant, it is also important to state **the exact place where the airstream is obstructed**. The **place of articulation** is usually labelled using the names of the articulators that approach each other or make contact while producing a consonant (cf. Fig. 3.4); we start at the front of the vocal tract and move backwards:

Fig. 3.7

place of articulation	production	examples
bilabial	produced by bringing both lips together	[p], [b], [m]
labiodental	made with the lower lip against the upper front teeth	[f], [v]
dental	produced with the tip of the tongue placed against or near the upper teeth, or between the front teeth (then also interdental)	[θ], [ð]
alveolar	articulated with the tip of the tongue at or near the small ridge behind the upper front teeth called the alveolar ridge	[t], [d], [s], [z], [n], [l]
postalveolar	made with the tongue approaching or touching the rear of the alveolar ridge or the area just behind it	[ʃ], [ʒ]
retroflex	articulated with the tip of the tongue curled back to come near or make contact with the hard palate	[ʈ]

palatal	made with the front of the tongue near or at the hard palate	[c], [j]
velar	produced by raising the back of the tongue to the velum (or soft palate)	[k], [g], [ŋ], [x]
uvular	made by moving the back or root of the tongue to the uvula	[ʀ]
pharyngeal	produced by retracting the root of the tongue into the pharynx	[ħ]
glottal	articulated by the vocal folds in the larynx	[h], [ʔ]

Place of articulation

Different sounds that share the same place of articulation are called **homorganic**. [p] and [b] are both bilabial sounds and are thus referred to as homorganic.

The third criterion used to provide unique and unambiguous descriptions of consonants is the so-called **manner of articulation**. We do not only have to state where the airflow is obstructed but also have to describe **the type or degree of closure** of the organs of speech involved, i.e. **how the airstream is modified** in the vocal tract to produce a certain consonant.

Manner of Articulation

| Fig. 3.8 |

manner of articulation	*production*	*examples*
plosive (or **stop**)	the speaker blocks (or stops) the airstream by forming a **complete closure** with the articulators, builds up air pressure and finally releases the air suddenly or "explosively" through the mouth	[p], [b], [t], [d], [k], [g], [ʔ]
fricative	a continuous airstream forces its way through a very narrow opening between the articulators and thereby produces audible **friction**	[f], [v], [θ], [ð], [s], [z], [ʃ], [ʒ], [h]
affricate	a single sound that is a **combination of a plosive and a fricative**; affricates begin with a complete closure and continue by slightly releasing the articulators, causing the air to escape relatively slowly through a narrow passage	[tʃ], [dʒ]
nasal	the velum is lowered so that the airstream partially or completely passes **through the nose**	[m], [n], [ŋ]
flap or tap	produced by striking the tongue quickly against the roof of the mouth, interrupting the flow of air very briefly	[ɾ]

trill	an articulator, such as the tongue-tip or the uvula, vibrates in the airstream	[r], [ʀ]
lateral fricative	the air escapes around the sides of a partial closure of the organs of speech through a narrow passage	[ɬ]
approximant	articulators approach but do not touch each other, leaving a wider opening than in the production of fricatives	[ɹ], [j], [w]
lateral approximant	made with air that escapes around the sides of a partial closure (like lateral fricatives), but no friction is produced as the opening is too wide (like approximants)	[l]

Manners of articulation

Some phoneticians assign consonants to two different groups, according to the degree of constriction in the vocal tract. Plosives, fricatives and affricates are said to be **obstruents**, as the airstream is either strongly or completely obstructed when they are articulated. The other types of consonants belong to the so-called **sonorants**, because they are produced with a relatively free airflow.

Three-Part Articulatory Description

Making use of these three major aspects of consonant description, we usually provide a **three-part articulatory description** in order to define a consonant precisely so that it cannot be confused with any other consonant. The **state of the glottis** (1) is mentioned first, followed by the **place of articulation** (2) and then the **manner of articulation** (3).

Example

Let us take the first sound in *van*, transcribed phonetically as [v], as an example: (1) When we touch our throat while we are producing this sound, we can feel our vocal cords vibrate, i.e. the sound is voiced. (2) The lower lip is placed against the upper front teeth, i.e. the place of articulation is labiodental. (3) The air forces its way through the very narrow opening between the lower lip and the upper front teeth producing audible friction, i.e. concerning the manner of articulation the sound is without doubt a fricative. The unique three-part articulatory description of [v] is thus: a *voiced labiodental fricative*.

In contrast to consonants, vowels are **articulated without any obstruction of the airstream** in the vocal tract. Vowels are essentially **always voiced** and **more sonorous than consonants**, i.e. they have a fuller tone than consonants and are perceived as louder and longer lasting.

Vowels

So how do we distinguish between different vowels? We need a completely different set of characteristics from the one we used for the description and classification of consonants. Vowels differ in **quantity**: they can be **short** or **long** (in the terminology of some phoneticians short vowels are referred to as **lax** and long vowels are referred to as **tense** vowels). Vowels also differ in **quality**, depending for the most part on the movements of the tongue: different parts of the tongue may be raised or lowered to modify the airstream in the vocal tract and the lips may be rounded or unrounded in order to produce different vowel qualities. The **description and classification of vowels** consists of the following **three criteria**:

| Fig. 3.9

	criterion	possibilities
1)	**height of the tongue (or: closeness)**	high (close), mid-high (close-mid), mid-low (open-mid) and low (open)
2)	**part of the tongue**	front, central and back
3)	**position of the lips**	rounded or unrounded

The description and classification of vowels

Some descriptions distinguish a fourth parameter, namely the position of the velum, i.e. the difference between **oral vowels**, produced with the velum raised and air escaping only through the mouth, and **nasal vowels**, produced with the velum lowered and some of the air passing through the nasal cavity. We will not employ this distinction here, as all English vowels are usually orals.

Vowels are also differentiated into **monophthongs** (or simple vowels or pure vowels) and **diphthongs** (or gliding vowels, because they exhibit a change in quality as they glide from one articulation to another during the production of the vowel).

Height of the Tongue

When phoneticians describe vowels they first look at the **height of the tongue** (or **closeness**). This parameter is used to describe **how high the tongue is raised** in the oral cavity (or **how close the tongue is placed with reference to the roof of the mouth**) to produce a certain vowel. We distinguish **high, mid-high, mid-low** and **low** or use the corresponding terms **close, close-mid, open-mid** and **open**. The two systems of terms are frequently used interchangeably, with high corresponding to close, mid-high to close-mid, mid-low to open-mid, and low to open. Both systems are presented as alternatives in the vowel charts in Fig. 3.15.

Part of the Tongue

The second element of a vowel description is the **part of the tongue** involved in the articulation. This parameter refers to the horizontal axis and tells us **which part of the tongue is raised** most to produce a certain vowel. On the horizontal axis three parts of the tongue are relevant for the articulation of vowels: the **front**, **central** and **back** areas.

Height of tongue and part of tongue are of course only relative terms. In order to describe and classify any vowel of any given language, we need a system with fixed points of reference against which the parameters of tongue height and tongue part can be measured. For this purpose, the English phonetician Daniel Jones (1881-1967) established a system of 18 numbered reference vowels, the so-called **cardinal vowels**. These artificial vowels mark the extreme positions of vowel articulation possible in the oral cavity and serve as reference points for all naturally occurring vowels. They are arranged in a **vowel chart** that reflects the space in the oral cavity where vowels are produced, as shown in Fig. 3.10. For example, cardinal number one [i] is the highest possible front vowel, with the front of the tongue raised as close to the roof of the mouth as possible without obstructing the airstream. Cardinal number five [ɑ], on the other hand, is the lowest possible back vowel. The cardinal vowels appear in pairs, with the symbol on the right representing a rounded vowel and the symbol on the left representing an unrounded vowel.

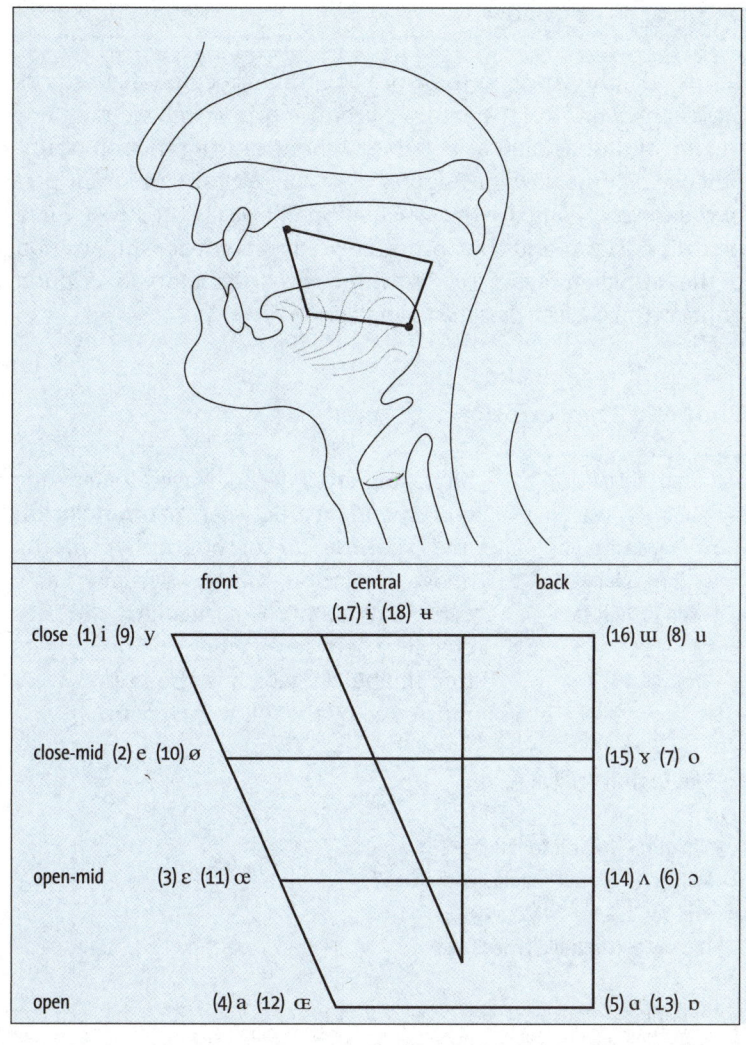

Fig. 3.10

The cardinal vowel chart (drawing from Davis 2007:35)

Vowel quality also depends on the **position of the lips**. Vowels are said to be **unrounded** when they are articulated with the lips in a neutral position, whereas vowels are referred to as **rounded** when they are produced with the lips pursed.

Position of the Lips

When describing vowels, we usually provide a **three-part articulatory description**. The **height of the tongue** (1) is mentioned first, followed by the **part of the tongue** (2) and then the **position of the lips** (3).

Three-Part Articulatory Description

Let us take the vowel in the word *feel*, transcribed phonetically as [iː], as an example: (1) When we produce this vowel, we raise our tongue almost as high as possible without causing friction or turbulence, i.e. the vowel is high or close. (2) We raise the front part of the tongue; compare the articulation of *fool*. (3) The lips are in a neutral position and thus unrounded; also compare the position of the lips when saying *fool*. The three-part articulatory description of [iː] is thus: a *high/close front unrounded* vowel.

3.1.3 | Phonetic Transcription

"The English have no respect for their language, [...]. They spell it so abominably that no man can teach himself what it sounds like. [...] German and Spanish are accessible to foreigners: English is not accessible even to Englishmen."

(George Bernard Shaw. 1916. *Pygmalion*. New York: Brentano. Preface)

Most languages do not have a one-to-one correspondence between **pronunciation and spelling** (or **orthography**). In the above quotation, George Bernard Shaw complains about the particularly wide discrepancy between spelling and pronunciation in English, which is also impressively illustrated by the following poem:

The English Tongue

When the English tongue we **speak**,
Why is **break** not rhymed with **freak**?
Will you tell me why it's **true**;
We say **sew** but likewise **few**;

And the maker of a **verse**;
Cannot rhyme his **horse** with **worse**?
Beard sounds not the same as **heard**;
Cord is different from the **word**;

Cow is **cow**, but low is **low**;
Shoe is never rhymed with **foe**.
Think of **hose** and **dose** and **lose**;
And of **goose** and also **choose**;

Think of **tomb** and **bomb** and **comb**;
Doll and **roll** and **some** and **home**.
And since **pay** is rhymed with **say**,
Why not **paid** with **said**, I **pray**?

We have **blood** and **food** and **good**;
Mould is not pronounced like **could**;
Wherefore **done** but **gone** and **lone**?
Is there any reason **known**?

I shall wonder ever **after**;
Why **slaughter** doesn't rhyme with **laughter**;
Thus in short, it seems to me,
Sounds and letters disagree.

Phonetic Transcription

The poem shows that we cannot rely on the traditional alphabetical spelling system when it comes to pronunciation in Present Day English. This means that we need a separate transcription system to represent speech sounds in writing, for example in dictionaries or textbooks for language learners. In such a system each sound must always be represented by the same symbol and there must be a separate symbol for each sound. **Phonetic transcription** provides such a system of one-to-one correspondence between sounds and symbols, the so-called **phonetic symbols**. Phonetic symbols are always enclosed in **square brackets** [ ] to distinguish them from letters, which are enclosed in **angled brackets < >**.

A whole set of phonetic symbols forms a **phonetic alphabet**. The best-known system that provides phonetic symbols for the sounds of any language is the **International Phonetic Alphabet (IPA)** (you will find a complete IPA chart on the inside of the front cover of this book). Most symbols of the IPA are similar to letters from the Roman alphabet, but the IPA also includes symbols from a variety of other sources. The IPA is used, with minor modifications, in most English-language dictionaries and other reference works. In many American publications, however, different transcription systems are used. The IPA is for the most part based on articulatory phonetics, i.e. the phonetic transcription of consonants and vowels depends on the way they are produced.

Consonant Transcription

The **IPA consonant chart** reflects the three-part articulatory description of consonants. Places of articulation are arranged on the horizontal axis and manners of articulation are placed along the vertical axis. Within the grid squares, voiceless consonants are positioned on the left and voiced sounds on the right:

Fig. 3.11

Manner of Articulation	Place of Articulation: Bilabial	Labio-dental	Dental	Alveolar	Post-alveolar	Retroflex	Palatal	Velar	Uvular	Pharyngeal	Glottal
Plosive	p b			t d		ʈ ɖ	c ɟ	k g	q ɢ		ʔ
Nasal	m	ɱ		n		ɳ	ɲ	ŋ	ɴ		
Trill	ʙ			r					ʀ		
Tap or Flap				ɾ		ɽ					
Fricative	ɸ β	f v	θ ð	s z	ʃ ʒ	ʂ ʐ	ç ʝ	x ɣ	χ ʁ	ħ ʕ	h ɦ
Lateral Fricative				ɬ ɮ							
Approxi-mant		ʋ		ɹ		ɻ	j	ɰ			
Lateral Approxi-mant				l		ɭ	ʎ	ʟ			

The IPA consonant chart (adapted from International Phonetic Association 1999:ix)
Symbols printed in blue indicate consonants used in RP or GenAm. Areas shaded in grey denote articulations judged impossible.

Consonants of English

Like all other languages, English does not make use of all consonants in the IPA chart. The following chart shows the most important consonants used in either **Received Pronunciation** (**RP**), long considered to be the most prestigious accent of British English, or in **General American** (**GenAm**), an idealization over a group of accents in the United States excluding Eastern and Southern accents, or in both. The consonants are grouped according to their manner of articulation. The four fricatives [s], [z], [ʃ] and [ʒ] form a subclass called **sibilants**.

Fig. 3.12

plosives					
[p]	*sport, supper, cup*	[t]	*stick, mostly, fit*	[k]	*skin, stick, unique*
[b]	*bite, bubble, globe*	[d]	*down, ladder, loved*	[g]	*get, bigger, egg*

nasals					
[m]	*mind, summer, sum*	[n]	*now, wind, sun*	[ŋ]	*singer, sung*

trill	
[r]	*right, true* (not in RP, but used in Scottish English in words such as *rat* and *true*)

tap or flap	
[ɾ]	*butter, rider* (not in RP, common in GenAm)

fricative					
[f]	*fun, office, photograph*	[θ]	*thick, ether, teeth*	[s]	*sit, descent, kiss*
[v]	*van, oven, prove*	[ð]	*these, either, teethe*	[z]	*zero, busy, jazz*
[ʃ]	*ship, nation, fish*	[ʒ]	*genre, vision, rouge*	[h]	*hat, who, behind*

approximants					
[ɹ]	*right, true* (common)	[ɻ]	*right, true* (GenAm)	[j]	*yes, view, few*

lateral approximants					
[l]	*light, silly*				

Consonants of English

Three other consonants of English that are not part of the IPA consonant chart but can nevertheless be accounted for by IPA symbols have to be mentioned. The consonants in question are represented by the symbols [w], [tʃ] and [dʒ].

[w] as in *water* is described as a **voiced labial-velar approximant**. It is special in that it has two places of articulation and does thus not fit into any of the squares of the IPA consonant chart. [w] and [j] both belong to the class of approximants and share some vowel-like qualities, as the air passes rather freely through the vocal tract when they are articulated. In fact, from a purely phonetic point of view these sounds are rather vowels than consonants. So why do we include them with the consonants? We will see below that [w] and [j] function like consonants in English and thus take an intermediate position between vowels and consonants (cf. 3.2.2). This is why they are frequently referred to as **semi-vowels** or **glides**.

[tʃ] and [dʒ] are so-called **affricates**, i.e. each of them is a single sound consisting of a combination of a plosive and a fricative (cf. 3.1.2). [tʃ] occurs in words like *church*, *feature* and *rich*. The voiced counterpart [dʒ] occurs in words such as *judge*, *magic* and *George*. — North American consonant descriptions differ from IPA mostly with respect to these affricates and the involved fricatives: [ʃ], [ʒ], [tʃ] and [dʒ] are usually transcribed as [š], [ž], [č] and [ǰ] respectively.

Some other important symbols from the IPA chart will be explained in the following table:

Fig. 3.13

plosives	
[ʔ]	• this sound is referred to as **glottal stop** • frequent in some accents of English, e.g. in Cockney: *bottle, what* • in Standard German this sound is always used at word boundaries when the following word starts with a vowel
fricatives	
[ç]	• not used in English • the final sound in the High German pronunciation of the word *ich* 'I'
[x]	• not used in RP or GenAm • found in the Scottish English pronunciation of words like *loch* • the final sound in the German pronunciation of the word *ach* 'alas'
[ʁ]	• not used in English • the first sound in the German pronunciation of the word *Rad* 'wheel' • the first sound in French *riz* 'rice'

Some other important consonant symbols

Vowel Transcription

Just like the IPA consonant system, the **IPA vowel chart** is based on articulatory description and thus on the cardinal vowel chart discussed above. It reflects the three-part articulatory description of vowels: the height of the tongue or closeness is arranged on the vertical axis and the part of the tongue involved in the articulation is shown on the horizontal axis. Lip rounding is indicated for the sounds that appear in pairs; the symbol to the right always represents a rounded vowel.

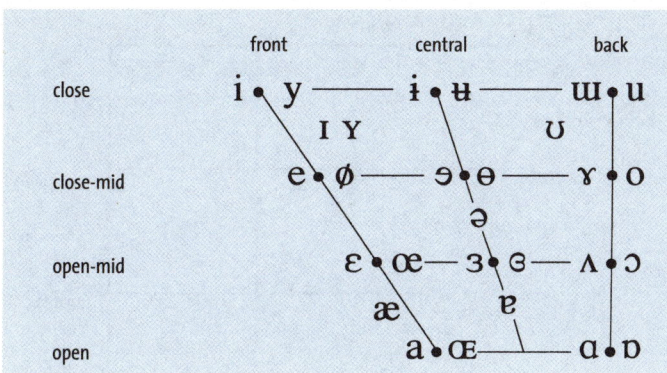

Fig. 3.14

The IPA vowel chart (International Phonetic Association 1999:ix)

Vowels of English

Of the numerous vowels included in the IPA vowel chart only a limited number are used in English. We will first look at the **monophthongs** of English before we turn our attention to the numerous **diphthongs**. The monophthongs of English can be distinguished into short and long vowels. These types, however, are not only distinguished by vowel length, but also by vowel quality, i.e. the positions of the tongue are different. Long vowels are usually followed by a **length mark** that consists of two vertical dots, although the length marks are not necessarily required in the IPA system because of the qualitative difference between, for example, [i] and [ɪ]. The monophthongs of RP and GenAm are thus as follows:

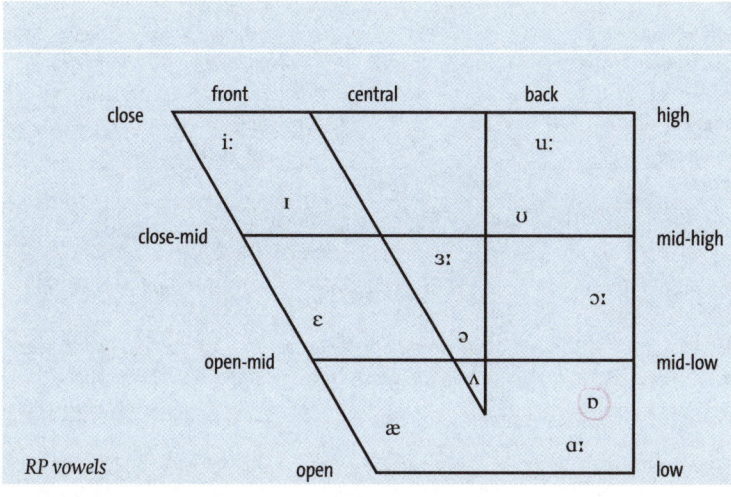

Fig. 3.15

RP and GenAm vowels (adapted from Meyer 2005:96-97, cf. Bibliography of Chapter 1)

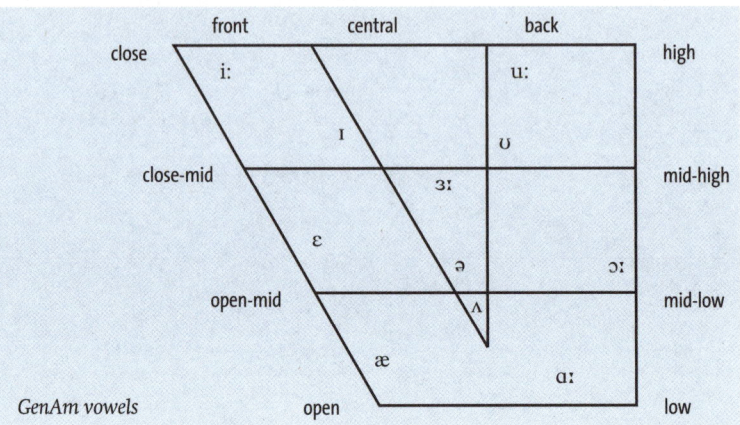

GenAm vowels

We can see in the above charts that vowel qualities are only approximate indications and the same symbol may represent slightly different vowel qualities in different languages or varieties of the same language. According to these vowel charts we can identify the following short and long vowels for RP and GenAm.

Fig. 3.16

IPA	three-part articulatory description	RP		GenAm	
		Short Vowels of English			
[ɪ]	mid-high high front unrounded	*bit, sin, income*			
[ɛ]	mid front unrounded	*let, guest*			
[æ]	mid-low low front unrounded		*bat, van*		*dance*
[ə]	mid central unrounded (always unstressed)	*teacher*	*about, bottom*	[ɚ] or [ər] *teacher*	
[ʌ]	mid-low central unrounded	*but, son*			
[ʊ]	mid-high high back rounded	*put, book*			
[ɒ]*	mid-low low back rounded	*pot, what*		–	
		Long Vowels of English			
[iː]	high front unrounded	*fee, tea, cream*			
[ɜː]	mid-high central unrounded	*bird, firm*		[ɝː] or [ɜːr] *bird, firm*	
[uː]	high back rounded	*food, two*			
[ɔː]	mid-low back rounded	*north, war, thought*		[ɔˑ] or [ɔːr] *north, war*	
[ɑː]	low back unrounded	*car, dance*	*father*	*pot,* [ɑˑ] or [ɑːr] *car*	

* RP only

Short and long vowels of English

In all of the above vowels, the so-called monophthongs, the vowel quality remains more or less constant throughout the production of the vowel, because the articulators stay in the same position. **Diphthongs** (or **gliding vowels**), on the other hand, are vowels that change their quality during their articulation. The articulators move or glide from one vowel position to another, changing the height of tongue, sometimes the part of tongue and sometimes lip rounding. This is why the transcription of diphthongs consists of a combination of two vowel symbols. For example, the vowel sound in *boy* is transcribed as [ɔɪ], i.e. first the back of the tongue is raised to a mid-low position and the lips are rounded, before the front of the tongue moves to a mid-high high position and the lips are unrounded.

There are **two different types of diphthongs in English**: (1) **Closing diphthongs**, which end in an [ɪ]-like or [ʊ]-like quality. This means that they rise to a rather close (or high) position towards the end of their articulation. (2) **Centring diphthongs**, which end in an [ə]-like quality that results from the loss of [ɹ] in the historical development of RP in words like *beer*. These diphthongs are all absent from GenAm, which is r-pronouncing (or rhotic). The following charts illustrate the articulatory movement during the pronunciation of the English diphthongs:

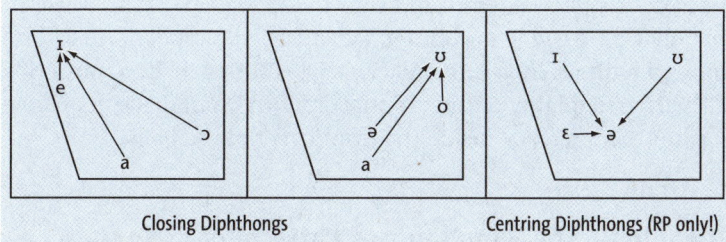

Closing Diphthongs   Centring Diphthongs (RP only!)

| **Fig. 3.17**

English diphthongs

The diphthongs depicted in these charts can be summarised and exemplified as follows:

Fig. 3.18

Closing Diphthongs rising to [ɪ]					
[eɪ]	*say, plate*	[aɪ]	*fly, pie, rye*	[ɔɪ]	*boy, toy*
Closing Diphthongs rising to [ʊ]					
[aʊ]	*how, loud*	[əʊ]	*bone, load* (RP only!)	[oʊ]	*bone, load* (GenAm only!)
Centring Diphthongs ending in [ə] (RP only!)					
[ɪə]	*here, beer*	[ɛə]	*hair, swear*	[ʊə]	*tour*

RP and GenAm diphthongs

Diacritics

So far we have encountered the IPA symbols for consonants and vowels. Occasionally, our phonetic transcription has to be more precise or we need to represent sounds slightly different from what we find in the IPA charts. In these cases we can modify the IPA symbols by the addition of little extra symbols, so-called **diacritics**. Diacritics are usually placed above, below or behind an IPA symbol. For example, we can show the extra puff of air immediately following the first sound in *pit* by adding a diacritic symbol: [pʰɪt]; we say that the initial [p] is aspirated. When a speaker does not release the closure at the end of the same word, another diacritic may be added to indicate the lack of plosion: [pʰɪt̚]. In section 3.2.1 we will encounter a velarised variant [ɫ] of the lateral approximant, as in *fool*; the diacritic [~] is added to [l] to transcribe the velarised quality of the sound. For a full list of diacritics please consult the IPA chart inside the front cover of the book.

3.2 | Phonology: The Function and Patterning of Sounds

Phonology is **"[a] branch of linguistics which studies the sound systems of languages. Out of the very wide range of sounds the human vocal apparatus can produce, and which are studied by phonetics, only a relatively small number are used distinctively in any one language."** (Crystal 2003:350)

Phonology is **concerned with the speakers' knowledge of the sound system of one specific language**. It is the branch of linguistics that studies the sounds used by a given language, the so-called **sound inventory**, and investigates the **function and (mental) organisation of these sounds** in the specific language in question.

There are **two branches of phonology**:

Fig. 3.19

	branch	field of study
1)	segmental phonology	Segmental phonology examines the function of **individual sounds** in a language, the so-called **segments**.
2)	suprasegmental phonology	Suprasegmental phonology is concerned with those **features of pronunciation that extend over more than one segment**.

Two branches of phonology

Segmental Phonology

3.2.1

When we split up our utterances into the individual sounds they are made up of, we identify the **segments**, hence the name **segmental phonology**. Unlike phonetics, segmental phonology is not concerned with the exact properties of speech sounds but with the function of these individual sounds in a certain language.

The speakers of a language know, consciously or unconsciously, which segments of their language **distinguish meaning**. For example, the words *light* and *bite* are distinguished only by their first sound (note that spelling is not important here!). The initial sounds in [laɪt] and [baɪt] are thus said to **contrast** (or to be **distinctive,** or to be **in opposition**). Contrasting units like this are called **phonemes** and form the basis of phonology. Phonemes are defined as **the smallest meaning-distinguishing units** in language.

Phonemes and Allophones

In order to identify the phonemes used by a particular language, as we have seen above, we have to find pairs of words that differ in only one sound and are different in meaning. These pairs are referred to as **minimal pairs**, the method is called the **minimal pair test**. We can identify both consonant and vowel phonemes with the help of this test. Other minimal pairs are for example: *fun* and *sun*, *sun* and *sum* or *sung*, *fish* and *fit*, *fee* and *tea*, *bit* and *but* or *bat*, and *sin* and *son*. All these contrasting sounds identified by the minimal pair test form the **phoneme inventory** of a language.

Fig. 3.20

Consonant phonemes of	
RP/GenAm	/p, b, t, d, k, g, f, v, θ, ð, s, z, ʃ, ʒ, tʃ, dʒ, h, m, n, ŋ, l, r, j, w/
Monophthong phonemes of	
RP	/iː, ɑː, uː, ɔː, ɜː, ɪ, ɛ, æ, ʊ, ʌ, ə, ɒ/
GenAm	/iː, ɑː, uː, ɔː, ɜː, ɪ, ɛ, æ, ʊ, ʌ, ə/
Diphthong phonemes of	
RP	/eɪ, aɪ, ɔɪ, aʊ, əʊ, ɪə, ɛə, ʊə/
GenAm	/eɪ, aɪ, ɔɪ, aʊ, oʊ/

The phoneme inventory of English

However, not all sounds that are phonetically different distinguish meaning in English and appear in minimal pairs. For example, most learners of English as a second or foreign language are taught at some point that there are two different "kinds of l" in many accents of English, namely the *clear l* and the *dark l*. The *clear l* is phonetically transcribed as [l] and occurs before a vowel or [j], e.g. in the words *lift* and *failure*. The *dark l*, on the other hand, is a velarised variant of the alveolar lateral approximant phonetically transcribed as [ɫ]. It is pronounced with an additional raising of the back of the tongue towards the velum, hence the name *velarised*, and occurs before a consonant or before silence, e.g. in words like *silk* and *feel*.

Fig. 3.21

Articulation of clear l vs. dark l

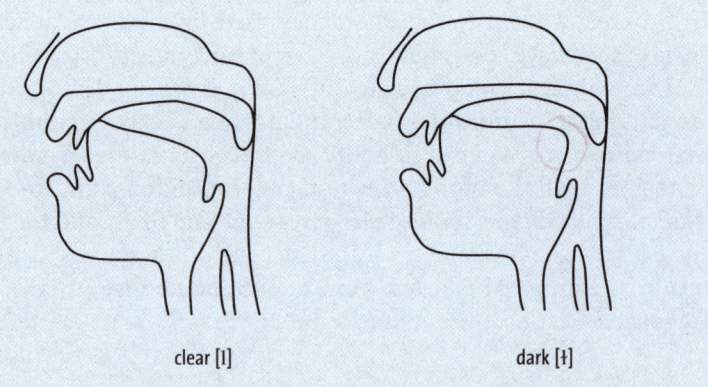

clear [l]   dark [ɫ]

In English, [l] obviously cannot occur where [ɫ] occurs and vice versa. This means that there cannot be any minimal pairs concerning [l] and [ɫ] and that they do not distinguish meaning in English. Native speakers will usually not be aware that there is a phonetic difference between the two sounds at all, to their mind they are the same sound. We can conclude that different phones that (1) **do not distinguish meaning** (or **are non-contrastive**), are (2) **regarded as "the same" sound** and are (3) **phonetically similar** are said to be **allophones** of the same phoneme. Allophones are thus different phonetic realisations (or phonetic variants) of what speakers of a language automatically and unconsciously group together into an abstract phonological unit called the phoneme. It is a convention that **phonemic symbols are enclosed by slashes / /**, whereas allophones are phonetic realisations and are as such enclosed by square brackets. We can conclude that [l] and [ɫ] are allophones of the phoneme /l/ in English:

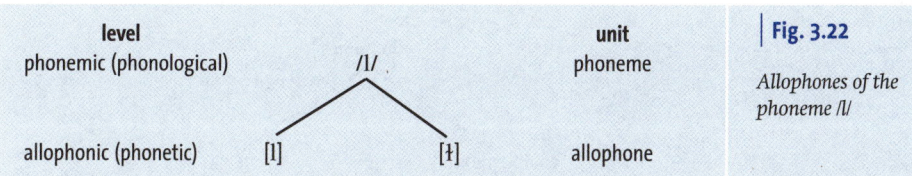

level		unit
phonemic (phonological)	/l/	phoneme
allophonic (phonetic)	[l] [ɫ]	allophone

Fig. 3.22

Allophones of the phoneme /l/

We have seen above that there are at least two allophones of /l/ in English and that the *clear l* [l] cannot occur where the velarised *dark l* [ɫ] occurs and vice versa. In cases like this, the occurrence (or **distribution**) of the different allophones is determined by the place within a word they can occur in and by the surrounding sounds, the so-called **phonetic context** (or **environment**). Since one of the allophones cannot occur where the other one does, we can say that their distribution is **predictable**. The two variants complement each other and are said to be in **complementary distribution**.

Distribution of Allophones

Fig. 3.23

/l/	distribution		
	before vowels and [j]	before consonants	before silence
[l]	yes	no	no
[ɫ]	no	yes	yes

The distribution of clear l vs. dark l

However, allophones do not always have to be in complementary distribution. The word-final voiceless bilabial plosive in words such as *ship* or *leap* may be realised in at least three different ways: (1) as [p], as in [ʃɪp] and [liːp], (2) with aspiration, transcribed as [pʰ], as in [ʃɪpʰ] and [liːpʰ], and (3) without release of the closure, transcribed as [p̚], i.e. [ʃɪp̚] and [liːp̚] (cf. 3.1.3: diacritics). The use of either of the three variants does not constitute a change of meaning. Generally speaking, we frequently have the choice between two or more different sounds that — like [p], [pʰ] and [p̚] — **occur in the same environment** and are not separate phonemes as they **do not distinguish meaning**, are **regarded as "the same" sound** and are **phonetically similar.** These allophones are said to be in **free variation.** [p], [pʰ] and [p̚] are thus **free variants** of the phoneme /p/.

Fig. 3.24

The distribution of allophones

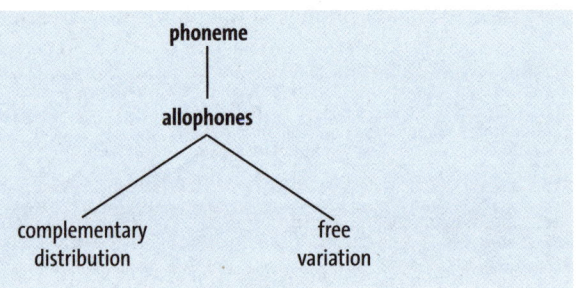

Some authors prefer another system that has a different two-way distinction: (1) allophones, which are by definition in complementary distribution, are opposed to (2) free variants. We will, however, not employ this system in this book.

Allophonic variation occurs in all languages, but it is important to note that the patterning of phonemes and allophones is language-specific, i.e. two sounds may be allophones of the same phoneme in one language and realizations of two separate phonemes in another.

Example

The voiced alveolar flap, transcribed as [ɾ], is a very common pronunciation variant of the phoneme /t/ in American English in words such as *city*, whereas /t/ is realised as [t] in words like *team*. [t] and [ɾ] are thus allophones of the phoneme /t/ in English.

We have seen that there are two different ways to transcribe spoken language: (1) **phonemic** (or broad) **transcription**, which focuses on the language system, ignores some detail and for which we use slashes and (2) **phonetic** (or narrow) **transcription**, which represents the actual pronunciation with a great deal of detail and for which we use square brackets. For example, the phonemic transcription of the English word lull /lʌl/ does not indicate the opposition of the initial *clear l* and the final *dark l*, whereas the phonetic transcription [lʌɫ] clearly marks the difference. Similarly, the three different variants [p], [pʰ] and [p˺] in the word *ship* are not contrastive and are thus ignored by the phonemic transcription /ʃɪp/. Depending on the amount of detail we need for a certain linguistic discussion, we choose a broad or a narrow description, with which we can represent as much detail as needed by using diacritics.

Phonetic and Phonemic Transcription

As shown above, (allo)phones and phonemes belong to different levels of language structure. Speakers store abstract phonemic forms in their minds and apply **phonological rules** to them to translate these mental entities into actual speech sounds:

Phonological Rules

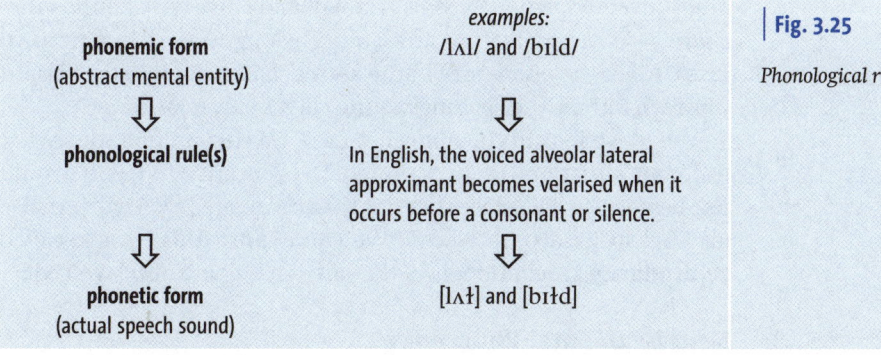

	examples:	
phonemic form (abstract mental entity)	/lʌl/ and /bɪld/	**Fig. 3.25** *Phonological rules*
⇩	⇩	
phonological rule(s)	In English, the voiced alveolar lateral approximant becomes velarised when it occurs before a consonant or silence.	
⇩	⇩	
phonetic form (actual speech sound)	[lʌɫ] and [bɪɫd]	

To describe the distribution of the allophones of /l/, the following phonological rule can be stated, trying to be as general as possible: [ɫ] occurs before consonants other than [j] and at the end of words; [l] occurs elsewhere.

When we look at minimal pairs such as *zeal* [ziːɫ] and *seal* [siːɫ] or *bid* [bɪd] and *bit* [bɪt], the only difference between the phoneme pairs /z/ and /s/, or /d/ and /t/, is a difference in voicing. With the place and manner of articulation being identical, voicing alone distinguishes the phonemes from each other. We are thus interested

Distinctive Features

in the presence, marked by plus (+), or absence, marked by (-), of the single **feature** of voicing. /z/ and /d/ are [+voiced] and /s/ and /t/ are [-voiced]. Features that distinguish one phoneme from another are called **distinctive features**. Individual sounds can be characterised by bundles of distinctive features, for example the voiced plosives in English:

Fig. 3.26

Distinctive features

	b	d	g
Plosive	+	+	+
Voiced (Lenis)	+	+	+
Labial	+	-	-
Alveolar	-	+	-
Velar	-	-	+

Each of the above phonemes differs from all the other phonemes in the chart by at least one distinctive feature. For example, /b/ and /d/ are both [+plosive, +voiced, and -velar], but /d/ is [-labial] and [+alveolar], whereas /b/ is [+labial] and [-alveolar]. Sounds that share at least one feature are said to belong to the same **natural class**. All of the phonemes in the above chart belong to the class of plosives, but only /d/ belongs to the class of alveolars.

When we look at the English nasals, we encounter a somewhat different situation. From a phonological point of view it would not be necessary to state that /m/, /n/ and /ŋ/ are [+voiced], because all English nasals are voiced. We can express this by a so-called **redundancy rule**: phonemes that are [+nasal] are also [+voiced].

3.2.2 | Suprasegmental Phonology

Phonology does not only deal with the individual segments speech is made up of. It also studies those phonological properties that extend over more than one segment, hence the name **suprasegmental phonology**. Suprasegmental phonology involves two different aspects: First, this type of phonology is concerned with the **combination of segments into larger units** such as **syllables**. Second, it studies the **phonological properties of longer stretches of speech** such as **stress, rhythm, tone** and **intonation**, often collectively referred to as **prosody**.

Syllables are **phonological units above the phoneme level** that can be vaguely defined as the smallest rhythmic unit of speech. Most people can intuitively count syllables in words without having an exact knowledge of what a syllable is. Words can consist of one syllable, i.e. they are **monosyllabic**, or two or more syllables, i.e. they are **polysyllabic**. The structure of a syllable is shown in the following figure with the monosyllabic word *stretch*:

Syllables

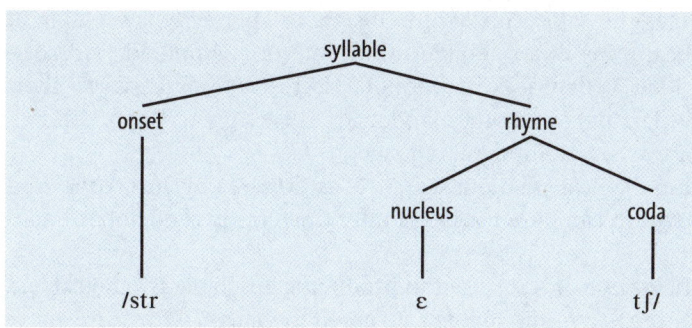

Fig. 3.27

Syllable structure

In English, all syllables contain a **nucleus** (or **peak**, **core** or **centre**) that is normally made up of a vowel. This vowel may be followed by a **coda** that consists of up to four consonants and is said to form the **rhyme** together with the nucleus. The nucleus may also be preceded by up to three consonants that form the **onset** of the syllable. Syllables that have an empty coda are referred to as **open syllables**, as opposed to the so-called **closed syllables**, which are "closed" by one or more consonants following the vowel.

Knowing about syllable structure now, we can add phonological aspects to our definition of vowels and consonants. **Vowels** are thus not only sounds that are produced without any obstruction of the airstream but **can also form the nucleus of a syllable**. In opposition to vowels, **consonants cannot form the nucleus of a syllable**. Occasionally, sonorant consonants can form a syllable by themselves in words such as *button* [bʌtn̩]; these consonants are called **syllabic** and indicated by the diacritic [ˌ]. **Semivowels** are special in that they are, on the one hand, **vowel-like in pronunciation** but, on the other hand, they can **never form the nucleus of a syllable** (cf. 3.1.3).

Suprasegmental phonology is also concerned with rules and restrictions regarding the combination of segments to form larger

Phonotactics

units such as syllables. The study of the possible combinations of phonemes in a language is referred to as **phonotactics**. All languages have such **sets of constraints** concerning the combination of phonemes, but the actual rules are language-specific and differ extensively between individual languages. English, for example, is fairly restrictive when it comes to the combination of consonants (or **consonant clusters**) at the beginning or at the end of syllables or words: /ps-/ and /kn-/ are not permissible onsets in English, whereas the same consonant clusters are perfectly acceptable at the beginning of a syllable in German, for example in *Psychologie* and *Knie*. Differences in phonotactic restrictions between their native language and other languages cause a great deal of difficulty for learners of foreign languages.

Prosody

Phonological phenomena such as **stress, rhythm, tone and intonation** can be subsumed under the term **prosody** of an utterance.

Stress and Rhythm

The degree of force used in producing a syllable is called **stress** (or **accent**). We distinguish **stressed** syllables, which are more prominent, and **unstressed syllables**, which are less prominent and often contain reduced vowels, such as /ə/ (schwa) and /ɪ/. The prominence of a syllable is achieved by increased loudness, frequently combined with increased length and higher pitch. Different types of stress play a role in English, most importantly **word stress** and **sentence stress**. In transcription, stress is marked by a raised vertical line ['] preceding the stress-bearing syllable.

In many languages, including English, the syllables of polysyllabic words are not pronounced with equal intensity. In longer polysyllabic words we can also distinguish **primary stress** ['] and **secondary stress** [ˌ]. Some languages have predictable stress placement, for example, stress is almost always placed on the first syllable of a word in Czech, on the next to last (or penultimate) syllable in Welsh and on the last syllable in French. The placement of **word stress in English**, however, is **generally not predictable**. This is mainly due to the fact that English has borrowed a large number of words from a multitude of languages in the course of its history (cf. 2.1). **Word stress can even be distinctive in English**, i.e. there are a number of minimal pairs that differ by stress placement only: for example, the word *import* is a noun when the stress is on the first syllable (RP: /ˈɪmpɔːt/) but a verb when the stress is on the second syllable (RP: /ɪmˈpɔːt/).

Sentence stress depends to a large part on the **rhythm**, i.e. on the distribution of stressed syllables in a sentence or an utterance. In many languages, stressed syllables occur in a sentence at fairly regular intervals of time. It does not matter how many unstressed syllables are between them. Languages such as English or German that have this kind of rhythm are said to be **stress-timed**. The opposite are languages like French or Italian, in which syllables are claimed to occur at rather regular intervals of time. The timing of these languages does not depend on whether the syllables are stressed or not. These languages are called **syllable-timed**. In English, many function words (such as determiners, auxiliaries, prepositions, pronouns and conjunctions) may carry no stress at all and become weakened (cf. 3.2.3). Sentence stress may also distinguish degrees of emphasis or contrast, as in *I would like some **strawberry** ice-cream*.

When we speak, our vocal folds can vibrate with different frequencies: the faster they vibrate, the higher the so-called **pitch**. All voiced speech sounds, particularly vowels, can thus be produced with different pitches. The role of pitch varies from language to language. In English, it does not make a big difference whether you say the word *beer* with a low pitch or a high pitch; it will still mean 'an alcoholic drink made from malt and flavoured with hops'. In many other languages, the meaning of a word can differ according to the pitch at which the syllables in the word are pronounced and the pitch movement within the word, the so-called pitch contour. These languages are called **tone languages** and include many African and Native American languages as well as many Asian languages such as Vietnamese, Thai or Chinese. In Mandarin Chinese /ma/ can mean, among other things, 'horse' and 'mother', depending on the tone. It can obviously have some very embarrassing consequences for foreign learners to get the tone wrong and there is even a tongue twister in Mandarin Chinese starting with *Mother is riding a horse*.

We will see that pitch does play a role in English, however, when we take a look at the phrase or sentence level. The pattern of rises and falls in pitch across a stretch of speech is called **intonation**. Languages that attach function to the pitch contour of a phrase or sentence are called **intonation languages**. In English, for example, intonation helps to mark the functions and boundaries of a syntactic unit and vaguely corresponds to punctuation in

Tone and Intonation

writing. Statements such as *She's gone* usually show a falling pattern towards the end of the phrase, whereas yes-no-questions such as *She's gone?* are characterised by a final rise. Intonation is also used to stress new information in an utterance or to express emotions and attitudes, for example interest, irony or sarcasm. It should be noted that there are not only differences in intonation between different languages but frequently also within the same language. The intonation patterns of RP and GenAm are markedly different in a number of respects.

3.2.3 | Connected Speech

So far, we have discussed the phenomena of phonetics and phonology mainly with the help of individual phones, phonemes, syllables and words. Except for sentence stress and intonation, we have not yet considered any of the processes and adjustments occurring in longer stretches of speech. We have looked at the forms of words the way they are pronounced in isolation, their so-called **citation form**, which is also the form we usually find in dictionaries. However, sounds and words undergo considerable changes when they occur in **connected speech**. We will now discuss the most important of these processes, namely **strong and weak forms**, **assimilation**, and **liaison**.

Strong and Weak Forms We already know from the section on stress above (cf. 3.2.2) that some words, especially function words, may carry no stress at all in an English sentence. The stressed (or accented) realizations of these words are termed **strong forms**, whereas the unstressed (or unaccented) versions are called **weak forms**. Weak forms are characterised by a **weakening** (or reduction) of the vowel to /ə/, /ɪ/ or /ʊ/ (recent studies suggest that the quality is often [i] rather than [ɪ] and [u] rather than [ʊ]), or an **elision** (or omission) of one or more sounds, or both. The weak form [əd] of *had* /hæd/ is the result of both the reduction of the vowel to [ə] and the elision of initial [h]. These changes are usually not reflected in spelling, with the exception of the contracted forms, for example *'m* or *'ve*, and fixed phrases such as *rock 'n' roll*. The following table is merely a selection of some of the most frequent weak forms:

| Fig. 3.28

	strong form	weak form(s)		strong form	weak form(s)
a	[eɪ]	[ə]	*have*	[hæv]	[(h)əv, ə, v]
am	[æm]	[(ə)m]	*he*	[hiː]	[(h)ɪ, hi, iː]
an	[æn]	[(ə)n]	*her*	[hɜː(r)]	[(h)ə(r), ɜː(r)]
and	[ænd]	[(ə)n(d)]	*me*	[miː]	[mɪ, mi]
are	[ɑː(r)]	[ər, ə, r]	*of*	[ɒv]	[əv, ə, v]
be	[biː]	[bɪ, bi]	*she*	[ʃiː]	[ʃɪ, ʃi]
but	[bʌt]	[bət]	*the*	[ðiː]	[ðə, ðɪ, ði]
can	[kæn]	[k(ə)n]	*they*	[ðeɪ]	[ðə]
do	[duː]	[də, dʊ, du, d]	*were*	[wɜː(r)]	[wə(r)]
had	[hæd]	[(h)əd, d]	*will*	[wɪl]	[(ə)l]
has	[hæz]	[(h)əz, z, s]	*you*	[juː]	[jʊ, ju]

Selected weak forms

The examples show that the realisation of different words can even become identical as a result of weakening and elision, for example *an* and *and* can both become /n/, and *the* and *they* can both be realised as /ðə/.

In connected speech, sounds often influence each other so that they become more like a neighbouring sound in terms of one or all of its articulatory features. This process is called **assimilation**. One of the main motivations for assimilation seems to be our wish to increase the ease of articulation (or minimise the effort) as we speak. When we pronounce, for example, the sequence *ten bats*, the usually alveolar nasal /n/ at the end of *ten* is realised as a bilabial nasal [m] because of the immediately following bilabial plosive /b/ in *bats*, i.e. the places of articulation become more alike. In cases like these, the assimilation moves backwards to the preceding segment, which is known as **regressive assimilation** (or **anticipatory assimilation**), because during the production of the preceding sound the organs of speech already anticipate the articulation of the following sound). Occasionally, but much rarer in English, one or more articulatory features of a preceding sound can influence the following sound. In phrases such as *Church Street*, the /s/ in *Street* can become identical with the /ʃ/ at the end of *Church*. This type of articulation is called **progressive** assimilation, because the assimilation moves forward to the following element. Assimilation by which sounds become more similar with each

Assimilation

other are called **partial assimilation**. When the assimilated sounds become identical we speak of **total assimilation**.

Another process that frequently occurs to increase the ease of articulation and improve fluidity is the insertion of a linking sound termed **liaison**. There are two well-known examples of liaison in English, particularly in RP and other so-called non-rhotic accents that do not normally articulate word-final *r* suggested by the spelling in words like *more* and *far*. A **linking r** is inserted only when the following word begins with a vowel, e.g. in phrases such as *far away* [fɑːr əweɪ]. Similarly, speakers of these accents often insert a so-called **intrusive r** between certain words, even when there is no <r> in the spelling, e.g. in phrases like *law and order* [lɔːrəndɔːdə].

3.3 | **Exercises**

1. Identify all the IPA symbols below which represent ...
  a)   plosives
  b)   fricatives
  c)   voiced sounds

[b]   [s]   [ʊ]   [w]   [ʃ]   [x]
[k]   [l]   [ɪ]   [θ]   [ŋ]   [d]

2. The following six drawings of the vocal tract depict the articulation of consonants of English. Identify the place and manner of articulation for each of the drawings. Then give the phonetic symbols of all English consonants which are produced in this way.

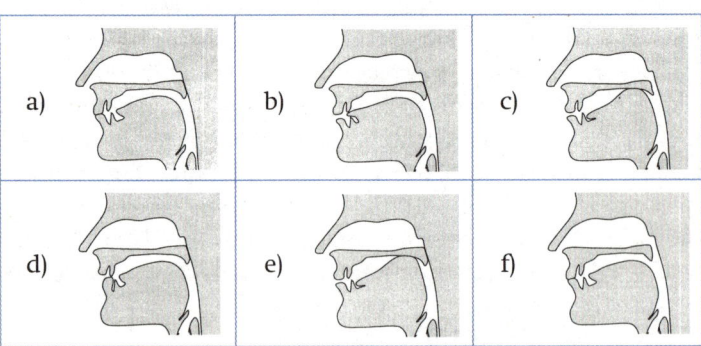

a)   b)   c)

d)   e)   f)

3. Which of the consonants in Exercise 2 are homorganic? Explain!

4. For each group of phones, state the articulatory feature or features they all share:
Example: [f], [s] and [x] are all fricatives and voiceless.

phones	feature(s)	phones	feature(s)
a) [m], [ŋ], [n]	_____	d) [f], [θ], [s], [ʃ]	_____
b) [k], [g], [ŋ], [x]	_____	e) [u], [i]	_____
c) [i], [e], [ɛ], [æ]	_____	f) [d], [n], [r], [l]	_____

5. After each of the following articulatory descriptions, write the corresponding phonetic symbol:
a) voiced alveolar fricative   [   ]
b) open-mid front unrounded vowel   [   ]
c) close back rounded vowel   [   ]
d) voiceless glottal plosive   [   ]
e) close-mid close front unrounded vowel   [   ]
f) voiceless postalveolar fricative   [   ]

6. Provide the articulatory description for the following phonetic symbols:
a) [ə]   b) [n]   c) [æ]   d) [t]   e) [ʊ]   f) [ɹ]

7. Give the conventional spelling or spellings for the following English words and phrases provided in broad transcription:

a)	/tʃiːt/	e)	/əˌsɪmɪˈleɪʃən/
b)	/sʌn/	f)	/lɪŋˈgwɪstɪks ɪz fʌn/
c)	/baɪt/	g)	/fəʊˈnetɪks tuː/
d)	/oʊld ˈɪŋglɪʃ/	h)	/ɪˈnʌf/

8. There are four main types of discrepancies between spelling and pronunciation in contemporary English, namely …
(1) the same spelling representing different sounds
(2) different spellings for the same sound
(3) the occurrence of so-called "silent letters" that are not pronounced at all
(4) the pronunciation of "phantom" letters not present in writing

All four types can be found in the poem *The English Tongue* on page 50-51. Please identify 2 examples each for types (1) through (3) and one example for type (4).

(Spelling is always put in angled brackets < >, whereas square brackets [ ] are placed around phonetic transcription.)

9. Find at least one further example for each of the four types of discrepancies between spelling and pronunciation mentioned in 8. Please do not take your example words from the poem!

10. The claim that *ghoti* could be an alternative spelling of *fish* is popularly attributed to George Bernard Shaw (1856-1950), Irish playwright and spelling-reform advocate. Think along the lines of Exercises 8 and 9 and explain how <ghoti> could theoretically represent [fɪʃ].

11. Find minimal pairs for the following pairs of English phonemes (Keep in mind that spelling is not important):

	phonemes	*minimal pair*
a)	/p/ - /b/	_____
b)	/iː/ - /uː/	_____
c)	/b/ - /m/	_____
d)	/n/ - /s/	_____
e)	/t/ - /d/	_____
f)	/ɪ/ - /æ/	_____

12. In Old English, [f] and [v] were in complementary distribution. Unlike Modern English, this means that [f] and [v] were allophones of the phoneme /f/ and that there were no minimal pairs involving these phones. Analyse the following data from the *Lord's Prayer* by looking at the phonetic environments and the position in which the allophones occur. Define the phonetic environments in which the two allophones of /f/ occur in Old English and try to state the resulting phonological rule, generalising as much as possible:

['fæder]   *fæder* 'father'
['heovon]   *heofon* 'heaven'
[hlaːf]   *hlaf* 'loaf (of bread)'
['yvele]   *yfele* 'evilly, badly'

Bibliography

Ashby, Patricia. 2005. *Speech Sounds*. 2nd edition. London. Routledge. *(A very manageable introduction to the description and classification of speech sounds)*

Carr, Philip. 1999. *English Phonetics and Phonology: An Introduction*. Malden: Blackwell. *(A concise but highly recommendable introduction to English phonetics and phonology)*

Clark, John & **Colin Yallop**. 2006. *An Introduction to Phonetics and Phonology*. 3rd edition. Oxford: Blackwell. *(A rather comprehensive introduction to phonetics and phonology)*

Crystal, David. 2008. *Dictionary of Linguistics and Phonetics*. 6th edition. Oxford. Blackwell. *(A comprehensive collection of linguistic and phonetic terminology)*

Davis, John F. 2007. *Phonetics and Phonology*. 7th edition. Stuttgart: Klett. *(A basic but very useful introduction to phonetics and phonology)*

Eckert, Hartwig & **William Barry**. 2005. *The Phonetics and Phonology of English Pronunciation*. 2nd edition. Trier: Wissenschaftlicher Verlag Trier. *(A self-study textbook for native speakers of German – with a CD-ROM)*

Giegerich, Heinz J. 1992. *English Phonology: An Introduction*. Cambridge: Cambridge University Press. *(Rather comprehensive overview of English phonetics and phonology)*

Gimson, Alfred C. 2008. *Gimson's Pronunciation of English*. 7th edition. Revised by Alan Cruttenden. London: Arnold. *(A comprehensive and systematic treatment of the pronunciation of English)*

International Phonetic Association. 1999. *Handbook of the International Phonetic Association: A Guide to the Use of the International Phonetic Alphabet*. Cambridge: Cambridge University Press. *(The comprehensive guide to the International Phonetic Alphabet)*

Jones, Daniel. 2006. *English Pronouncing Dictionary*. 17th edition. Edited by Peter Roach, James Hartman & Jane Setter. Cambridge: Cambridge University Press. *(A comprehensive and up-to-date guide to the pronunciation of English)*

McMahon, April. 2002. *An Introduction to English Phonology*. Edinburgh: Edinburgh University Press. *(A concise overview of English phonology)*

Pullum, Geoffrey K. & **William A. Laduslaw**. 1996. *Phonetic Symbol Guide*. 2nd edition. Chicago: University of Chicago Press. *(A comprehensive treatment of all phonetic symbols)*

Roach, Peter. 2001. *Phonetics*. Oxford: Oxford University Press. *(A very short introduction to phonetics)*

Roca, Iggy & **Wyn Johnson**. 1999a. *A Course in Phonology*. Malden: Blackwell. *(A comprehensive textbook on phonology)*

Roca, Iggy & **Wyn Johnson**. 1999b. *A Workbook in Phonology*. Malden: Blackwell. *(A workbook accompanying the textbook)*

Rogers, Henry. 2000. *The Sounds of Language: An Introduction to Phonetics*. Harlow: Pearson. *(A good overview of English phonetics and phonology)*

Skandera, Paul & **Peter Burleigh**. 2005. *A Manual of English Phonetics and Phonology: Twelve Lessons with an Integrated Course in Phonetic Transcription*. Tübingen: Narr. *(A very approachable and hands-on introduction to English phonetics and phonology – with a CD-ROM)*

Upton, Clive et al. 2003. *The Oxford Dictionary of Pronunciation for Current English*. Oxford: Oxford University Press. *(Paperback edition of this current and comprehensive record of the pronunciation of both British and American English)*

Wells, John C. 2008. *Longman Pronunciation Dictionary*. 3rd edition. Harlow: Pearson Longman. *(An up-to-date guide to the pronunciation of English)*

Interesting Links
Speech Accent Archive
<http://accent.gmu.edu>
International Dialects of English Archive
<http://web.ku.edu/~idea/>

Morphology $\mid$ **4**

Abstract

Morphology examines how words are created, structured and changed. When Johann Wolfgang von Goethe coined the word morphology (meaning 'the study of the form or shape') for a new science concerned with the anatomies of animals and plants at the end of the 18th century, he could not possibly predict that linguists would later adopt his term for the study of the "anatomy" of words. In this chapter, we will look at the forms and functions of the smallest meaning-bearing units of language known as morphemes and at the most relevant morphological processes.

4.1 | Morphology and Grammar

Talking about **morphology** means talking about **words** and their "anatomy". Morphology studies the internal structure of words. But what is a word? Consider the following sentence: *The students borrowed the books from the library.* How many words are there in this sentence? And how can we decide what to count? A first suggestion would be to consider the physical properties of the items in question, namely their spelling and their pronunciation. In written language, most **orthographic words** are preceded by a space and followed by a space or a punctuation mark. However, English words compounded of two or more elements may separate their elements either by hyphens or, confusingly, by spaces as well. You may try and replace *books* with the compound *morphology books* in the above example: From a linguistic point of view, the new sentence *The students borrowed the morphology books from the university library* contains just as many words as the first sentence, although there are more items between spaces. In spoken language, so-called **phonological words** are even less easy to recognise because speakers of English usually do not leave pauses between their words. Another suggestion for the identification of words would be to interpret them as **linguistic signs**, that is, as arbitrary combinations of a sound image such as /bʊk/ and a concept such as 📖. This works more smoothly with **content words** like *student*, *borrow*, *book* and *library* than with **function words** like *the* and *from* that can less easily be imagined. Additionally, according to a very general definition, words can be defined as grammatical units that function according to grammatical rules. Therefore, morphology is also called the **grammar of words**.

As you will have noticed, *students*, *books* and *borrowed* differ from *student*, *book* and *borrow* in that they contain the elements -*s* or -*ed*. These elements are not words but alter the meaning of *student*, *book* and *borrow* by adding grammatical information such as [+plural] or [+past], provided that they are attached at the appropriate place: Constructions such as *stu-s-dent, *s-book or *ed-borrow are not acceptable in English.

If we consult a dictionary of English to check the words in the sentence *The students borrowed the books from the library*, we will discover that the only items with entries of their own are *the*, *from* and *library*. We will neither find *students* nor *books*, nor will we find *borrowed*. Instead, we will find *student*, *book* and *borrow*. Most dictionaries will also inform us that *student* and *book* are nouns and that *borrow* is a verb. If we are native speakers or proficient non-native speakers of English, however, we do not need to consult any dictionary to understand the above sentence. We will simply use what linguists call our **mental dictionary**, or **mental lexicon**. Just as any written dictionary, our mental dictionary contains information about the meaning of words, combined with information about their grammatical properties.

How many words are there in the sentence *The students borrowed the books from the library*? Most speakers of English would probably opt for six, because they would count the function word *the* only once, although it occurs three times. However, journalists and other people who regularly have to produce texts with a maximum or minimum length, expressed in a fixed number of words, might rather opt for eight. The first interpretation corresponds to what linguists define as **word types**, i.e. 'particular words', whereas the second interpretation corresponds to what linguists define as **word tokens**, i.e. 'occurrences of words'. Imagine a political newspaper article containing twenty different nouns, such as *parliament*, *government*, *debate* and *opposition*. The **type frequency** of nouns in this newspaper article is exactly twenty, because these nouns represent twenty different word types. However, their **token frequency** will probably be much higher than twenty, because some of these nouns are likely to occur more than once, so that the token frequency of nouns in the whole article might be e.g. thirty-five nouns in various grammatical forms. Accordingly, our example sentence *The students borrowed the books from the library* contains only six word types, namely various grammatical forms of the four content words *student*, *borrow*, *book* and *library* and the two function words *the* and *from*, but eight word tokens, because the function word *the* appears three times.

Word Types and Word Tokens

Words are distinct from units of sound such as phonemes and syllables in that they carry meaning. They are also distinct from sentences in that they are stored in our mental lexicon as lexical entries, or **lexemes**. Other than sentences, words are usually not made up on demand. They may be grammatically modified for the production of grammatically correct sentences, but their lexicon entries will remain unchanged. However, speakers of English and other languages may create new words easily. In doing so they follow rules most of which they have never been taught. These

Words, Sounds and Sentences

rules are part of the speakers' linguistic competence. Linguists differ in their views as to whether the rules are stored together with individual lexemes or separately. Because we know these rules, no matter where exactly they are stored, we are able to understand spoken and written language even if there are obvious mistakes. Consider the following sign from a beach in North Tenerife:

Fig. 4.1

Playa peligrosa
Dangerous beach

The correct English translation of the Spanish warning *Playa peligrosa, fuertes corrientes* would be *Dangerous beach, strong currents*. The translator changed the order of the noun phrases and coined the expression *danger beach*, using the noun *danger* like an adjective, or like the first part of a compound noun composed of two nouns, such as *danger area*, *danger list* or *danger money*. Although *danger beach* is not a common English expression, other than the three compound nouns *danger area*, *danger list* or *danger money*, we are able to interpret this compound noun because we know and recognise the grammatical rules for combining words even if they are incorrectly applied.

Grammatical Rules

What else do we know about grammar? When we hear a word that is familiar to us, we know whether it is a noun, a verb, an adjective or a member of other word classes, and how it may be used to build larger constructions. We also know how we can modify a word if we want it to carry some particular grammatical information. For instance, we know that the regular plural of English nouns is formed by adding the ending -*s*. Therefore, we will form the plural of *e-mail* accordingly (even though the noun *mail* is chiefly used in the singular), for instance if we want to complain to a friend that somebody is currently flooding us with *e-mails*. We also know that the verb *e-mail* is related to the verb *mail*. From our knowledge about the grammatical properties of verbs we will conclude that the verb *e-mail* may also occur in several tenses, in active and passive constructions, as well as in a simple and a progressive form. This is useful if we want to inform our friend that the person with the unpleasant writing urge has, after all, stopped flooding us with *e-mails*, in other words: stopped *e-mailing* us. But does our knowledge also work with unfamiliar or invented words? Take a look at the following familiar verbs:

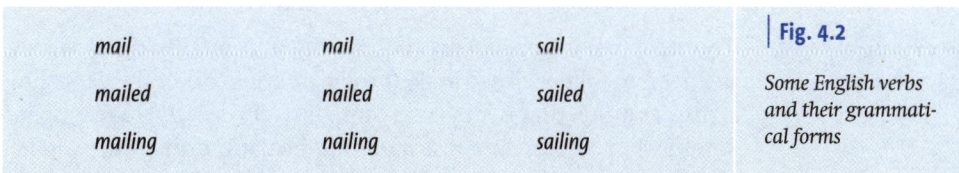

mail	nail	sail
mailed	nailed	sailed
mailing	nailing	sailing

Fig. 4.2

Some English verbs and their grammatical forms

Although you have probably never heard the invented verbs *e-nail* or *e-sail* before and only have some vague idea of what they might mean, you can easily build grammatically correct forms such as *e-nailed* and *e-nailing*, or *e-sail* and *e-sailing*. Obviously, speakers' knowledge about the grammatical properties of words exists independently of their knowledge of single words. This knowledge can be applied to familiar and unfamiliar words alike.

However, our ability to create new words has its limits. Not all word classes accept new members. There are **open classes** that frequently adopt new members, and **closed classes** that usually do not adopt new members. This corresponds to an important distinction between two groups of word classes. The first group contains word classes such as nouns (e.g. *student*), verbs (e.g. *borrow*), adjectives (e.g. *new*) and adverbs (e.g. *quickly*). These word classes are called **content words**. They are also known as **lexical classes**. Lexical classes are usually open, because they regularly adopt new members. The second group contains word classes such as determiners (e.g. *the*), prepositions (e.g. *from*), quantifiers (e.g. *every*) and conjunctions (e.g. *and*). These word classes are called **function words**. They are also known as **grammatical classes**. Grammatical

Open and Closed Word Classes

classes are usually closed, as they rarely adopt new members. You may test this with a little experiment: Find out how many new content words and how many new function words you can invent in five minutes, and discuss the result with a friend.

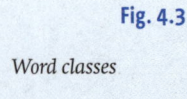

Fig. 4.3

Word classes

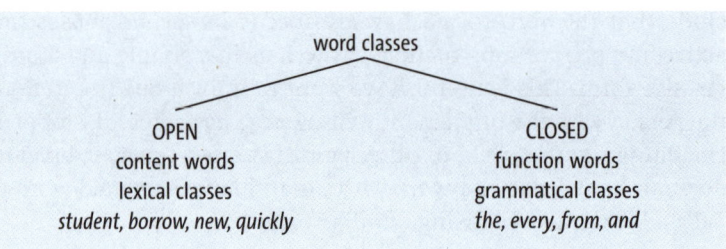

Morphemes

To understand more about the making and modifying of words, we need to take a closer look at their internal structure. Morphologists assume that words are not only physically made up of sounds, but also of smallest **meaning-bearing units**. The linguistic term for any smallest meaning-bearing unit of language is **morpheme**. Morphemes may carry lexical information but also grammatical information. Take an English word that consists of a single morpheme, such as the noun *book*. If we want to say that a particular book is a very small book, we may turn it into a *mini-book*, or *minibook* (the spelling is irrelevant here), by adding *mini-* at the beginning of *book*. If we want to talk about more than one book, or mini-book, we may add the plural marker *-s* at the end of these nouns, so that we can talk about *books*, or *mini-books*. *Book*, *mini-* and *-s* are all individual morphemes. The morpheme *mini-* is used to create a new word from an existing word by adding lexical information, whereas the morpheme *-s* is used to add the grammatical information [+plural].

Morphemes and Words

How many morphemes may occur in a word? The minimum number of morphemes in a word is exactly one, as in *book*. As to the maximum number of morphemes, there is no limit, at least not theoretically. For instance, Modern German is a language that frequently combines a comparatively high number of morphemes in one word. This has often been ridiculed by speakers of other languages, for instance by the American author Mark Twain (1835-1910). In "The Awful German Language", Twain does his best to deride "the ponderous and dismal German system of piling jumbled compounds together", as he calls it. "The Awful German Language" contains numerous examples from Twain's collection of German compound nouns, such as *Freundschaftsbezeigungen* ('declarations of friendship'), *Unabhängigkeitserklärungen* ('declarations of independence') and *Generalstaatsverordnetenversammlungen* (Twain's satirical translation: 'General-statesrepresentativesmeetings'). Had Twain lived until the end of the 20th century, he might have been delighted by *Rindfleischetikettierungsüberwachungsaufgabenübertragungsgesetz*. This German compound noun was coined by the authorities of Mecklenburg-Vorpommern as the name of a new law for the inspection of beef and shortlisted for "Word of the Year" by the German Language Society in 1999. But there are famous long words in English, too. One much-quoted example is *antidisestablishmentarianism*. Especially in English media language, even whole phrases are turned into words by creatively using hyphens, as in *ex-madam-now-action-movie-transsexual*, one of the many journalistic neologisms in the online database of the Research and Development Unit for English Studies (RDUES) at the University of Liverpool. A little warning: This collection is great but also includes non-serious material and puns such as the entry on *ebloody*:

ebloody
If ebooks have ejackets then I can perhaps add an ewarning about ebloody estrong elanguage.

As we have seen above, some morphemes are identical with words, such as *mail*. They can combine with other morphemes or stand alone. Therefore, these morphemes are called **free morphemes**. Others, such as plural endings, or the morpheme *un-* in words such as *unkind* only appear in combination with free morphemes and never on their own. Therefore, they are called **bound morphemes**.

Free and Bound Morphemes

All bound morphemes are **affixes**, that is, morphemes that are attached to other morphemes. Affixes play an important role in various morphological processes. On the one hand, we use affixes to express grammatical information such as [+plural], as in *book ~ books*. On the other hand, we use affixes to build new words. For instance, the noun *reader* is derived from the verb *read* by adding the affix *-er*. The relationship between the morphemes in a word can be represented in a tree diagram. *N* means noun, *V* means verb, and *Af* stands for affix:

Affixes

Fig. 4.4

Morpheme representation in a tree diagram

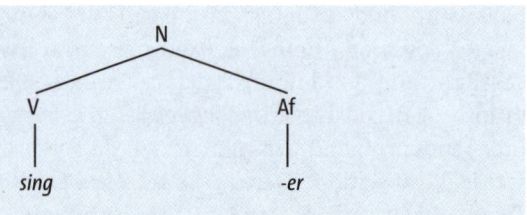

The same relationship can also be represented in square brackets:

Fig. 4.5

$$[_N[_V sing][_{Af} er]]$$

Morpheme representation in square brackets

An even more simplified and frequently found form of representation is *sing-er*.

Types of Affixes

As indicated above, there are different types of affixes with different functions. **Lexical or derivational affixes** are used in **word formation processes**, i.e. for the creation of new words, whereas **grammatical or inflectional affixes** are used in **inflectional processes**, i.e. processes that add grammatical information. In contemporary English, affix classes tend to be closed. Of course, no one knows how English will form its plural or its past tense 500 years from now, or which new derivational affixes will then be **productive**, i.e. able to form new words, in word formation processes, but generally languages are more likely to create new content words than new function words or new affixes.

Unique Morphemes

Some bound morphemes appear only in particular words. For instance, *cran-* and *huckle-* appear only in *cranberry* and *huckleberry*. Such morphemes are called **unique morphemes**. One may wonder why berries seem to attract unique morphemes, because they do so in languages other than English, too. For instance, the German nouns *Himbeere* ('raspberry') and *Brombeere* ('blackberry') contain the unique morphemes *Him-* and *Brom-*. In Modern German, there is a superficial similarity to *Brom*, the German expression for the chemical element *bromine*, but this noun has nothing to do with the *Brombeere* and is pronounced differently. Many unique morphemes have developed diachronically from free morphemes we no longer recognise today.

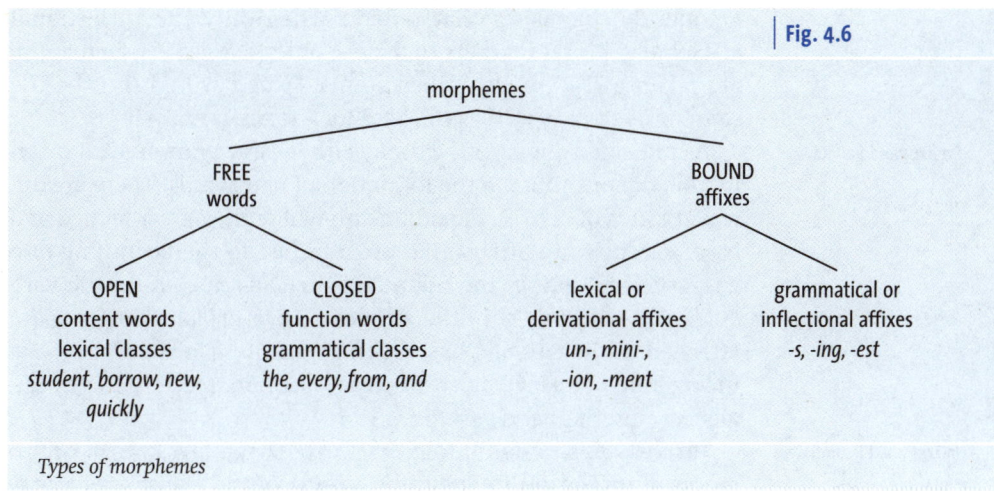

Fig. 4.6

Types of morphemes

Not only do linguists have names for the items that are attached to words, they also have special terms for the particular elements of words that they are attached to. Unfortunately, this terminology is not always used consistently. Most linguists call any form to which an affix is attached a **base**. If a word is stripped of all its affixes, both derivational and inflectional, the remaining part is called the **root**. Roots are always single morphemes that cannot be morphologically analysed any further. In this common terminology, the word *speakers* is analysed into an inflectional suffix *-s* and its base *speaker*, which itself consists of the derivational suffix *-er* and its base *speak*. *Speak*, however, is not only the base of *-er* but also the root of the word *speaker* at the same time, as it cannot be morphologically analysed any further.

Roots, Bases and Stems

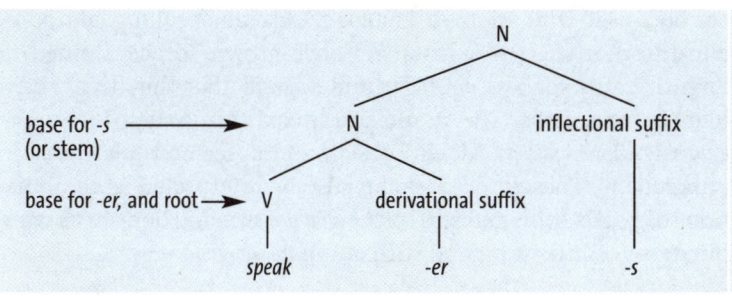

Fig. 4.7

Root and base(s)

Frequently, the bases that remain when only the inflectional affixes (e.g. plural markers such as -s, or tense markers such as -ed) are taken away are also called **stems**. *Speaker* would thus be the stem of *speakers* as well as the base for the suffix -s.

Prefixes and Suffixes

As indicated above, affixes may either carry grammatical information or contribute to the formation of new words. There are different kinds of affixes, depending on where they are attached to a base. **Prefixes** are affixes that are attached to the beginning of a base, such as *anti-* in the noun *antihero* (*anti-hero*), *dis-* in the verb *disarm* (*dis-arm*), or *un-* in the adjective *unfair* (*un-fair*). **Suffixes** are attached to the end of a base, such as *-ness* in *sadness* (*sad-ness*), *-ing* in weeping (*weep-ing*), or *-est* in *deepest* (*deep-est*). Most affixes of English are prefixes and suffixes.

Infixes and Circumfixes

Infixes are inserted into a base. One of the few known occurrences of **infixation** in English is Eliza Doolittle's *absobloominglutely* (*absolutely+blooming*, inserted in the middle) in her famous Cockney song "Wouldn't it be loverly" in *My Fair Lady,* the musical based on Bernard Shaw's play *Pygmalion*. In English, the only linguistic items that are used for infixation are swear words such as *blooming, bloody* or *fucking*. Other than "real" affixes, these infixes are not bound morphemes, but free morphemes or morpheme combinations. **Circumfixes** are attached both to the beginning and to the end of a base. Consequently, some linguists prefer to interpret circumfixes as a combination of a prefix and a suffix. A typical example is the German past participle. Many German verbs build this verb form by attaching both the prefix *ge-* and the suffix *-(e)t* or *-(e)n* to the root of the verb, such as *sagen* ('say') ~ *gesagt* (*ge-sag-t*) ('said'), *fragen* ('ask') ~ *gefragt* (*ge-frag-t*) ('asked') and *geben* ~ *gegeben* (*ge-geb-en*) ('given'). There are no circumfixes in English. However, this type of affix may occur when English words are borrowed into another language. German-speaking computer and internet users, for instance, have grown so accustomed to English verbs such as *download* and *upgrade* that they treat them like German verbs. The results are mixed forms such as *gedownloadet* (*ge-download-et*) ('downloaded') and *upgegradet* (*up-ge-grade-t*) ('upgraded'). These processes may also be interpreted as combinations of prefixation and suffixation (*ge-download-et*) or even as combinations of infixation and suffixation (*up-ge-grade-t*).

Morphemes and Allomorphs

In Chapter 3 "Phonetics and Phonology" we discussed the distinction between phonemes and their allophones. Just as phonemes are realised as different allophones, morphemes are realised as different **allomorphs**. Allomorphs are variants of morphemes. Consider our example *e-mails* from section 4.1. Would you pronounce the plural ending *e-mail[s]* or *e-mail[z]*? If you are a native speaker or a proficient non-native speaker of English, you would probably instinctively pronounce it *e-mail[z]*. In doing so, you would have applied one of the best-known **morphophonological rules** of English. Morphophonological rules are responsible for the actual realisation of morphemes depending on the phonological context. The morphophonological rule you intuitively applied determines how the English plural morpheme *-s* for the regular plural is pronounced in different phonological environments. Compare the plural forms *texts*, *e-mails* and *faxes* and the different pronunciations of the plural marker as [-s] in *texts*, [-z] in *e-mails* and [-ɪz] in *faxes*: You will notice that voiceless [-s] occurs after a voiceless sound such as [t] in *text*, voiced [-z] occurs after a voiced sound such as [l] in *e-mail*, and [-ɪz] occurs after the sibilant [s] in *faxes*. Note that [z] and [s] denote sounds associated with different phonemes, namely /z/ and /s/, not allophones of the same phoneme. These particular rules do not apply within morphemes, only at morpheme boundaries. If [l] and [s] occur within the same morpheme, as in *else* [els], their combination is perfectly legitimate. Generally, the complementary distribution of the three **phonologically conditioned allomorphs** of the English plural morpheme is as follows:

Phonemes and Morphemes

Environment	Examples	Allomorph
• bases that end in a voiceless consonant that is not a sibilant	*texts*	[-s]
• bases that end in a vowel or in a voiced consonant that is not a sibilant	*e-mails*	[-z]
• bases that end in a voiced or voiceless sibilant, i.e. [s], [z], [ʃ] or [ʒ]	*faxes*	[-ɪz]

| Fig. 4.8

Phonologically conditioned allomorphs of the English plural marker

However, allomorphs are not always affixes and may involve internal sound changes, as in the English plural forms *women* or *men*. Occasionally, there is no physical allomorph at all, as in the plural of *sheep* or *aircraft*. In such cases, some linguists say that the plural is realised by a so-called **zero-allomorph**.

4.3 | Morphological Processes

Inflection and Word Formation

As we have seen in the previous sections, morphology describes the processes that create or change words. There are two major groups of morphological processes. **Inflectional processes** are the morphological processes that add grammatical information to existing words. Some linguists use the term morphology only for such processes. Morphological processes that create new words are called **word formation processes**. In English, as indicated above, the most important word formation processes are **derivation** and **compounding**.

Fig. 4.9

Morphological processes

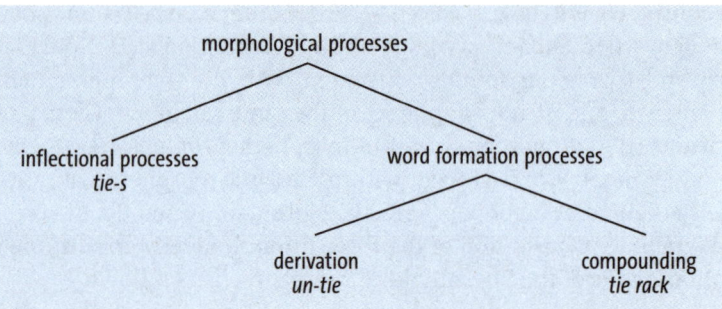

4.3.1 | Inflection

Inflection

Modern English has only relatively few inflectional affixes, other than languages such as German, Russian or Japanese, which have significantly more. All inflectional affixes of English are suffixes:

Nouns	Plural -s	the texts
	Possessive -'s	the teacher's text
Verbs	3rd person singular present indicative -s	she writes well
	-ing-form	she is studying
	Past tense -ed	he e-mailed
	Past participle -ed	they have called
Adjectives	Comparative -er	the longer one
	Superlative -est	the longest one

Fig. 4.10

Inflectional suffixes of Modern English nouns, verbs and adjectives

However, English shows many inflectional irregularities. Consider the following poem:

For a laugh, or a smile

We'll begin with a box, and the plural is boxes;
but the plural of ox is oxen not oxes.
One fowl is a goose, but two are called geese,
yet the plural of moose should never be meese.
You may find a lone mouse or a nest full of mice;
yet the plural of house is houses, not hice.
If the plural of man is always called men,
why shouldn't the plural of pan be called pen?
If I spoke of my foot and showed you my feet,
and I gave you a boot, would a pair be called beet?
If one is a tooth and a whole set are teeth,
why shouldn't the plural of booth be called beeth?
Then one may be that, and three would be those,
yet hat in the plural would never be hose,
and the plural of cat is cats, not cose.
We speak of a brother and also of brethren,
but though we say mother, we never say methren.

Many of the plural forms in this poem mark the changes in number internally (*goose ~ geese, foot ~ feet*). This kind of **internal change** reflects traces of other types of plural formations that were productive in earlier periods of English. When a morpheme is replaced with an entirely different morpheme to mark a grammatical contrast, this is called **suppletion**, as in *go ~ went*. Occasionally, it is hard to determine from a purely synchronic point of view whether a form originates from suppletion or from internal changes. This is the case with verbs like *bring ~ brought* or *find ~ found*. The formation of their past tense is sometimes called **partial suppletion**.

4.3.2 | **Word Formation**

Heads

Unlike inflectional processes, word formation processes may make words change their lexical class (or part of speech). Usually, the right-hand morpheme in a complex English word determines its lexical class. This determining morpheme is often called the **head**. In English, the most productive word formation processes are **derivation** and **compounding**.

Derivation

When a new lexeme is formed by adding an affix to an existing word, this morphological process is called **derivation**. The English language uses mainly **prefixes** and **suffixes** for its derivational processes.

Prefixes

Derivational prefixes modify the meaning of English words without any changes regarding their lexical class. Many English prefixes are of Latin or Greek origin. The following survey lists a selection of some types of information that prefixes may add to English words. Many bases of these words are of Latin or Greek origin as well:

Fig. 4.11 |

Derivational prefixes

In English, prefixes may inform about, e.g.

quantity

mono-	'one'	*monograph, monosyllabic*
poly-	'many'	*polysyllabic, polygraph*

the kind of involvement

co-	'together, jointly'	*coexistence, cooperate*
contra-	'against, opposite'	*contradiction, contraindication*

evaluations

mis-	'badly, wrongly'	*miscalculate, mislead*
pseudo-	'false, deceptive resemblance'	*pseudoartist, pseudoprophet*

place or direction

ad-	'toward'	*adjoin, admeasure*
sub-	'under, below'	*subdivision, subtitle*

measurement

hyper-	'over, to excess'	*hyperactive, hypersensitive*
hypo-	'under, slightly'	*hypotactic, hypotoxic*

negation and opposite

dis-	'apart, reversal, lacking'	*disorder, dislike*
un-	'not'	*unbearable, uneven*

time and duration

post-	'after, behind'	*postdate, postcolonial*
re-	'anew, again, back'	*regenerate, restore*

Only derivational suffixes can make English words change their lexical class. For instance, the derivational suffix *-ly* turns most adjectives into adverbs (e.g. *quick-ly, beautiful-ly*). Additionally, derivational suffixes may produce new words with different meanings. For instance, the suffixes *-er* and *-ee* may combine with the verb *interview* to create two different nouns, one for the person who does the interviewing, and one for the person who is being interviewed: An *interviewer* (*interview-er*) is somebody who interviews an *interviewee* (*interview-ee*).

Suffixes

In English, derivational suffixes may form, e.g.

Fig. 4.12

Derivational suffixes

agentive nouns from verbs or adjectives

-er	'agent'	*singer, teacher*
-ist	'one connected with, or agent'	*cyclist, typist*

abstract nouns from verbs or adjectives

-al	'act of'	*renewal, revival*
-ness	'state, condition, quality of'	*bitterness, fairness*

verbs from adjectives and nouns

-en	'to become'	*darken, deafen*
-ify	'to cause to (be)'	*purify, beautify*

adjectives from verbs or nouns

-able	'fit for doing, fit for being done'	*agreeable, understandable*
-less	'without, free from'	*faultless, fearless*

adjectives from names

-(i)(a)n	'belonging to'	*Shakespearean, Victorian*
-ist	'supporting'	*Marxist, Bushist*

As derivational processes may be repeated or combined, we distinguish simple and complex derivations, depending on the degree of complexity involved. Sometimes it is not easy to decide which process occurred first. Consider the noun *unkindness*:

Fig. 4.13

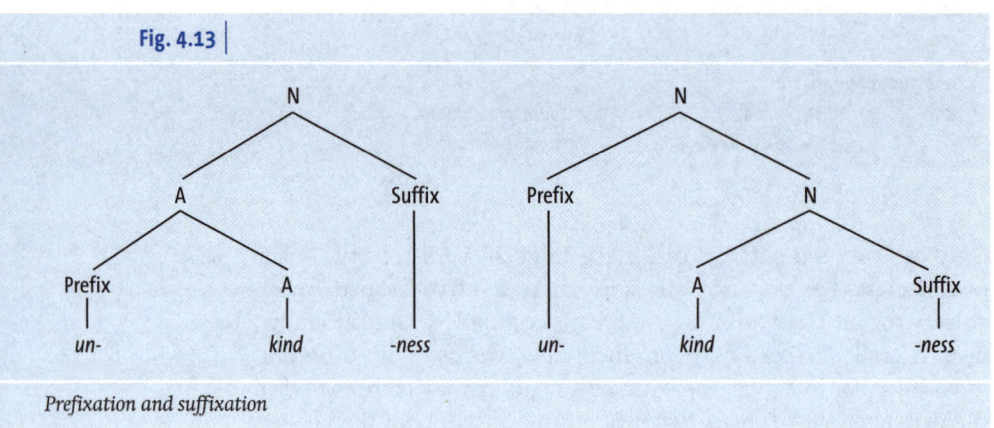

Prefixation and suffixation

Is the adjective *unkind* the base to which the nominalisation suffix *-ness* is attached, or is the negative prefix *un-* attached to the noun *kindness*? At first sight, both interpretations may be possible. However, the English prefix *un-* tends to combine with adjectives, not with nouns. Therefore, the first interpretation to the left is more appropriate.

Conversion

Conversion occurs when a word comes to belong to a new word class without the addition of a physical affix. Therefore, this process is sometimes also called **zero-derivation**. For instance, many English words exist both as nouns and as verbs, such as *smell*, *taste*, *hit*, *walk*, *bottle*, *interview*, or, more recently, *text*, the latter nowadays referring to the sending of electronic text messages via mobile phones. It is sometimes hard to determine which grammatical category they belonged to first. Proper names may be converted, too. Prominent examples are *Boycott* (N) ~ *boycott* (V), or *Bogart* (N) ~ *bogart* (V), as the following slightly modified extract from the *Oxford English Dictionary Online* shows:

bogart, *v.*
Slang.
[< the name of Humphrey Bogart (1899-1957), U.S. film actor. In sense 1, with allusion to the series of strong, tough characters played by Bogart. In sense 2,

with allusion to Bogart's frequent on-screen smoking, esp. to the long drags
he took on cigarettes. Cf.: **1951** *Western Folklore* **10** 172 *To pull a Bogart*, to
act tough.]

1. *trans. U.S.* (esp. in African-American usage): To force, coerce; to bully, intimi-
   date. [...]
2. *trans.* orig. and chiefly *U.S.* To appropriate (a marijuana cigarette) greedily
   or selfishly. Hence more generally: to take or use most of; to steal. Also
   occas. *intr.*
   Popularized by the 1969 U.S. Film *Easy Rider*, the soundtrack of which
   featured the song *Don't Bogart Me* by Fraternity of Man.
   (Draft Entry June 2010)

Compounding is another major word formation process. This
process combines at least two existing words to form a new word.
Many English tongue-twisters make use of compounds, such as:

> She sells **seashells** by the seashore.
> The shells she sells are surely **seashells**.
> So if she sells shells on the **seashore**,
> I'm sure she sells **seashore shells**.

In English, most compound words are nouns, verbs or adjectives.
There are only a few compounds in other lexical classes, such as
the preposition compounds *into* and *onto*. Usually, the head of a
compound, i.e. the element furthest to the right, determines its lexical class. English compounds may be written either as one word,
with or without a hyphen, or as two words. Consider the following
noun compounds, verb compounds and adjective compounds:

Compounding

| Fig. 4.14

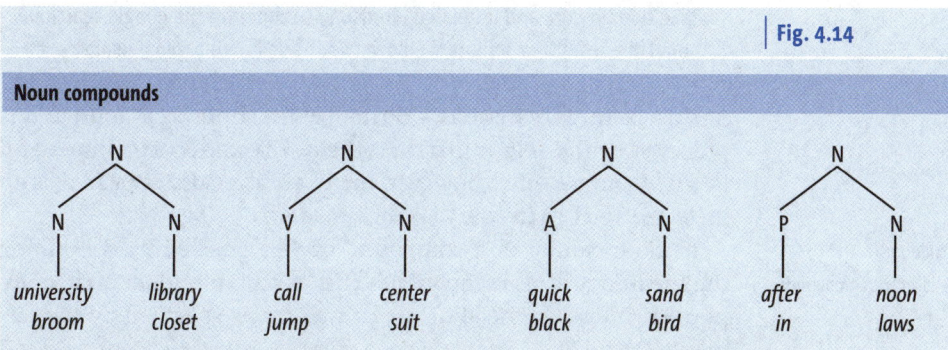

Noun compounds

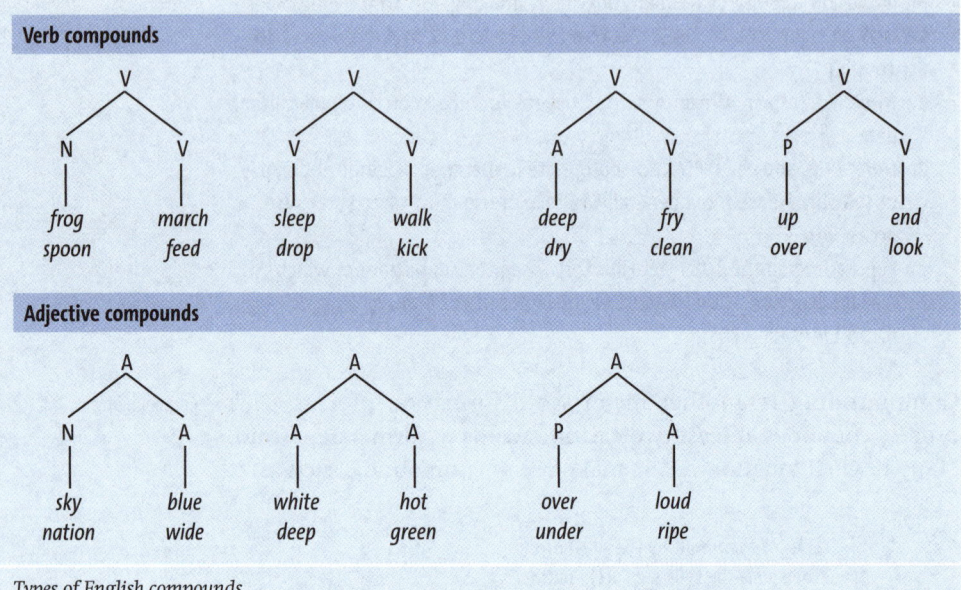

Verb compounds

V	V	V	V
N — V	V — V	A — V	P — V
frog / march	sleep / walk	deep / fry	up / end
spoon / feed	drop / kick	dry / clean	over / look

Adjective compounds

A	A	A
N — A	A — A	P — A
sky / blue	white / hot	over / loud
nation / wide	deep / green	under / ripe

Types of English compounds

Occasionally, it is hard to determine the compound type, especially with neologisms. In such cases, we may try to identify the lexical class by considering the grammatical properties of the head. For instance, the word *whack*, which functions as the head of the compound *googlewhack*, can be a verb as well as a noun. In the RDUES database of neologisms, *googlewhack* is listed with an example sentence in which it appears as a noun:

googlewhack
Take two obscure and unrelated words, type them into the google search bar and if the result is a solitary web page you have found a **googlewhack**.

In this example, *googlewhack* obviously functions as a noun and is preceded by the determiner *a*. As the media started to comment on this new online sport, however, the word soon also appeared as an inflected verb, as in *have you googlewhacked?*

Endocentric and
Exocentric Compounds

If the meaning of a compound can be guessed by combining the meanings of its components, it is called an **endocentric compound**. Often, the head of the compound is specified by the elements to the left. For instance, a *morphology book* is a special kind of book, *garlic sauce* is a special kind of sauce, and *winter holiday* is a special kind of holiday. Most examples in Fig. 4.14 are endocentric compounds. **Exocentric compounds** such as *blackbird, bluebottle* or *redneck* have meanings that cannot be guessed by combining the meaning of their components. A *blackbird* is only a black bird when it is male, because female blackbirds have brownish plumage. A *bluebottle* can be either a flower or a fly and a *redneck* belongs to a particular social group in the U.S.A. To distinguish compounds from non-compound combinations of adjectives and nouns, you may try the following **conjunction test**: In non-compound combinations such as *black bird, blue bottle* or *red neck*, you may insert another adjective into the phrase with the help of a conjunction such as *and* or *or* to build phrases such as *a black and brown bird, a blue or green bottle* or *a red and pimpled neck*. This is not possible with compound nouns. In many cases, the consideration of word stress can be of help. In spoken English, the compounds *bláckbird, blúebottle* or *rédneck* are all stressed on their first element, whereas the elements of the non-compound combinations *black bírd, blue bóttle* or *red néck* are stressed on their second element.

Other types of word formation processes include blending, clipping and back-formation. **Blends** combine non-morphemic parts of words into a new word, as in *brunch* (**br**eakfast+**lunch**), *motel* (**mot**or+**hotel**) or *chunnel* (**ch**annel+**tunnel**). There are borderline cases between compounding and blending in which at least one of the words remains intact: Users of electronic media will be familiar with blends such as *emoticon* and *netiquette*, which gained popularity during the last decade of the 20th century, as the *Oxford English Dictionary Online* documents:

Blends, Clipping and Back-Formations

emoticon, *n.*
Computing.
[Blend of **EMOTION** *n.* and **ICON** *n.*]
A representation of a facial expression formed by a short sequence of keyboard characters (usually to be viewed sideways) and used in electronic mail, etc., to convey the sender's feelings or intended tone. Examples are the sequences :-) and :-(representing a smile and a frown respectively.
1990 *N.Y. Times* 28 Jan. I. 39/4 Emoticon - typographical device used to indicate tone or emotion in a posting. **1994** *Observer* 13 Feb. (Life Suppl.) 8/3 Hence the development of 'netiquette', essentially on-line codes of behaviour, and 'emoticons' or 'smileys', little text ideograms which are used to signal

sense (e.g. :-) to show good intentions, ;-) a wink to indicate irony). **1997** *Vancouver Sun* 29 Jan. D13/3 Mitchell and Murphy ask their clients to convey their emotions within square brackets rather than using the normal e-mail emoticons. **2001** *Guardian* (Electronic ed.) 24 Feb., Imagine the horrors of being poised over your mobile phone and suddenly forgetting the necessary emoticon. (Draft Entry June 2001)

Clipping is a word formation process that creates new words by shortening existing words, as in *prof* from *professor*, *ad* from *advertisement*, *plane* from *aeroplane*, *flu* from *influenza* or (in British English) *pram* from *perambulator*. **Back-formations** are special types of clipping where a supposed or real affix is removed and the result looks as if the longer word had been derived from the shorter word. For instance, *edit* is a back-formation of *editor*, and *baby-sit* is a back-formation of *baby-sitter*.

Initialisms, Alphabetisms and Acronyms

Another type of shortening process results in so-called **initialisms**, which can be subdivided into **alphabetisms** and **acronyms**. Initialisms usually consist of the first letters of the words that make up the name of something. Whereas **alphabetisms** such as *U.S.A.*, *EU*, *BBC*, *CNN* or *SMS* are spoken as individual letters, **acronyms** such as *UNESCO*, *NATO*, *AIDS*, *radar* or *laser* are pronounced as single words. Mixed cases such as *CD-ROM* are also possible.

Word Formation across Languages

Word formation is also possible across languages. English often adopts morphemes from Latin or classical Greek, for example in medical terminology:

cardi(o)- *The heart.* [Greek *kardia*, heart.]
The medical study of the heart is **cardiology**, practised by a **cardiologist**; an **electrocardiogram** (Greek *graphein*, write), or ECG, is a record or display of a person's heartbeat, created by an **electrocardiograph**. Several adjectives relate to the heart as part of the wider body system; these include **cardiovascular** (Latin *vasculum*, a little vessel) for the heart and its blood vessels, **cardiopulmonary** (Latin *pulmo*, *pulmon-*, lung) for the heart and lungs, and **cardiothoracic** (Greek *thorax*, chest) for the heart and chest. Outside medicine the most common compound is **cardioid** for a heart-shaped curve in mathematics. (based on Quinion 2002:37)

New words may also be formed with morphemes from living languages such as German (*sitz bath*, *sitz mark*), and occasionally even from names:

franken- *Genetically modified.* [The first element of the name of Baron Victor *Frankenstein*, from Mary Shelley's novel *Frankenstein, or the Modern Prometheus* of 1818.]

Activists sometimes describe genetically modified foods as *Frankenstein foods*, evoking Baron Frankenstein's creation of a living being, in popular under-standing a terrifying monster who turns on his creator and destroys him. The first element of his name appears in various invented words – such as **frankenfood**, **frankencrop**, and **frankenfruit** – with the technology known generically as **frankenscience** (all are often written with initial capital letter). They are all deeply pejorative. (Quinion 2002:87-88)

Word manufacture or **coinage** is used, for example, to create product names such as *Weetabix*, *Sellotape*, or *Marmite*. It is also used by writers of fiction for characters or items that exist only within their texts, for example *hobbit* in John R.R. Tolkien's *The Lord of the Rings*. And last but not least, there are special coinages that do not mean anything at all but occasionally are famous nevertheless, such as *supercalifragilisticexpialidocious* from the Walt Disney film *Mary Poppins*, or the amazing inventions in James Joyce's *Finnegans Wake*, such as the word that symbolises Tim Finnegan's great fall from his ladder:

Inventing New Words

Bothallchoractorschumminaroundgansumuminarumdrumstrumtrumi-
nahumptadumpwaultopoofoolooderamaunsturnup!

Exercises

| 4.4

1. How many word types and word tokens are there in the sentence *The birds sang and the bells rang*? How many of these can you find in a dictionary?

2. The following words are made up of two morphemes. Isolate them and decide for each one whether it is free or bound. Where applicable, decide what kind of affix is involved and whether it is inflectional or derivational.

   a) *cats*   e) *signpost*
   b) *unhappy*   f) *rejoin*
   c) *milder*   g) *greedy*
   d) *bicycle*   h) *hateful*

3. Divide the words below into their component morphemes and describe the morphemes as you did in Exercise 2. — Note: words may consist of one, two, or more than two morphemes.
   a) *comfortable*
   b) *reconditioned*
   c) *senseless*
   d) *rationalisation*
   e) *environmental*
   f) *thickeners*

4. In each group of words that follows, identify the lexical categories of the bases and the lexical categories of the whole words.
   a) *government, speaker, contemplation*
   b) *fictional, childish, colourful*
   c) *calmest, lovelier, sillier*

5. Identify the bound affixes in the following groups of words and name the lexical category of their bases. Then say whether the affix changes their lexical category, and if so, say to what.
   a) *spiteful, healthful, truthful*
   b) *unsure, untrue, unimportant*
   c) *retake, review, relive*

6. Bontoc is a language spoken in the Philippines. Which morphological process is used to produce the following verb forms? Describe it in detail, using the appropriate terminology.
   a) [fikas] 'strong'
   b) [kilad] 'red'
   c) [bato] 'stone'
   d) [fusul] 'enemy'
   e) [fumikas] 'he is becoming strong'
   f) [kumilad] 'he is becoming red'
   g) [bumato] 'he is becoming stone'
   h) [fumusul] 'he is becoming an enemy'
   (adapted from Bergmann et al. 2007:178, cf. Bibliography of Chapter 1)

7. There are many euphemisms for dismissing employees. Analyse the following examples regarding the word formation processes that created them.
   a) *career change opportunity*
   b) *decruitment*
   c) *outplacement*

8. Compare with the help of a dictionary: *catfish, shellfish, selfish, swordfish.* Are these words endocentric or exocentric compounds (or maybe something completely different)?

9. Identify the morphological processes involved in the creation of the following neologisms (adapted from *Urban Dictionary*):
    a) *Airplane Talker*
       May 24, 2010 Urban Word of the Day
       noun
       1) A person who stands within the confines of your personal space bubble (causing extreme discomfort) to hold an ordinary conversation, like someone sitting next to you on an airplane would.
          Your friend, over there, is a total airplane talker.
       2) A person who speaks louder than the current conversation calls for, as if they are trying to talk over a plane's engines.
    b) *fat finger*
       May 7, 2010 Urban Word of the Day
       verb
       The act of performing a typo. Often used when referring to password typos.
       I thought the server was down, but I just fat fingered my password.
       You didn't get my email? I must have fat fingered the address.
    c) *ash hole*
       April 18, 2010 Urban Word of the Day
       noun
       1) The small opening in the volcanic ash clouds that allows airliners to fly through without any chance of danger.
          We were stranded at Heathrow Airport for hours until the airline found some ash hole to fly through.
       2) The opening at the top of a volcano from which forth spews volcanic ash.

Bibliography | 4.5

Aronoff, Mark & **Kirsten Fudeman**. 2005. *What is Morphology?* Malden, MA: Blackwell. *(A beginner-friendly introduction with many valuable examples and exercises)*

Bauer, Laurie. 1983. *English Word-Formation.* Cambridge: Cambridge University Press. *(A standard reference book)*

Bauer, Laurie. 2003. *Introducing Linguistic Morphology*. 2nd edition. Edinburgh: Edinburgh University Press. *(Updated version of a standard introductory textbook)*

Bauer, Laurie. 2004. *A Glossary of Morphology*. Edinburgh: Edinburgh University Press. *(An excellent overview of current terminology)*

Booij, Geert. 2007. *The Grammar of Words. An Introduction to Linguistic Morphology*. 2nd edition. Oxford: Oxford University Press. *(Ambitious and comprehensive)*

Carstairs-McCarthy, Andrew. 2001. *An Introduction to English Morphology: Words and their Structure*. Edinburgh: Edinburgh University Press. *(Accessible and thorough)*

Coates, Richard. 1999. *Word Structure*. London: Routledge. *(Very beginner-friendly and basic)*

Haspelmath, Martin. 2002. *Understanding Morphology*. London: Arnold. *(Extensive treatment of languages other than English)*

Katamba, Francis. 2004. *English Words. Structure, History, Usage*. 2nd edition. London: Routledge. *(Profound and highly readable)*

Katamba, Francis & **John Stonham**. 2006. *Morphology*. 2nd edition. London: Palgrave Macmillan. *(Updated version of a standard reference book)*

Lieber, Rochelle. 2010. *Introducing Morphology*. Cambridge: Cambridge University Press. *(A lively and motivating introduction to morphology)*

Oxford English Dictionary Online. 2010. <www.oed.com> *(The most comprehensive dictionary of the English language)*

Plag, Ingo. 2003. *Word-Formation in English*. Cambridge: Cambridge University Press. *(Critical and user-friendly)*

Quinion, Michael. 2002. *Ologies and Isms. Word Beginnings and Endings*. Oxford: Oxford University Press. *(A collection of 1.250 productive English affixes)*

Quirk, Randolph et al. 1985. *A Comprehensive Grammar of the English Language*. London: Longman. *(Still one of the most important reference grammars)*

Spencer, Andrew & **Arnold Zwicky**, eds. 2001. *The Handbook of Morphology*. Oxford: Blackwell. *(Expert articles on central issues in morphology including the relationships between morphology and other linguistic disciplines)*

Stockwell, Robert & **Donka Minkova**. 2001. *English Words: History and Structure*. Cambridge: Cambridge University Press. *(Combines language history and the study of word formation for beginners)*

The Oxford Dictionary of Abbreviations. 2nd edition. 1998. *(The most comprehensive dictionary of abbreviations available)*

Further References

Burridge, Kate. 2004. *Blooming English. Observations on the Roots, Cultivation and Hybrids of the English Language*. Cambridge: Cambridge University Press. *(Brilliant scientainment)*

Quinion, Michael. 1996-2010. *World Wide Words*. <http://www.worldwidewords.org> *(A website that should deny access to anybody with deadlines to meet)*

Research and Development Unit for English Studies at the University of Liverpool (RDUES). 2004-2010. *Neologisms in Journalistic Text*. <http://rdues.uce.ac.uk/neologisms.shtml> *(Another temptation)*

Twain, Mark. 1880. "The Awful German Language." In: Twain, Mark. *A Tramp Abroad*. Appendix D. Hartford, Conn.: American Publishing Company. *The Project Gutenberg EBook* 119. Release date June 2004. Posting Date June 2, 2009. <http://www.gutenberg.org/files/119/119-h/119-h.htm> *(Unflattering but to the point)*

Urban Dictionary 1999-2010. <http://www.urbandictionary.com> *(A user-created online dictionary)*

Syntax

Contents

Abstract

Syntax examines how words are combined to form larger grammatical units such as phrases, clauses and sentences. This chapter outlines the basic rules and principles that enable speakers to recognise and produce syntactical structures.

5.1 | Syntactic Categories

The term *grammar* is commonly used to refer to the characteristics of morphology and syntax of a language. The previous chapter on morphology was devoted to the structure of words. **Syntax** is concerned with **the combination of words into phrases, clauses and sentences**. Sentences are structured **hierarchically**. This means that the "building blocks" of sentences are arranged on several levels, with systematic relationships between them: **Words** are combined into **phrases**, phrases are combined into **clauses**, and clauses may either constitute **sentences** by themselves or be combined to build more complex sentences (cf. 5.3 below). The following figure illustrates the hierarchical relationships within sentences:

Fig. 5.1

Words, phrases, clauses and sentences

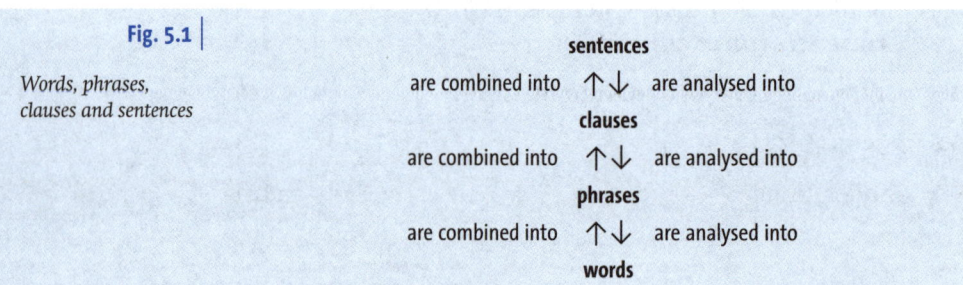

	sentences	
are combined into	↑↓	are analysed into
	clauses	
are combined into	↑↓	are analysed into
	phrases	
are combined into	↑↓	are analysed into
	words	

Determining Syntactic Categories

Syntax classifies words into different **syntactic categories** (or **word classes**, or **parts of speech**). This classification goes back to the description of Greek and Latin in antiquity. From the chapter on morphology in this book, we are already familiar with most of these categories, such as nouns, verbs, adjectives, adverbs and prepositions. We also have an idea about their meaning and know the inflectional properties of the categories that are inflected. But these are only two of the three criteria that linguists traditionally use to determine the syntactic category of a word. The three criteria are **meaning, inflection** and **distribution**. Meaning is a notional criterion, whereas inflection and distribution are formal criteria. Meaning refers to the semantic description of the word classes, for example stating that all words which name persons, objects and places are nouns. Inflection refers to the morphological properties of a word, such as the plural and possessive forms of a noun. The distribution of a word depends on its syntactic properties, including its potential positions and functions within a phrase, clause or sentence.

We may try to determine the category of the word *teacher* by first applying the meaning criterion. A *teacher* is a person and we know that words naming persons, objects and places are generally nouns. According to its meaning, the word *teacher* is thus a noun. Secondly, we could check which inflections may occur with the word *teacher*. *Teacher* may occur in the plural form *teachers*, as in *Mary loves all her teachers*, and the possessive form *teacher's*, as in *the teacher's book*. Words that have a plural and a possessive form are generally nouns (cf. Fig. 4.10), i.e. the second test confirms that teacher is most likely a noun. Thirdly, we may check the distribution of *teacher* in sentences. This works most conveniently by finding words in a given sentence for which we can substitute *teacher*. In the sentence *The student went quickly to the new pub*, we can substitute both *student* and *pub* by *teacher*, as in *The student went quickly to the new teacher* or *The teacher went quickly to the new pub*. *Teacher* occurs with both a determiner in *the teacher* and an adjective in *the new teacher*, which are typical distributions for English nouns. We can now safely say that teacher is a noun.

As has been shown by the example above, the identification of a word's category may be fairly straightforward and simple. The noun *teacher* fulfils each of the three criteria, so that their combination may occasionally seem redundant. However, combining the criteria is advisable, since all syntactic categories contain words which may cause problems with single tests. Consider the noun *intelligence*. From the point of view of meaning, nouns are traditionally defined as words referring to persons, objects or places (see above). *Intelligence*, however, is an abstract entity, i.e. the criterion of meaning only works if the definition is expanded to include abstract entities as well. This is why some linguists prefer not to employ the criterion of meaning at all.

In the case of abstract nouns such as *intelligence*, inflection is not a very helpful criterion either, because many abstract nouns do not appear in the plural or in the possessive. Inflection is generally a somewhat problematic criterion in Modern English, because the English language has lost most of its inflections in

Applying Criteria

Comparing Criteria

the course of its history (cf. Fig. 2.12). Additionally, some words belong to several different word classes and may thus show inflectional properties of more than one syntactic category.

Abstract nouns such as *intelligence* can be best identified by checking their distribution, i.e. whether they can appear in contexts that are characteristic for nouns. The abstract noun *intelligence* can occur both after a determiner such as *the* and after an adjective such as *immense*. We can easily imagine contexts like *the intelligence of mice* or *thanks to their immense intelligence*. In this case, the distribution test yields convincing results for the identification of *intelligence* as a noun. Unfortunately, distribution alone does not always help to safely determine the category of a word either. For instance, most English nouns may occur with determiners (*a frog, the pond*), except for so-called **proper nouns** naming persons or places: **the London* is impossible except in sentences like *What I saw was different from the London I remembered*. All in all, the safest method for identifying the category of an English word is usually a combination of all three tests.

Major Syntactic Categories of English

Highly simplified, the meaning, inflection and distribution of the major syntactic categories of English can be summarised as follows:

Fig. 5.2

syntactic category	meaning	inflection	distribution
▸ noun (N)	▸ person, object, place, abstract entity	▸ plural ▸ possessive	▸ subject or object of a sentence ▸ may follow a determiner ▸ may be modified by an adjective ▸ *The **students** went quickly to the new **pub***
▸ verb (V)	▸ act, event, state, emotion	▸ 3rd person singular present indicative ▸ *-ing*-form ▸ past tense ▸ past participle	▸ predicate of a sentence ▸ usually follows the subject, may precede an object ▸ combines with auxiliaries ▸ may be modified by an adverb ▸ *The students **went** quickly to the new pub*
▸ adjective (Adj)	▸ quality, attribute	▸ comparative ▸ superlative	▸ modifies nouns ▸ occurs before a noun, may be preceded by a determiner ▸ *The students went quickly to the **new** pub*

► adverb (Adv)	► quality, attribute	► ∅	► modifies verbs, adjectives, adverbs and prepositions ► *The students went **quickly** to the new pub*
► preposition (Prep)	► location, direction, relation	► ∅	► occurs before a noun or a determiner ► *The students went quickly **to** the new pub*

Main syntactic categories of English

Other syntactic categories are, for instance, pronouns (Pro) such as *she* or *they*, determiners (Det) such as *a*, *the*, and *some*, and conjunctions (Con) such as *and* and *or*. It is important to note that many words can belong to more than one syntactic category, e.g. the word *text*, which can be both a noun and a verb (cf. 4.3.2).

Sentence Types | 5.2

Words from different syntactic categories are combined to form sentences with different structures and functions. Compare the following four sentences:

(1) *Anna is singing.*
(2) *Is Anna singing?*
(3) *Sing!*
(4) *How beautifully Anna is singing!*

When we utter one of these sentences, we do so with a particular communicative purpose. Those intentions are

Communicative Intentions

(1) to inform someone of something
(2) to get information about something
(3) to get someone to do something
(4) to express our attitude about something

These four intentions correspond to the four major functional sentence types:

Major Functional Sentence Types

(1) declarative sentence
(2) interrogative sentence

(3) imperative sentence
(4) exclamatory sentence

English sentences have characteristic word orders for each of these sentence types. In our examples, we can observe the following word order patterns:

(1) noun – auxiliary verb – verb in *ing*-form
(2) auxiliary verb – noun – verb in *ing*-form
(3) verb by itself
(4) wh-expression – adverb – noun – auxiliary – verb in *ing*-form

Such a linear representation does not reveal much about the relationships between the individual words that make up the sentences. In the following section, we will take a closer look at some of these relationships and different ways of representing the syntactic make-up of declarative sentences.

5.3 | Building Sentences

As previously stated, sentences are made up of words, phrases and clauses. At the word level, the sentence *Anna sang a song yesterday* can be analysed as follows:

Fig. 5.3

Syntactic analysis of a sentence at the word level

$[_N$ *Anna*$]$ $[_V$ *sang*$]$ $[_{Det}$ *a*$]$ $[_N$ *song*$]$ $[_{Adv}$ *yesterday*$]$

Constituents and Constituency Tests

Our intuition, however, tells us that certain words in a sentence belong more closely together than others. For instance, we would intuitively say that the words in the group *a song* are more closely related than the words in the sequences *sang a* or *song yesterday*. Groups of words that belong together and function as a single unit in a sentence are called **constituents**. Constituents can be identified by a number of different **constituency tests**.

Substitution

Constituents may be identified as units in a sentence by the **substitution test**. A word or a group of words form a constituent, if they can be replaced by a pronoun such as *she*, *he*, *it*, *they*, *her*, *him* etc. In the sentence *Anna sang a song yesterday*, *Anna* can be replaced by the pronoun *she*, and *a song* can be replaced by the pronoun *it*. The word *Anna* and the group *a song* thus must be constituents of this sentence.

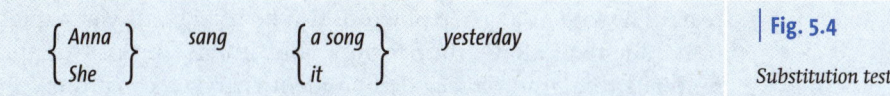

Fig. 5.4

Substitution test

Another test for constituency is the **coordination test**. A word or a group of words are a constituent of a sentence, if we can use a conjunction such as *and* or *or* to join them to another word or group of words. For instance, *Anna* could be coordinated with *Jack*, and *a song* could be joined to *an aria*, i.e. *Anna* and *a song* must be constituents of our example sentence. Sequences of words which do not belong to a single unit, such as *song yesterday*, fail this test.

Coordination

$$\left\{\begin{array}{l} Anna \\ Anna\ and\ Jack \end{array}\right\} \quad sang \quad \left\{\begin{array}{l} a\ song \\ a\ song\ and\ an\ aria \end{array}\right\} \quad yesterday$$

Fig. 5.5

Coordination test

Optional constituents may be identified by applying the **deletion test**. If a word or group of words can be deleted from a sentence, it must be an optional constituent. In our example sentence *yesterday* can be deleted, hence *yesterday* must be a constituent of this sentence:

Deletion

Anna sang a song yesterday

Anna sang a song ~~yesterday~~

Fig. 5.6

Deletion test

A fourth test for constituency is the **movement test**. Words or groups of words which can be moved to a different position within the sentence are constituents of this sentence. For instance, *yesterday* can be moved to the beginning of our example sentence and thus must be a constituent.

Movement

Fig. 5.7

Movement test

Anna sang a song yesterday

Yesterday, Anna sang a song

Questions

A fifth test for constituency is the **question test** (or **stand-alone test**). If a word or a group of words can be used to answer a question and stand alone, they form a constituent. In our example sentence, the group *a song* can be identified as a constituent by asking the following question:

Fig. 5.8

Question test

Question: *What did Anna sing yesterday?*

Answer: *A song*

There is no question that has *song yesterday* as its answer, except questions such as *What did you just say?* or *Which example are we supposed to discuss?* to which the answer could indeed be *song yesterday*. These latter questions are known as **metalinguistic** (or **metadiscursive**) questions because they refer to the language itself. Such questions are not useful in constituency tests, because they can be applied to anything said or written in a particular context.

As a result, we can say that our example sentence has the following major constituents (the traditional terminology describing their functions in the sentence is supplied in brackets, cf. Fig. 5.9 below): *Anna* (the subject), *sang* (the predicate), *a song* (an object), as well as the optional constituent *yesterday* (an adverbial).

Syntactic Elements and their Functions

We have already used the terms for some of the traditional syntactic elements such as subject, predicate, object and adverbial above, assuming that most of us are familiar with them. In addition to the obligatory elements **subject** and **predicate**, English sentences can also contain **objects**, **complements** and **adverbials**. Fig. 5.9 provides simplified definitions for each of the main elements of sentences, which are probably similar to the definitions many of us learned in school:

| **Fig. 5.9**

Syntactic elements and their functions

subject (S) A syntactic element which is traditionally seen as representing someone or something of which something is said, e.g. *John* in ***John** came*, ***John** helped me*, ***John** was freed*, ***John** is my friend*, or *the car* in ***The car** is red*, ***The car** was scratched*, and so on. Subjects can also be constructions with the *ing*-form of verbs, e.g. *knowing him* in ***Knowing him** helped me*, or clauses, e.g. *that he is worried* in ***That he is worried** is obvious*.

predicate (P) Some linguists use the term predicate to refer to that part of a clause or sentence which represents what is said of (or predicated of) the subject, e.g. *bought a coat in London* in *My friend **bought a coat in London***. Other linguists use the term predicate to refer to the verb only, e.g. *bought* in *My friend **bought** a coat in London*. We will follow the latter convention in this book.

object (O) An element which characteristically represents someone or something, other than the person or thing represented by the subject, that is involved in actions, processes and similar activities. There are **direct objects**, such as *him* in *I met **him***, and **indirect objects**, such as *her* in *I'll give **her** a flower*. Direct objects, such as *him* in the first example and *a flower* in the second example, are immediately involved in a subject's activities, whereas indirect objects, such as *her* in the second example, benefit from or receive the direct objects involved in these activities.

complement (C) A syntactic element seen as 'completing' the construction of another element, frequently the subject and the object. A subject complement thus completes the subject, e.g. *happy* in *He seems **happy***, whereas an object complement completes the object, e.g. *happy* in *That will make him **happy***.

adverbial (A) A syntactic element usually providing information about the time, place or manner of the action or state referred to in a sentence. Represented by adverbs such as *tomorrow*, adverbial phrases such as *on Monday*, or adverbial clauses such as *when I'm ready*. Cf. *I'll do it **tomorrow** / **on Monday** / **when I'm ready***.

(adapted from Matthews 2007)

The syntactic elements described in Fig. 5.9 are used to build clauses and sentences. A **sentence** can be loosely defined as an independent syntactic unit which usually begins with a capital letter and ends with a full stop/period, question mark or exclamation mark/exclamation point in writing. Up to this point, there has been no need to be more specific or distinguish between clauses and sentences, as our example *Anna sang a song yesterday* contains a subject as well as a predicate and is both a clause as well as a sentence. A **clause** is a constituent with one subject-predicate structure and may either constitute a sentence by itself or be combined with other clauses to form a sentence. Clauses thus contain a subject and a predicate, e.g. *Anna (S) sang (P)*,

Clauses and Sentences

and may contain other optional syntactic elements, e.g. the object *a song* in *Anna (S) sang (P) a song (O)*. Sentences which consist of one clause only, i.e. which contain only one subject-predicate structure, are called **simple sentences**. A clause which makes up a simple sentence must be capable of standing on its own and is thus called a **main clause** (or **independent clause**).

Sentences, however, can consist of more than one clause. To form such non-simple sentences, the obligatory main clause may either be combined with one or several main clauses to form a **compound sentence**, or with at least one **subordinate clause** (or **dependent clause**), which cannot stand on its own, to form a **complex sentence**.

Fig. 5.10

Simple and non-simple sentences

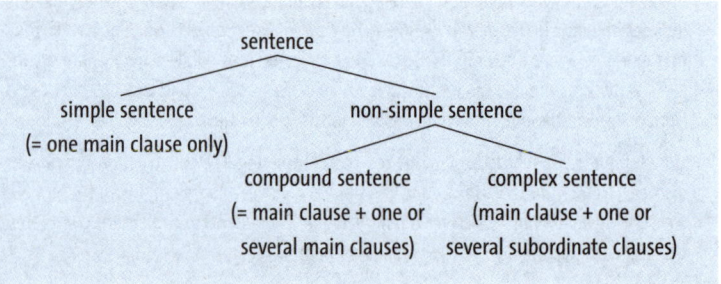

Coordinating conjunctions such as *and*, *but* and *or* are commonly used to join two or more main clauses to form a compound sentence. In contrast, complex sentences often contain a subordinating conjunction such as *although*, *because* and *when*, or a relative pronoun such as *who* and *which*.

Fig. 5.11

Compound and complex sentences

compound sentence

Anna sang a song   *and/but*   *her brother played the guitar.*

main clause   coordinating conjunction   main clause

complex sentences

Anna sang a song,   *although she was ill.*

main clause   subordinate clause containing a subordinating conjunction

The police questioned the woman   *who had witnessed the accident.*

main clause   subordinate clause containing a relative pronoun

According to the verb form used in the predicate of a clause, clauses can be divided into **finite clauses** and **non-finite clauses**. Finite clauses contain a verb element that is marked for tense, such as *sang* in *Anna sang a song yesterday*, as well as person and number, such as *sings* in *Anna sings a song every day*. Finite clauses can serve as main clauses and subordinate clauses, e.g. *although she was ill* in the sentence *Anna sang a song, although she was ill* (cf. Fig. 5.11).

Finite and Non-Finite Clauses

In contrast, the verb element in non-finite clauses lacks markers for tense, number and person. The infinitive with *to*, the present participle and the past participle are non-finite verb forms. Non-finite clauses can only occur in subordinate function, such as the subordinate clauses *you to stay* in *I want you to stay*, *leaving the country* in *Leaving the country, they waved their fans goodbye*, and *defeated by the Spanish team* in *Defeated by the Spanish team, the German team flew home on an Airbus A380*.

After having taken a close look at words and clauses, we can now turn to the **phrase level**, i.e. the level between the word level and the clause level (cf. Fig. 5.1). Phrases are different from words in that they may consist of more than one word, and different from clauses in that they do not have a subject-predicate structure. Let us consider a simple sentence first. *Anna sang* is a sentence that consists of only one main clause. The noun *Anna* is the subject and the verb *sang* is the predicate.

The Phrase Level

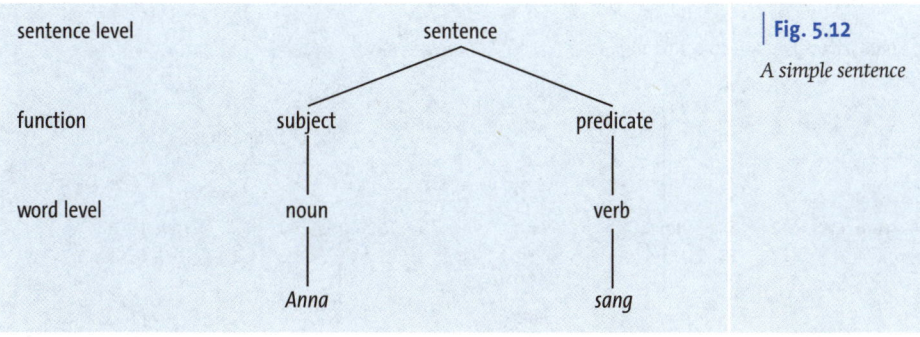

Fig. 5.12

A simple sentence

To indicate that both the noun *Anna* and the verb *sang* are not only words belonging to different syntactic categories but also phrases (very simple phrases, in this case, but we will encounter more complex phrases soon), we may switch from a functional to a formal point of view and say that the sentence *Anna sang* consists of the **noun phrase** *Anna* and the **verb phrase** *sang*.

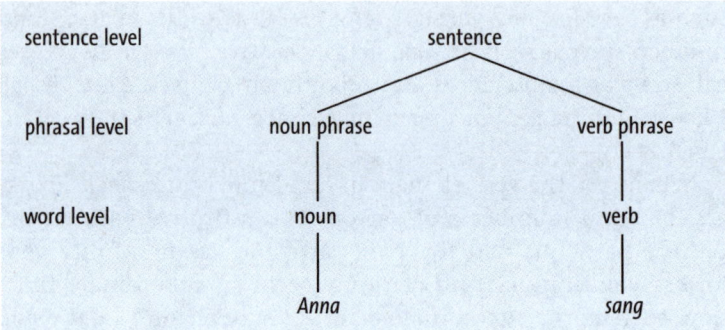

Fig. 5.13

A simple sentence revisited

We may use the term **subject noun phrase** to distinguish this function of noun phrases from other functions, such as an **object noun phrase**. Consider the sentence *Anna sang a song*. The noun phrase *Anna* is the subject. The verb phrase, however, does not only contain the verb *sang*, but also the object noun phrase *a song*, which consists of the determiner *a* and the noun *song*.

Fig. 5.14

sentence level   sentence

phrasal levels   subject noun phrase   verb phrase

                                                object noun phrase

word level   noun   verb   determiner   noun

                  Anna   sang   a   song

A sentence with a subject and an object

Most linguists prefer to use only abbreviations in tree diagrams, such as S for sentence, NP for noun phrase, VP for verb phrase, N for noun, V for verb, and Det for determiner (cf. Fig. 5.2). According to these conventions, our example sentence from Fig. 5.14 is usually represented as follows:

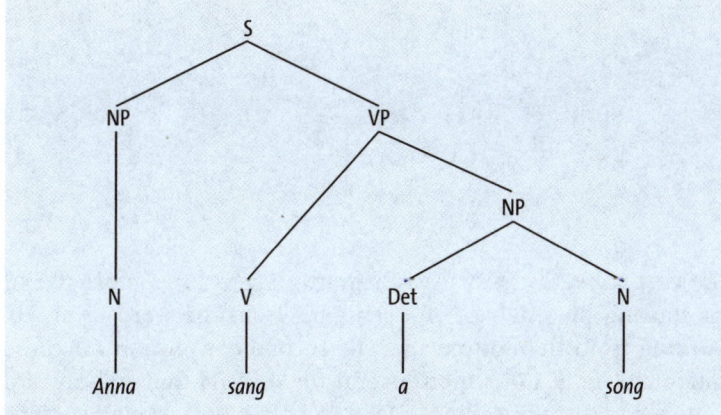

Fig. 5.15

A sentence with a subject and an object (common representation)

Tree diagrams, as illustrated in Fig. 5.15, and similar representations of sentences are widely used today. Alternatively, the elements of a sentence may also be represented in a linear fashion by enclosing them in labelled square brackets:

[$_S$ [$_{NP}$ [$_N$ *Anna*]] [$_{VP}$ [$_V$ *sang*] [$_{NP}$ [$_{Det}$ *a*] [$_N$ *song*]]]]

Fig. 5.16

A sentence with a subject and an object (representation in labelled square brackets)

Some linguists use an alternative form of tree diagram that emphasises the relationships between the constituents by breaking up the linear representation of the sentence as a string of words:

Fig. 5.17

A sentence with a subject and an object (alternative tree diagram)

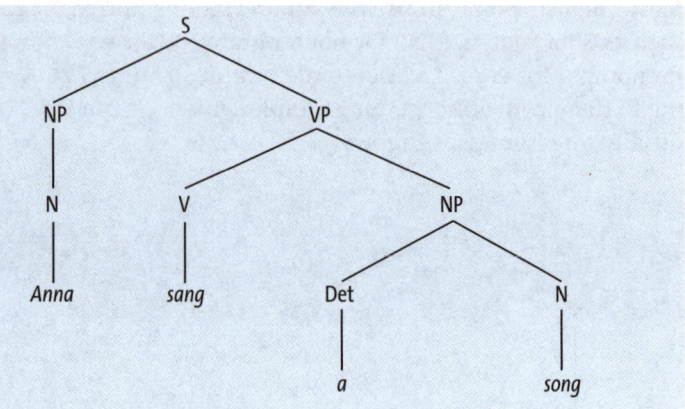

The first convention for tree diagrams (Fig. 5.15) is more useful for starting the analysis of a sentence from the word level, i.e. working from the bottom up. The second convention for these diagrams (Fig. 5.17) is more useful for starting the analysis of a sentence at the phrasal level. Within both conventions, simplifications are possible.

Simplifications

To simplify tree diagrams, linguists sometimes leave out the internal structure of selected phrases. These phrases are then represented with so-called "clothes hangers":

Fig. 5.18

Some sentences with a subject and an object (simplified representation)

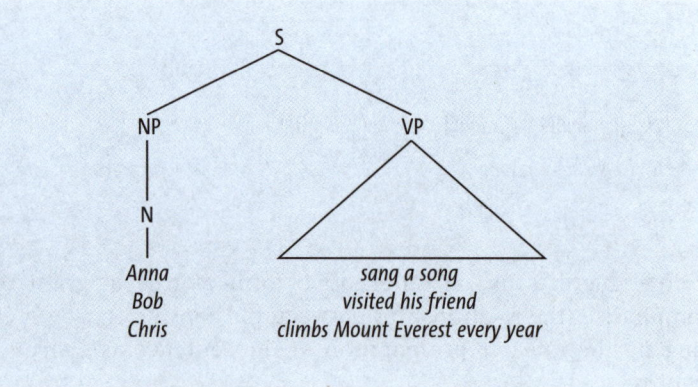

Phrases and Heads

Phrases can be divided into **simple phrases**, i.e. phrases consisting of one word only, and **complex phrases**, i.e. phrases consisting of two and more words. The subject noun phrase *Anna* in the sentence *Anna sang a song* is thus a simple phrase. In the similarly structured sentence *The talented soprano sang a song*, the subject noun phrase *the talented soprano* is a complex phrase (cf. also 5.4).

The name of a phrase is determined by its **head** around which it is built, i.e. a phrase built around a noun or a pronoun is a noun phrase (NP), a phrase built around a verb is a verb phrase (VP), and a phrase built around an adjective is an adjective phrase (AdjP) etc. As we know from the section on compounding in the chapter on morphology, the head of a complex word determines the word's syntactic class and, accordingly, its grammatical properties. Similarly, the heads of syntactic phrases determine the grammatical properties of the phrase. For instance, since nouns and pronouns can function as subjects and objects in clauses, noun phrases headed by nouns and pronouns can also function as subjects and objects. Along the same lines, verb phrases are headed by verbs and can function as the predicate of sentences, adjective phrases are headed by adjectives and can modify nouns, and so on. The relationship between all types of phrases and their heads is summed up in the following blueprint:

An XP is a phrasal constituent **headed** by an X.

Fig. 5.19

Phrases and their heads

Characteristic Phrase Structures and Clause Structures of English

| 5.4

Each language has its characteristic phrase structures and clause structures. In the acquisition of their first language, children master these characteristic structures at a very early age. For instance, during the two-word stage, which begins around eighteen months, children start to use their native language's characteristic order of subject noun phrase and verb phrase:

Some Examples for Language-Specific Structures

Fig. 5.20

*Word order at the
two-word stage
in first language
acquisition (adapted
from Peccei 2005)*

English	German	Finnish	Samoan
Bambi go	*Puppe kommt*	*Seppo putoo*	*Pa'u pepe*
	'doll come'	'Seppo fall'	'fall doll'
subject NP + VP	subject NP + VP	subject NP + VP	VP + subject NP

However, before we can take a closer look at the characteristic clause structures of English, we need to discuss some of the typical phrase structures. We will now take a look at the internal structure of some simple and complex phrases.

Noun Phrases

In English, a **simple noun phrase** consists of a single proper noun (e.g. *Anna*, *Bob*, or *Chris*), a single plural noun without a determiner (e.g. *boats*, *cars*, or *bikes*), or a single pronoun (*he*, *she*, *they*). In contrast, a **complex noun phrase** contains at least one additional constituent such as a determiner phrase and/or an adjective phrase before the head noun, and a relative clause and/or a prepositional phrase after the head noun.

Fig. 5.21

*Constituents of
complex noun phrases*

determiner phrase	adjective phrase	head noun	relative clause / prepositional phrase
every	*long*	*holiday*	*that we plan*
(all) the	*red (and green)*	*candle(s)*	*on (and under) the table*

Determiner Phrases, Adjective Phrases and Prepositional Phrases

Fig. 5.21 shows that determiners, adjectives and prepositions may also head complex phrases, i.e. **determiner phrases** (DetP) may contain more than one determiner (e.g. *all* and *the*), **adjective phrases** (AdjP) may contain more than one adjective (e.g. *red* and *green*), and **prepositional phrases** (PrepP) may not only contain more than one preposition (e.g. *on* and *under*), but also noun phrases (e.g. *the table*). As the following example shows, elements of the same category are frequently linked with a **coordinating conjunction** such as *or* or *and*:

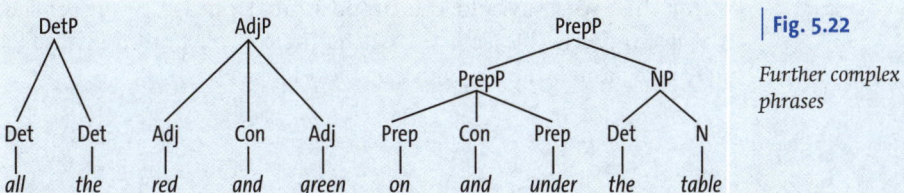

Fig. 5.22

Further complex phrases

As we have just seen, most constituents of phrases may occur more than once. Accordingly, we may produce phrases of nearly infinite complexity. Repeatable rules that can be applied over and over again are called **recursive**. We may, for example, integrate several prepositional phrases into a noun phrase. When we add the prepositional phrase *with the hat* to the noun phrase *the lady*, the result is the complex noun phrase *the lady with the hat*:

Recursivity

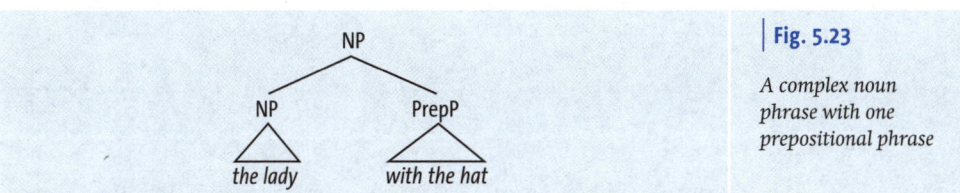

Fig. 5.23

A complex noun phrase with one prepositional phrase

We may repeat this procedure and add the prepositional phrase *with the feather* to the noun phrases *the hat* in the prepositional phrase *with the hat*, thus expanding the noun phrase *the lady with the hat* to *the lady with the hat with the feather*:

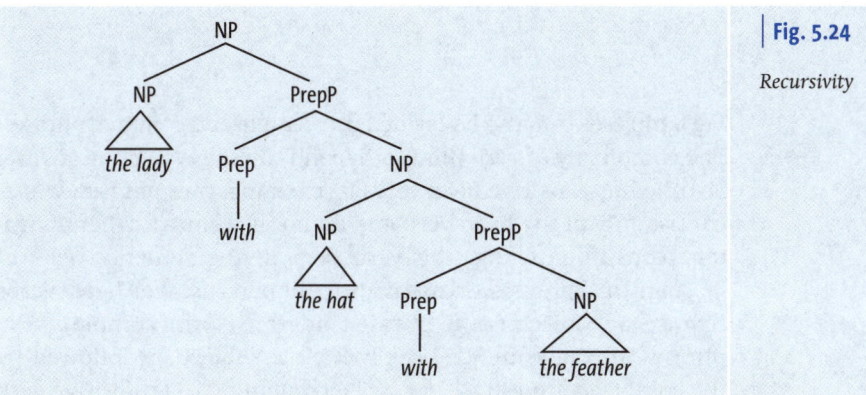

Fig. 5.24

Recursivity

After this, we may add the prepositional phrase *on the brim* to the noun phrase *the feather*, creating the complex noun phrase *the lady with the hat with the feather on the brim*:

Fig. 5.25

Recursivity continued

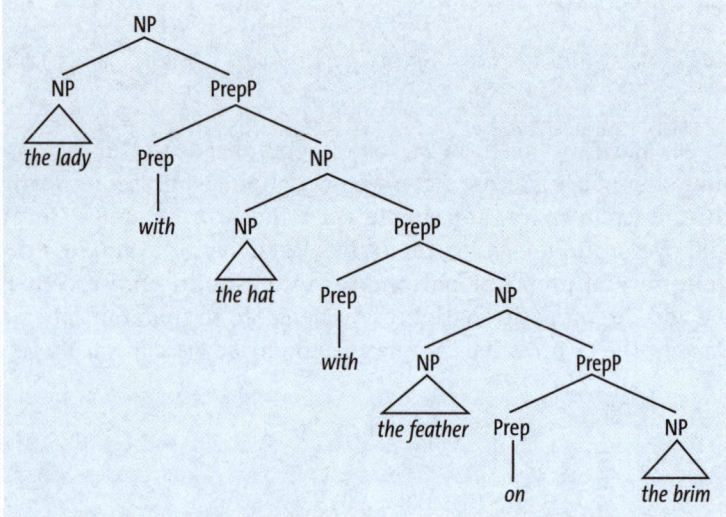

Complex phrases may also be represented in labelled square brackets:

Fig. 5.26

Recursivity continued (representation in labelled square brackets)

[NP the lady [PrepP with [NP the hat [PrepP with [NP the feather [PrepP on [NP the brim]]]]]]]

Verb Phrases

Verb phrases can also be divided into simple and complex phrases. The complexity of verb phrases depends on the type of head verb. So-called **intransitive** head verbs form simple verb phrases, which consist only of the head verb and do not need any further obligatory constituents, e.g. the verb *sleep* in the sentence *She was sleeping*. In contrast, **transitive** (or monotransitive) head verbs require an object noun phrase and thus form complex verb phrases. In the sentence *I love books*, the subject *I* is followed by the complex verb phrase *love books*, containing the transitive verb *love*, which requires an object, in this case *books*. **Ditransitive** head verbs need two object noun phrases, a direct object and an indirect object (cf. Fig. 5.9). In the sentence *We sent them a parcel*, the subject *we* is followed by the ditransitive verb *send*, which requires a direct object such as *a parcel* and an indirect object such as *them*. The most widely-known types of head verbs are illustrated in Fig 5.27. It is important to note that many verbs belong to several different transitivity types. For instance, the verb *sing* can be used intransitively (e.g. *Anna sang*), monotransitively (e.g. *Anna sang a song*) and ditransitively (e.g. *Anna sang him a song*).

verb type	required other constituents	example verbs	example clause
INTRANSITIVE	none	*sleep, swim, sing*	*She was sleeping*
TRANSITIVE (or MONOTRANSITIVE)	one object NP	*love, hate, sing*	*I love books*
DITRANSITIVE	two object NPs	*send, give, offer, sing*	*We sent them a parcel*

Fig. 5.27

Some types of head verbs

Corresponding to the types of head verbs illustrated in Fig. 5.27, there are a limited number of characteristic **clause patterns** found in declarative sentences in English. In Fig. 5.28, we will represent some of these basic patterns, using S for subject, P for predicate, and O for object (cf. Fig. 5.9).

Some Basic English Clause Patterns

verb type	example clause	clause pattern
INTRANSITIVE	*She was sleeping*	SP
TRANSITIVE (or MONOTRANSITIVE)	*I read a book*	SPO
DITRANSITIVE	*We sent them a parcel*	SPOO

Fig. 5.28

Some basic clause patterns

The patterns illustrated in Fig. 5.28 are characteristic of English declarative clauses and the reason for the classification of English as a so-called **SPO-language** (or **SVO-language**).

In another research tradition, the syntactic structure of verb phrases is described with the help of an analogy from chemistry. Just as chemical elements may form bonds with a certain number of other chemical elements, **predicates** may combine with a certain number of so-called **syntactic arguments**. This relationship is known as **valency**. Within this research tradition, the subject noun phrase is seen as one syntactic argument among others. This means that predicates with intransitive verbs, which do not require any arguments other than a subject noun phrase, are interpreted as **monovalent**, predicates with transitive (or monotransitive) verbs, which require the two arguments subject and object, as **divalent**, and predicates with ditransitive verbs, which require the three arguments subject, direct object and indirect object, as **trivalent**:

Fig. 5.29

Valency: Some types of predicates and their arguments

predicate type	examples	arguments
MONOVALENT	*She was sleeping*	*she*
DIVALENT	*I read a book*	*I, a book*
TRIVALENT	*We sent them a parcel*	*we, a parcel, them*

Additionally, there is a group of English verbs such as *rain* or *snow* which form predicates that do not require a subject in the sense of 'someone or something of which something is said' (cf. Fig. 5.9). These verbs regularly trigger the use of the so-called "dummy *it*", as in *It is raining*, to fill the subject slot of a sentence. Verbs from this group do not require a syntactic argument and are thus interpreted as **avalent**, because the "dummy *it*" is not considered a "real" argument.

In addition to the basic types of head verbs and corresponding clause patterns outlined above, there are further verb types and clause patterns which are relevant for English. **Copular verbs** (or "linking verbs") such as *be* and *become* are followed either by a subject complement such as *the President of the United States* in *He became the President of the United States* or by an adverbial such as *too early* in *We were too early*. **Complex transitive verbs** such as *find* or *put* form clause patterns with a combination of an object such as *clause patterns* and a complement such as *fascinating* in the clause *We find clause patterns fascinating*, or an object such as *the book* and an adverbial such as *on the shelf* in *I put the book on the shelf*:

verb type	required other constituents	example verbs	example clauses	
COPULAR	one complement	*become, be*	*He became the President of the United States*	**Fig. 5.30** *Further types of head verbs*
	or an adverbial		*We were too early*	
COMPLEX TRANSITIVE	one object NP and one complement	*find, put*	*We find clause patterns fascinating*	
	or one object NP and an adverbial		*I put the book on the shelf*	

Corresponding to the types of head verbs illustrated in Fig. 5.30, there are further characteristic clause patterns shown in Fig. 5.31, containing complements (C) and adverbials (A) as additional syntactic elements (cf. Fig. 5.9).

Further English Clause Patterns

verb type	example clause	clause pattern	
COPULAR	*He became the President of the United States*	SPC	**Fig. 5.31** *Further clause patterns of English*
	We were too early	SPA	
COMPLEX TRANSITIVE	*We find clause patterns fascinating*	SPOC	
	I put the book on the shelf	SPOA	

In terms of valency, copular verbs form divalent predicates, i.e. they require two arguments, whereas complex transitive verbs form trivalent predicates, i.e. they require three arguments. The following figure gives an overview of the seven characteristic clause patterns of English, including the corresponding verb types and their valency:

Fig. 5.32

The seven basic clause patterns of English

verb type	example clause	valency	clause pattern
INTRANSITIVE	*She was working*	monovalent	SP
TRANSITIVE (or MONOTRANSITIVE)	*I read a book*	divalent	SPO
DITRANSITIVE	*We sent them a parcel*	trivalent	SPOO
COPULAR	*He became the President of the United States*	divalent	SPC
	We were too early	divalent	SPA
COMPLEX TRANSITIVE	*We find clause patterns fascinating*	trivalent	SPOC
	I put the book on the shelf	trivalent	SPOA

The clause patterns shown in Fig. 5.32 correspond to what is frequently referred to as the characteristic **word order** of English. Word order, or more precisely the order of constituents of a sentence and the word order within these constituents, is particularly important in analytic languages such as Modern English (cf. 2.1.4). As English has lost most of its inflections in the course of its history, word order is now essential for the expression of grammatical relations within sentences. A change in the order of constituents almost invariably leads to a change in meaning: *John loves Shirley* does not mean the same as *Shirley loves John*. Changes in word order can also result in a violation of the sentence structure rules of a particular language: **Loves Shirley John* is considered impossible in English and thus marked with an asterisk. Strings of words which do not conform to the syntactic rules of a particular language are called ungrammatical. We will look at grammaticality in the following section.

5.5 | **Grammatical Rules and Grammaticality**

Grammaticality

Human memory is limited and speakers cannot store all possible words and sentences of a language in their brains. Instead, they store words and grammatical rules, which enable them to produce, understand and make judgements about an unlimited number of sentences based on a limited set of means. Children acquire this largely subconscious knowledge when they acquire their native language. Without necessarily being able to explain why, native speakers can usually intuitively tell the difference between a **grammatical sentence**, i.e. a sentence that obeys the grammatical rules of the language in question, and an **ungrammatical string of words**, i.e. a string of words that violates the grammatical rules of the language. Consider a famous example coined by Noam Chomsky more than half a century ago:

Colourless green ideas sleep furiously.
*Furiously sleep ideas green colourless.

Native speakers as well as proficient non-native speakers of English will identify the first sentence as grammatical, although it does not make much sense, whereas they will judge the structure of the second example ungrammatical in English. Some linguists also use the terms *well-formed* for grammatical sentences and *ill-formed* for ungrammatical sequences of words. We will avoid these terms here because descriptive linguistics generally avoids value judgements (cf. 1.3).

The unconscious knowledge native speakers have of the grammatical rules of the language they grow up with is called **competence**. On the basis of their competence, they are able to state that the sentence *Colourless green ideas sleep furiously* conforms to the grammatical rules of English, while **Furiously sleep ideas green colourless* does not. Competence, however, is not the same as actual language behaviour. What humans actually produce in their spoken or written utterances may or may not reflect their competence. Particularly in spoken discourse, humans often do not strictly follow the syntactic rules of a language although they are familiar with them. This happens either unintentionally, due to impairing factors such as distractions, or deliberately, for the sake of certain effects. Actual language behaviour is called **performance**.

Competence and Performance

Crystal (2003:191) observes that "native speakers of English quite often say that they 'don't know' any grammar, or that foreigners speak English better than they do". Such statements are not merely a matter of being polite to non-native speakers. In fact, native speakers are often unable to explain the grammatical rules of their language because, as stated above, their linguistic

Knowing Grammar and Knowing About Grammar

knowledge is largely subconscious. They "**know their grammar**" but **do not necessarily know much *about* it**, i.e. they are often not able to formulate the rules governing their linguistic choices. Non-native speakers, on the other hand, often learn these rules consciously, as most of us know from personal experience.

Generative Approaches to Syntax

The fairly recent **generative** approaches to syntax pay particular attention to the subconscious rules that constitute our competence and allow us to generate an unlimited number of sentences. Generative approaches originated with Noam Chomsky in the 1950s. One of these approaches, the so-called **principles-and-parameters framework**, which was initiated by Chomsky at the end of the 1970s, assumes that there are general (or universal) **principles** that are common to all languages, and individual **parameters** which differ from language to language. For example, one general principle says that declarative sentences must contain a subject. The subject of a sentence in English is usually explicitly expressed by means of a noun phrase, whereas it may appear either explicitly or implicitly in other languages: For instance, the Italian sentence *Parla francese* ('she speaks French') is perfectly grammatical without an explicit subject, whereas most speakers of English would consider the literal equivalent *Speaks French* to be ungrammatical. Languages such as Italian are known as null-subject languages, whereas languages such as English are considered non-null-subject languages. The corresponding parameter is known as the Null Subject Parameter, which states whether the subject has to be expressed explicitly. The position of syntactic elements within sentences, such as the position of the predicate, is another parameter which differs between languages (cf. Fig. 5.20).

"**Whenever the literary German dives into a sentence, that is the last you are going to see of him till he emerges on the other side of his Atlantic with his verb in his mouth.**"

(Mark Twain. *A Connecticut Yankee in King Arthur's Court*. 1889)

Syntax, Grammar and Meaning

As we have seen in this chapter, it is our conscious or subconscious knowledge of grammatical rules that allows us to not only judge whether a sentence is grammatical, but also helps us to interpret its meaning. We will take a closer look at the meaning and meanings of words, phrases and sentences in the next chapter.

Exercises

1. Determine the syntactic categories of the words in the following sentences. Represent your results as in Fig. 5.3.
   a) *Bob called a friend.*
   b) *She called him a genius.*
   c) *The baby cried.*
   d) *The students sent the teacher some very interesting suggestions.*

2. Why is *call* a verb? Apply all three relevant criteria and give
   reasons.

3. Determine the sentence types.
   a) *Twinkle, twinkle, little star!*
   b) *How I wonder what you are!*
   c) *Is the little star twinkling?*
   d) *The little star is twinkling.*

4. Determine whether *a book* is a constituent in the sentence
   John read a book last night by applying constituency tests.

5. Identify all simple and complex phrases in the following sentences.
   a) *April is a cruel month.*
   b) *Midnight shakes the memory.*
   c) *I met a traveller from an antique land.*

6. Represent the sentence *John read a book*
   a) with the help of a tree diagram.
   b) using labelled square brackets.

7. Represent the complex noun phrase *the husband of the lady with
   the cat*
   a) with the help of a tree diagram.
   b) using labelled square brackets.

8. Analyse the example sentences of exercise 1 and in each
   identify
   a) the verb type.
   b) the clause pattern.
   c) the valency of the verb.

9. Which of the following examples based on poems by T. S. Eliot are grammatical sentences? Give reasons.

a) *Houses rise fall and*

b) *Houses live and die*

c) *We are the hollow men*

d) *The we are hollow men*

5.7 | Bibliography

Aarts, Bas. 2008. *English Syntax and Argumentation.* 3rd edition. Houndmills: Palgrave Macmillan. *(Thorough but accessible)*

Börjars, Kersti & **Kate Burridge.** 2010. *Introducing English Grammar.* 2nd edition. London: Hodder Education. *(Beginner-friendly and lively)*

Burton-Roberts, Noel. 1997. *Analysing Sentences. An Introduction to English Syntax.* 2nd edition. London: Longman. *(Comprehensive and clear)*

Chomsky, Noam. 1995. *The Minimalist Program.* Cambridge, MA: MIT Press. *(A milestone in generative grammar)*

Chomsky, Noam. 1957. *Syntactic Structures.* Berlin: de Gruyter. *(The vantage point of generative grammar)*

Crystal, David. 2003. *The Cambridge Encyclopedia of the English Language.* 2nd edition. Cambridge: Cambridge University Press. *(Very illustrative and appealing)*

Fabb, Nigel. 2005. *Sentence Structure.* 2nd edition. London: Routledge. *(Contains a wealth of useful exercises)*

Gelderen, Elly van. 2010. *An Introduction to the Grammar of English.* Revised edition. Amsterdam: Benjamins. *(Excellent for beginners)*

Haegeman, Liliane & **Jacqueline Guéron.** 1999. *English Grammar. A Generative Perspective.* Oxford: Blackwell. *(Substantial and clear)*

Huddleston, Rodney. 1984. *Introduction to the Grammar of English.* Cambridge: Cambridge University Press. *(Traditional but strongly aware of theoretical discussions)*

Huddleston, Rodney & **Geoffrey K. Pullum.** 2002. *The Cambridge Grammar of the English Language.* Cambridge: Cambridge University Press. *(An advanced comprehensive reference grammar)*

Matthews, Peter. 2007. *The Concise Oxford Dictionary of Linguistics.* Oxford: Oxford University Press. *(Very helpful as a first orientation)*

Miller, Jim. 2008. *An Introduction to English Syntax.* 2nd edition. Edinburgh: Edinburgh University Press. *(Basic and accessible)*

Quirk, Randolph et al. 1985. *A Grammar of Contemporary English.* London: Longman. *(Still one of the most comprehensive traditional reference grammars)*

Radford, Andrew. 2004a. *Minimalist Syntax. Exploring the Structure of English.* Cambridge: Cambridge University Press. *(Very thorough, with extensive workbook sections and practical hints)*

Radford, Andrew. 2004b. *English Syntax. An Introduction.* Cambridge: Cambridge University Press. *(Abridged version of Minimalist Syntax, suitable for ambitious beginners)*

Tallerman, Maggie. 2005. *Understanding Syntax.* 2nd edition. London: Arnold. *(Very accessible and beginner-friendly)*

Verspoor, Marjolijn & **Kim Sauter.** 2000. *English Sentence Analysis.* Amsterdam: Benjamins. *(Great for absolute beginners, accompanied by an exercise CD-ROM)*

Further References

Eliot, T. S. 1963. *Collected Poems 1909-1962.* New York: Harcourt Brace. *(Thought-provoking and rich in linguistic challenges)*

Peccei, Jean. 2005. *Child Language.* <http://childlanguage.homestead.com> *(A beginner-friendly site with many useful links)*

Twain, Mark. 1889. *A Connecticut Yankee in King Arthur's Court.* New York: Webster. *The Project Gutenberg EBook* 86. Released August 20, 2006. <http://www.gutenberg.org/files/86/86-h/86-h.htm>

Semantics

Contents

Abstract

Semantics is the systematic study of meaning in human language. It is concerned with the linguistic meaning of words, phrases and sentences. Other than pragmatics (cf. Chapter 7), semantics deals mainly with context-independent meaning.

6.1 | The Study of Meaning

What do linguists mean when they say that they study meaning? Linguists working in the field of **semantics** are interested in **meaning in human language** (or **linguistic meaning**). For thousands of years, philosophers have been concerned with more general questions of meaning and the nature of meaning, but we will only address linguistic meaning here.

We have seen in Section 1.3 that there is an arbitrary but systematic relationship between the form and the meaning of each word in a certain language. According to Saussure, each linguistic sign (or word) consists of two inseparably connected parts, namely a sound sequence (or signifier) and a concept (or signified). The speakers of a certain language or language variety are aware of the generally agreed-upon meaning(s) of words. As we know, with only a few exceptions such as onomatopoeic words, these meanings are only a matter of convention.

Branches of Semantics

In order to be able to communicate with others in a particular language, we must learn and adhere to the agreed-upon meanings of words, and the ways in which words are combined to form larger meaningful units such as phrases and sentences (cf. Chapter 5). Accordingly, semantics can be split up into two major branches: **lexical semantics** is concerned with the meaning of words and the meaning relationships among words, whereas **sentential semantics** (or **phrasal semantics**) deals with the meaning of syntactic units larger than words, i.e. phrases, clauses and sentences, and semantic relationships between them.

6.2 | Lexical Semantics

In Chapter 4 on morphology, we have seen that words are made up of one or more so-called morphemes, defined as the smallest meaning-carrying units in language. In lexical semantics we will discuss the meaning of words, keeping in mind that words may consist of several morphemes.

Meaning Relations Among Words | 6.2.1

The words of a certain language or variety can be semantically related to one another in a number of different ways. We will now take a look at the most important of these **meaning relations** (or **sense relations**).

Synonymy

Imagine you have to write an essay describing the process of buying your first house. What can you do to avoid using the word *buy* over and over again? One strategy would be to choose other verbs with the same or nearly the same meaning, such as *purchase* or *acquire*. *Buy*, *purchase* and *acquire* are said to be **synonyms**, the semantic relation between them is termed **synonymy**. Synonyms are traditionally defined as words with the same meaning. It is, however, rare for words to have exactly the same meaning (or perfect synonymy). Many linguists claim that it would be uneconomical for one language to have two or more words with exactly the same meaning and thus prefer to define synonymy as **extensive semantic similarity**. For example, synonyms may differ with regard to stylistic level (*buy ~ purchase*, cf. the example sentences in *Style* in Section 8.2), or social or regional variety (e.g. BrE *lift* ~ AmE *elevator*).

		Fig. 6.1
car ~ automobile	*begin ~ commence*	
worker ~ employee	*informal ~ casual*	*Some pairs of synonyms in English*
house ~ domicile	*eat ~ consume*	

Lists of synonyms can be looked up in a **thesaurus**. Thesauruses are dictionaries in which words with similar meanings are grouped together. The most famous thesaurus of the English language is *Roget's Thesaurus*. It does not only provide lists of synonyms, but can also help us to find the opposite of synonyms, namely antonyms.

Antonymy

Word pairs that are opposite in meaning are called **antonyms**. The semantic relationship between them is referred to as **antonymy**. Antonyms are opposites with respect to at least one component of their meaning, but share all other aspects of their meaning. For example, the verbs *come* and *go* are opposites with respect to direction but both involve the notion of movement. To specify the "kind of oppositeness", linguists distinguish several major types of antonyms.

Word pairs like *present ~ absent* or *dead ~ alive* are referred to as **complementary pairs. Complementary antonymy** is characterised by an either-or relationship between the two members of such a pair, and by the fact that the negative of one of the words is synonymous with the other. For example, a person can be either *present* or *absent* and either *dead* or *alive*. Furthermore, *not present* is synonymous with *absent* and *not absent* is synonymous with *present*, just as *not dead* is synonymous with *alive* and *not alive* is synonymous with *dead*.

Antonym pairs such as *hot ~ freezing* or *small ~ large* belong to a different type of antonymy. Pairs like these are referred to as **gradable pairs**, while the type of antynomy is accordingly called **gradable antonymy**. In these cases, the opposite of one of the words is not necessarily synonymous with the other. We all know from our favourite fast food place that drinks do not only come in *small* and *large*, but that there is at least a *medium* in between. So *not large* is not necessarily synonymous with *small*, just as *not hot* is not necessarily synonymous with *freezing*. Gradable antonymy is sometimes also referred to as **polarity**, because gradable pairs are often opposite poles of a continuum of expressions, with one or more intermediate stages between them:

Fig. 6.2

Gradable antonymy

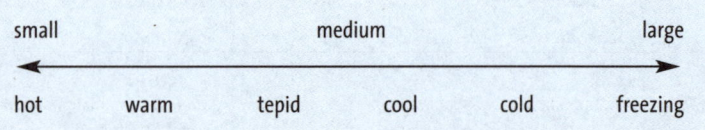

The example shows that there is obviously not an either-or relationship between gradable antonyms. In gradable pairs, more of one is less of the other. More smallness is less largeness and hotter is less freezing. Most gradable pairs are pairs of adjectives that do not by themselves provide an absolute scale but are always related to the expression they modify. For example, even a *large bee* is still much smaller in absolute size than a *small horse*.

Some pairs of gradable antonyms show an asymmetry with respect to their usage conditions. This means that one of the words can appear in more contexts than the other. When we ask questions like *How **old** are you?* and *How **high** is the skyscraper?*, we automatically use *old* not *young* and *high* not *low*. The expressions with the wider range of uses, here *old* and *high*, are called **unmarked**, whereas the expressions with the more limited range of uses, here *young* and *low*, are referred to as **marked**. We say that these gradable antonyms differ with respect to **markedness**.

Another type of antonymy can be illustrated by pairs like *teacher ~ pupil* and *buy ~ sell*. The words in these pairs are called **relational opposites**, as they describe the same situation from opposite perspectives. If X is Y's *pupil*, then Y is X's *teacher*, and if X *buys* something from Y, then Y *sells* something to X. For example, nouns derived from verbs by adding the bound derivational suffixes *-er* and *-ee* respectively are usually relational opposites. If X is Y's *employee*, than Y is X's *employer*. Or think about the pair *interviewer ~ interviewee* we have discussed in the section on word formation (cf. 4.3.2).

The fourth and last type of antonymy we would like to address here shows in pairs such as *come ~ go* and *rise ~ fall*. We have said above that *come ~ go* are opposites with respect to the direction of a movement. The same holds true for the pair *rise ~ fall*. Pairs like these that describe the opposite directions of a movement are thus called **directional opposites**.

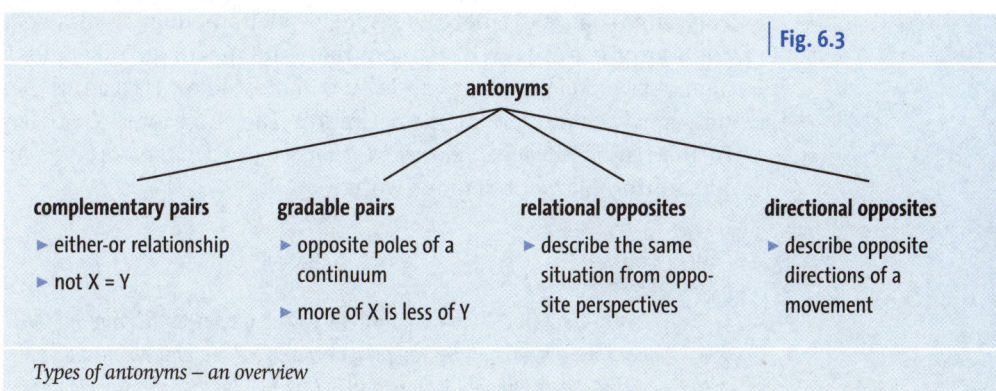

| Fig. 6.3

Types of antonyms – an overview

From the point of view of word formation, there are a number of different ways to form antonyms: We have seen above that we can add *-er ~ -ee* to some verbs to produce opposite nouns, as in *interviewer ~ interviewee*. Other morphological ways to form antonyms include the addition of the prefixes *un-, in-, non-, dis-* and *mis-*, as in *able ~ unable, sane ~ insane, sexist ~ non-sexist, honest ~ dishonest* and *behave ~ misbehave.*

Knowing a word involves both knowing the pronunciation and the meaning of the word. This corresponds to Saussure's model of the linguistic sign, which always consists of a sound sequence (= form) as well as a concept (= meaning). However, there are sound sequences that have two or more different meanings. When the individual meanings of a sound sequence are historically and/or semantically related, we speak of one **polysemous** word that has a range of different meanings. When the individual meanings of a sound sequence are unrelated, we speak of separate words that are **homophones**.

According to the above distinction, **homophony** occurs where one form has two or more completely distinct meanings, as in /raɪt/ representing both *right* and *write*. Homophones are thus different words with the same pronunciation. In dictionaries, homophones are usually represented by separate entries. Spelling is completely irrelevant. *Write* and *right* are homophones just like *bank* 'the side of a river' and *bank* 'a financial institution', because each of the two pairs consists of different words with an identical pronunciation.

On the other hand, as we have said above, **polysemy** occurs where one lexeme has a range of different but related meanings. Polysemy is an extremely widespread phenomenon, as it is very common for words to have more than one meaning. Take a look at any page of a dictionary and you will most likely find a number of words with more than one definition. The entry for the verb *buy* in the *Oxford Advanced Learner's Dictionary* (*OALD*) can serve as an illustration for a polysemous word:

buy /baɪ/ *verb*
WITH MONEY
1 **~ sb sth| ~ sth (for sb)** to obtain sth by paying money for it: [vnn, vn] *He bought me a new coat. He bought a new coat for me.* [vn] *Where did you buy that dress? I bought it from a friend for £10.* [v] *If you're thinking of getting a new car, now is a good time to buy.* [vn-adj] *I bought my car second-hand.* OPP sell
2 [vn] (of money) to be enough to pay for sth: *He gave his children the best education that money can buy. Five pounds doesn't buy much nowadays.*
3 [vn] to persuade sb to do sth dishonest in return for money SYN bribe: *He can't be bought* (= he's too honest to accept money in this way).

OBTAIN

4   [vn] [usually passive] to obtain sth by losing sth else of great value:
   Her fame was bought at the expense of her marriage.

BELIEVE

5   [vn] (informal) to believe that sth is true, especially sth that is not very
   likely: *You could say you were ill but I don't think they'd buy it* (= accept
   the explanation).

Both polysemy and homophony refer to a single form that has
two or more meanings. Such words with more than one meaning
are called **ambiguous**, and accordingly polysemy and homophony
are said to create **lexical ambiguity**. The sentence *She has bought it*
could mean either that she has obtained something by paying
money for it or, metaphorically, that she believes something she
has heard to be true (cf. the definitions 1 and 5 in the above entry
for *buy* from the *OALD*). In this case, we cannot tell which of the
two possible meanings of *buy* the speaker or writer of the sentence
intended. The sentence is ambiguous. Many puns and jokes are
based on ambiguity. Consider the following example:

   *Is life worth living? It depends on the **liver**.*

In our example, *liver* is used as an ambiguous noun that either
means 'a large organ in our body' or 'a person who lives'. In the
second rather exceptional meaning, *liver* is interpreted as a noun
that is derived from the verb *live* by adding the derivational suffix
-er. In our explanation of the ambiguity in this example, we have
just used the lexically ambiguous term *organ* that can either refer
to a body part or a musical instrument. In this case, however, it
becomes immediately clear from the context that *organ* refers to a
body part, as it would be very unlikely for a musical instrument
the size of an organ to be "in our body". This shows that the surrounding words and the wider context usually make the intended
meaning clear. Thus, we can say that on the one hand lexical
ambiguity is extremely widespread, but on the other hand it rarely
causes real comprehension problems in everyday speech.

   Homophony and polysemy have so many things in common
that it is in many cases difficult if not impossible to distinguish
between these two types, especially from a purely synchronic
point of view. It is not always clear where to draw the line and

decide whether two meanings are related or unrelated. Etymological information, i.e. information about the history of individual words, can provide some clues, but there is no general agreement on how far back in time we should go in our research and how similar the meanings have to be in order to be called "related".

Words that are spelled the same but have different meanings are referred to as **homographs**, such as *bank* 'a financial institution' and *bank* 'the side of a river', or *dove* /dʌv/ the bird and *dove* /doʊv/, the past tense of the verb *dive* in American English. This relationship is called **homography**. Homographs that are not pronounced identically, such as *dove* /dʌv/ and *dove* /doʊv/ are also called **heteronyms**. This means that all heteronyms are homographs, but not all homographs are also necessarily heteronyms. All homographs that are not heteronyms are pronounced the same and thus homophones, such as *bank* 'a financial institution' and *bank* 'the side of a river'. The following table should help to clarify the distinctions between the somewhat overlapping semantic terms we have looked at so far:

Fig. 6.4

	Synonymy	Antonymy	Polysemy	Homophony	Homography	Heteronymy
same/similar meaning	yes	no	no	no	no	no
pronounced identically	no	no	yes	yes	irrelevant	no
same spelling	no	no	yes	irrelevant	yes	yes
historically related	irrelevant	irrelevant	yes	no	irrelevant	irrelevant

Some semantic relations among words

Unfortunately, not all linguists use these semantic labels in exactly the same way. In addition to the terms outlined in Fig. 6.4, some linguists use the term **homonymy**, which is employed in one of two ways. It is either used synonymously with homophony or employed in a narrow sense to refer only to those words that have both identical pronunciations and spellings. Employing the latter definition, some linguists would systematically distinguish the homophones *right* and *write* from the **homonyms** *bank* 'a financial institution' and *bank* 'the side of a river'.

The last semantic relation we want to look at here involves **hierarchies** in the vocabulary. When the meaning of one word is included in the meaning of another, we speak of **hyponymy**. For example, words like *peach*, *orange* and *mango* are **hyponyms** of the more general expression *fruit*. This means that *peach*, *orange* and *mango* are subordinate to the term *fruit*. The term *fruit* itself, on the other hand, is called a **hyperonym**, because it is superordinate to the more specific terms *peach*, *orange* and *mango*.

Hyponymy, Hyperonymy, and Meronymy

Hyperonym (superordinate)   *fruit*

Hyponym (subordinate)   *peach*

Fig. 6.5

Hyponymy and hyperonymy

A different kind of hierarchical relationship is involved in **part-whole relations**. A *pit* (or *stone*) is a part of a *peach* just as the *trunk* and the *branches* are parts of a *tree*. *Pit* is thus a so-called **meronym** of *peach*, and *trunk* and *branch* are meronyms of *tree*. Meronymy is different from hyponymy in that it refers to terms for parts of real objects, whereas hyponymy refers to a hierarchy between sets of words. This means that a *peach* is not a part of an actual *fruit* but that the word *peach* is an element in the semantic class of *fruit*.

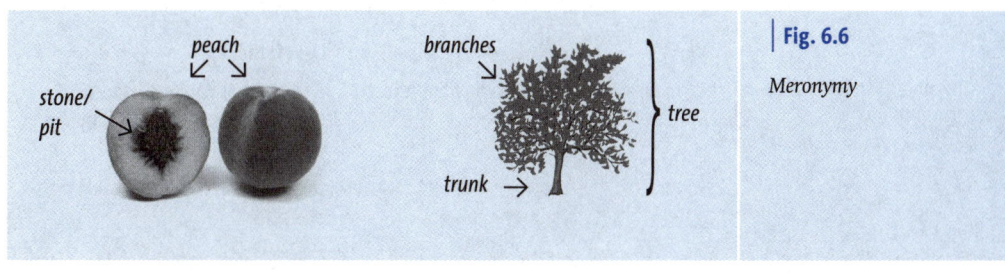

peach

branches

stone/ pit

trunk →

tree

Fig. 6.6

Meronymy

Word Meaning

6.2.2

In the previous section, we have seen that linguists have developed a relatively precise system to describe meaning relations among words. We have also said earlier that humans have been interested in meaning for thousands of years. However, we still do not know much about the nature of meaning and how meaning is represented in the human mind. Let us now take a look at some well-known proposals concerning the meaning of expressions, keeping in mind that many questions regarding meaning are still unanswered and that the terminology is not yet standardised and still under discussion.

Three pairs of terms play an important role in semantic analysis: **connotation ~ denotation**, **sense ~ reference** and **intension ~ extension**. Generally speaking, the first term in each pair relates to the language-internal (or intra-linguistic) side of meaning, whereas the second terms relate to language-external (or extra-linguistic) reality.

Connotation and Denotation

When we hear a word, usually a number of associations come to our mind. For example, for most people who live in the southern part of Germany near the Alps, the word *winter* evokes associations of snow, ice, freezing cold, slippery roads, skiing, and the like, which are also called the **connotation** of the expression. In this case, *winter* is defined within the network of words that we think of when we hear the term *winter*.

In contrast with connotation, **denotation** refers to the relationship between a linguistic expression and the concrete language-external entities to which it refers. The denotation of *winter* is found in its dictionary definition of 'the season between autumn and spring'.

Fig. 6.7

Connotation and denotation

Word	Connotation (selected)	Denotation
labrador	friend, companion, etc.	one breed of 'canine quadrupeds', i.e. four-legged animals belonging to the dog family
winter	snow, ice, freezing cold, slippery roads etc.	the season between autumn and spring

Sense and Reference

The **sense** of an expression is the meaning it has within a language. It is essentially defined by its relations with other expressions, i.e. within its network of synonyms, antonyms etc. (cf. 6.2.1). The **reference** of a word, on the other hand, is defined as its direct relation to the extra-linguistic world. Reference is the relationship between an expression and the persons, objects, entities or states of affairs in the real world to which it refers. The sense of the term *cow* is 'a large four-legged animal kept on farms to produce milk or beef', whereas the reference are all the cows out there in the world, no matter what colour or size they are. The pair sense ~ reference can also be explained by using an analogy with money, because money is also a symbolic system. When you point to all the things you can buy with 50 cents, you are indicating what would be called the **referents** of 50 cents in language. To describe 50 cents by indicating its position in the monetary scale would be its sense: five times a dime (10 cents), twice a quarter (25 cents) or half a dollar.

The distinction of sense and reference, however, has its limitations. There are some words that clearly have a sense, but no obvious referents in the real world, such as *unicorns* and *dragons*. There may also be more than one expression to talk about the same referent, just think of the phrases *the leader of the Republican Party* and *the President of the United States*. The expressions differ in sense but may well refer to the same referent, e.g. currently to George W. Bush. This example also indicates that an expression with one particular sense may be used to refer to different entities in the real world and that these referents may change over time (cf. Fig. 6.8). The sense of *the President of the United States* remains constant, whereas in this case the referents have to change periodically, as it is required by law that no president can serve more than two terms:

Sense	Referents	
'the elected political leader of the United States of America'	in 1789: George Washington	**Fig. 6.8**
	in 2000: Bill Clinton	*Sense and referents over time*
	in 2010: Barack Obama	
	in the future: ?	

Intension and Extension

The **intension** of an expression is the set of semantic properties which define it. For example, the term *bird* evokes language-internal definitions like 'animate' and 'not human' that are part of its intension. The notion of intension is thus very similar to the notion of sense. Linguists now frequently specify the sense/intension of an expression by indicating its so-called **semantic features** (or **semantic properties**). *Bird* could be characterised by the semantic features [+animate], [-human], [+wings] and [+feathers], whereas the intension of *child* can be described as [+animate], [+human] and [+young]. In this approach, a word's intension is broken down into semantic components, which is why this approach is called **componential analysis**. The componential analysis of words allows us to group entities into natural classes. For example, all animals are part of a class that is defined by the semantic features [+animate, -human], while *child*, *baby*, *girl* and *boy* can be placed in a class characterised by the features [+animate, +human, +young]. Intensions are often said to correspond to mental images.

Extension, on the other hand, refers to the class of entities to which an expression can be applied. The extension of the term *bird* would be a list of entities including *robin, dove, parrot, duck, ostrich* etc., but also the mythical bird *phoenix*. The extension of an expression can be defined as the class of its potential referents. Of course, the extension of an expression can change over time as well, as indicated in the following figure:

Fig. 6.9

Extension and intension

Word/Phrase	Extension	Intension
bird	robin, dove, parrot, duck, ostrich etc., but also phoenix	all animals that fit the defining properties of birds, i.e. [+animate], [-human], [+wings], [+feathers]
capital of Massachusetts	Boston	city which is the seat of state government
pope	Benedict XVI (2010)	leader of the Roman Catholic Church
President of the United States	Barack Obama (2010)	the elected political leader of the United States of America

To sum up, we can say that the corresponding pairs connotation ~ denotation, sense ~ reference and intension ~ extension are parts of an attempt to explain the organisation of our mental lexicon, i.e. how words and meaning are represented and processed in our mind.

6.2.3 | Conceptualisation and Categorisation

So far, we have looked at the definition and analysis of meaning from a predominantly language-internal perspective. This kind of semantic analysis is called **structural semantics**, as it is essentially based on the assumption that every linguistic element is integrated into the structure of the language system through a network of relations. Current lexical semantics is still to a large extent committed to these structuralist assumptions and the view that language is a system of related and interdependent elements.

In the 1930s, structuralist assumptions of the relation of words were applied to a then new approach called the **semantic field theory**. This theory holds that words do not exist in isolation but form a so-called **semantic field** (or **lexical field**) with other semantically related words. Colour terms are often cited as an example of a semantic field. According to this theory, for example, the English terms *red* and *blue* are related in that they are both colours, i.e. they are hyponyms of the term *colour*.

Since the 1980s, however, the more recent approach of **cognitive semantics** sees language as part of our cognitive ability through which we organise and classify all aspects of our experience. This view is based on the assumption that meaning is linked to the way we group all kinds of perceptions and phenomena into **conceptual categories**. Categorisation and conceptualisation are based on the comparison of new things with ones we already know and the resulting cognitive construction of similarities between different entities.

Concepts differ with respect to the question of how clear-cut the boundary of the concept is. The concept referred to by the expression *the President of the United States* is rather clear-cut: only one person can be the elected leader of the United States of America. Other concepts are not so straightforward, just imagine words like *tall* or *strong*. How tall does a person have to be to be called *tall*, or how much weight does a person have to be able to lift to be called *strong*. Some people clearly fall into the category *strong* and others clearly do not, but there are also a lot of borderline cases for which we are unable to decide definitively whether or not they count as *strong*. The notion of "strength" obviously does not have a clear-cut boundary and is thus called a **fuzzy concept**. Fuzziness of this kind is characteristic of the human conceptual system.

Fuzzy Concepts

Many concepts do not only have fuzzy boundaries, their members can also be **graded** according to their **typicality**. For example, even assuming that we all think along the lines of the dictionary definitions and imagine *birds* as 'creatures that are covered with

Prototypes

feathers, have two wings and two legs, and the majority of which can fly', we still have a feeling that some of these animals are more birdlike than others. Our intuition tells us that *robins* and *sparrows* are more typical and thus better examples of birds than are *penguins* or *ostriches*. This intuitive grading of the members of the concept *bird* reflects the fact that many concepts have an internal structure. In this case, *robins* are felt to be one of the most **prototypical** members of the concept *bird*, whereas *ostriches* and *penguins* are considered less typical and thus more peripheral examples. **Prototypes**, such as *robins* for the concept *bird*, are cognitive reference points. Due to the important role prototypes play in cognitive semantics, the term **prototype semantics** is sometimes used as an alternative.

Fig. 6.10

Birdiness rankings (Aitchison 2003:56)

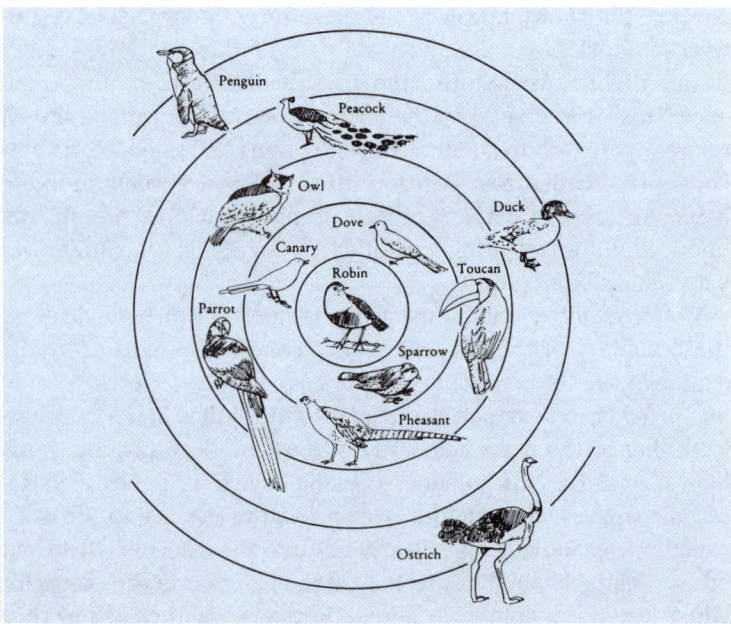

Metaphor

Another important notion of cognitive semantics is the assumption that the concepts expressed by language are interconnected and make up a huge network. In many cases, one concept can be understood in terms of the other. This type of interconnection is called **metaphor**. We are all familiar with the term metaphor as referring to literary devices. In the linguistic sense, however, metaphors are a part of the conceptual system that is shared by all human beings. The use of metaphors is so common that most of them are frequently not even noticed by many speakers. For example, at least in Western languages, the notion of *time* is often treated in everyday language as if it were a concrete valuable commodity. This is illustrated in the following examples from English:

(1) *Home cleaning tips and tricks to **save** time*
(2) *Ideas on how to **spend** time with your kids*
(3) ***Invest** your time **profitably** and study linguistics*
(4) *Time is **money***

Sentence Meaning | 6.3

So far, we have essentially concentrated on the meaning of words. Most of the time, however, we communicate in larger units such as phrases and sentences. The meaning of phrases and sentences is studied in **sentential semantics** (or **phrasal semantics**). The analysis of phrase and sentence meaning is based on the so-called **Principle of Compositionality**:

The meaning of a phrase or a sentence is determined by the meaning of its component parts and the way they are combined structurally.	**Fig. 6.11**
	The Principle of Compositionality

Meaning Relations Among Sentences | 6.3.1

Similar to words, sentences have meanings that can be analysed in terms of their relation to the meaning of other sentences. We will now look at three important types of semantic relations among sentences.

Two sentences that have the same meaning are said to be **para-phrases** of each other. Common ways to produce paraphrases are, for instance, to replace one word with a synonymous expression, as in the example sentences (5a) and (5b), or to rephrase an active sentence in the passive voice or vice versa, as in the pair of sentences (6a) and (6b).

Paraphrase

Fig. 6.12

Pairs of paraphrases

(5a) *We have just bought a fairly expensive house*

(5b) *We have just purchased a fairly expensive house*

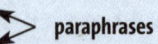 **paraphrases**

(6a) *The dog chased the cat*

(6b) *The cat was chased by the dog*

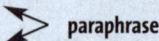 **paraphrases**

Sentences (a) and (b) in the above examples are very similar in meaning and one cannot be true without the other sentence also being true. Pairs of sentences that are true under the same circumstances are said to have the same **truth conditions**. The type of semantics that approaches meaning by employing the notion of truth is called **formal semantics**. The part of the meaning of a sentence that can be said to be either true or false is called the **proposition** (or **propositional content**).

At the sentence level, paraphrases are the equivalent of synonyms at the lexical level. As with synonyms, many linguists hesitate to speak about sentences with identical meanings, as there is a minor stylistic difference between (5a) and (5b) and a subtle difference of emphasis between (6a) and (6b) (for *buy* ~ *purchase* cf. 6.2.1 and 8.2). These linguists claim that paraphrases, like synonyms, are never perfect and that we are actually concerned with sentences that have very similar meanings.

Entailment

There are also cases in which the truth of one sentence **entails** (or implies) the truth of another sentence. The relation between such sentences is accordingly referred to as **entailment**. In each of the following pairs of sentences, the meaning of sentence (a) entails the meaning of sentence (b):

Fig. 6.13

Entailment

(7a) *The cat killed the mouse*

(7b) *The mouse is dead*

> **entails**

(8a) *Anna likes every single kind of fruit*

(8b) *Anna likes oranges*

> **entails**

Paraphrases, as in (5a) and (5b), and (6a) and (6b), have the same truth conditions and always entail each other. The entailment involved is symmetrical. The entailment in the pairs (7a) and (7b), and (8a) and (8b) is of a different kind: it is asymmetrical. (7a) entails that (7b) is true and (8a) entails that (8b) is true but the reverse does not follow. We cannot conclude from our knowledge that the mouse is dead that it was necessarily a cat which killed it. Similarly, Anna could like oranges but hate peaches.

The entailment in the pair (8a) and (8b) is the result of the lexical meaning relation between the terms *fruit* and *orange*. *Orange* is a hyponym of *fruit* (cf. 6.2.1). So if it is true that she really likes all kinds of fruit, she must like oranges as well, as they are members of the class of fruit. There are many examples of entailment that are based on hyponymy between lexical items. For example, the sentence *Cheeky is a dog* entails the sentence *Cheeky is an animal*, as *dog* is a hyponym of *animal*.

In contrast to paraphrases, there are pairs of sentences which **contradict** each other. This means that the truth of one sentence implies the falseness of the other, as illustrated in the pairs (9a) and (9b), and (10a) and (10b):

Contradiction

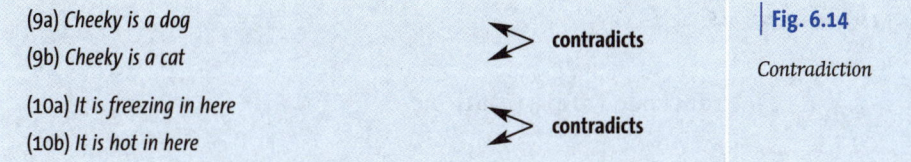

(9a) *Cheeky is a dog*
(9b) *Cheeky is a cat*

contradicts

(10a) *It is freezing in here*
(10b) *It is hot in here*

contradicts

Fig. 6.14

Contradiction

If the sentence (9a) is true, i.e. if it is true that Cheeky is a dog, then it cannot be true that sentence (9b) is true as well, as it is impossible for one animal to be a dog and a cat at the same time. The sentences contradict each other, because if one of the sentences is true, the other is necessarily false. We say that there is a **contradiction**, which could also be called "negative entailment".

The pair of sentences (10a) and (10b) in Fig. 6.14 follows the same logic. It cannot be hot and freezing in the same room at the same time. In this case, the contradiction is based on the use of a pair of antonyms, namely *hot* and *freezing* (cf. 6.2.1). Antonymy can thus be one source for contradiction between sentences.

Fig. 6.15

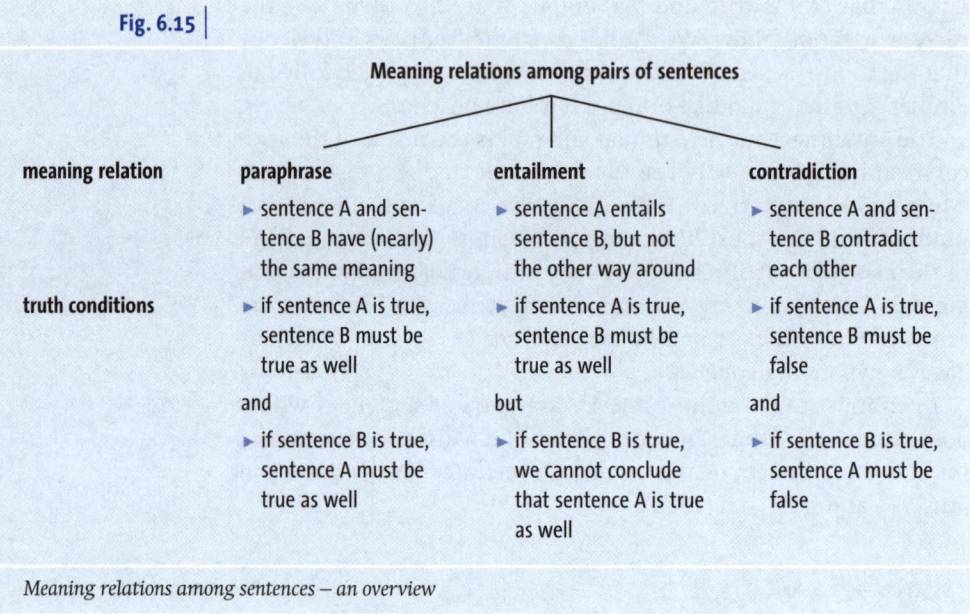

meaning relation	paraphrase	entailment	contradiction
	▸ sentence A and sentence B have (nearly) the same meaning	▸ sentence A entails sentence B, but not the other way around	▸ sentence A and sentence B contradict each other
truth conditions	▸ if sentence A is true, sentence B must be true as well	▸ if sentence A is true, sentence B must be true as well	▸ if sentence A is true, sentence B must be false
	and	but	and
	▸ if sentence B is true, sentence A must be true as well	▸ if sentence B is true, we cannot conclude that sentence A is true as well	▸ if sentence B is true, sentence A must be false

Meaning relations among pairs of sentences

Meaning relations among sentences – an overview

6.3.2 | Sentence Interpretations

After having looked at the most important meaning relations between sentences, we will now turn to some selected cases of **sentence interpretation**.

Sentence Meaning and Syntax

The above-mentioned Principle of Compositionality states that the meaning of a sentence depends on the meaning of its components and the way these components are combined (cf. 6.3). This principle emphasises the importance of lexical semantics as well as syntax for the interpretation of sentence meaning. We are all familiar with the fact that the syntactic structure of a sentence is relevant to its meaning in a number of ways. Most fundamentally, the same words can be combined differently to form sentences with entirely different meaning. Consider the following pair of examples, involving two fictional characters from the animated comedy series *South Park*: Kenny McCormick, who routinely gets killed in each episode of the series, and Eric Cartman, one of his friends:

(11) *Eric kills Kenny*
(12) *Kenny kills Eric*

Although sentences (11) and (12) are made up of exactly the same words and *kills* is inflected in exactly the same way in both sentences, it still requires no further explanation that the sentences mean something completely different. A mere change in word order, i.e. exchanging the subject and the object, creates semantically quite distinct sentences. As in most cases, the Principle of Compositionality proves to be valid in this example.

Sometimes, however, even identical strings of words can have more than one possible meaning. The phrase *rich women and men* allows two different interpretations (or **readings**). *Rich* can be interpreted as a property of both the women and the men in question, or of just the women alone. Figure 6.16 shows that the two readings of the phrase are due to a structural difference. Phrases and sentences that have more than one possible meaning are thus said to be **structurally ambiguous**.

Structural Ambiguity

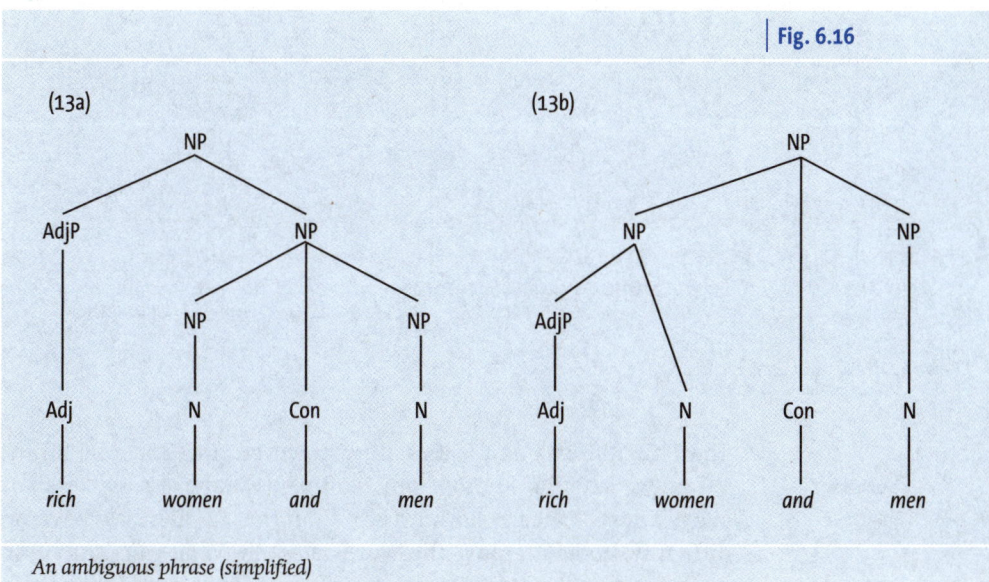

| Fig. 6.16

An ambiguous phrase (simplified)

The structure of example (13a) in Fig. 6.16 indicates that both the women and the men are rich, whereas the structure in example (13b) represents the reading that the adjective *rich* only applies to the women. But **structural ambiguity** does not only occur in simple phrases, it can also be found in whole sentences. Consider the sentence *Anna saw tourists with binoculars*. In one interpretation, the preposition phrase *with binoculars* modifies the noun *tourists*, i.e. Anna noticed tourists who had binoculars with them. In the other possible reading, the preposition phrase *with binoculars* modifies the verb, i.e. Anna saw the tourists by using a pair of binoculars. The tourists thus have the binoculars in example (14a) in Fig. 6.17, whereas it is Anna who uses binoculars to see the tourists in (14b):

Fig. 6.17

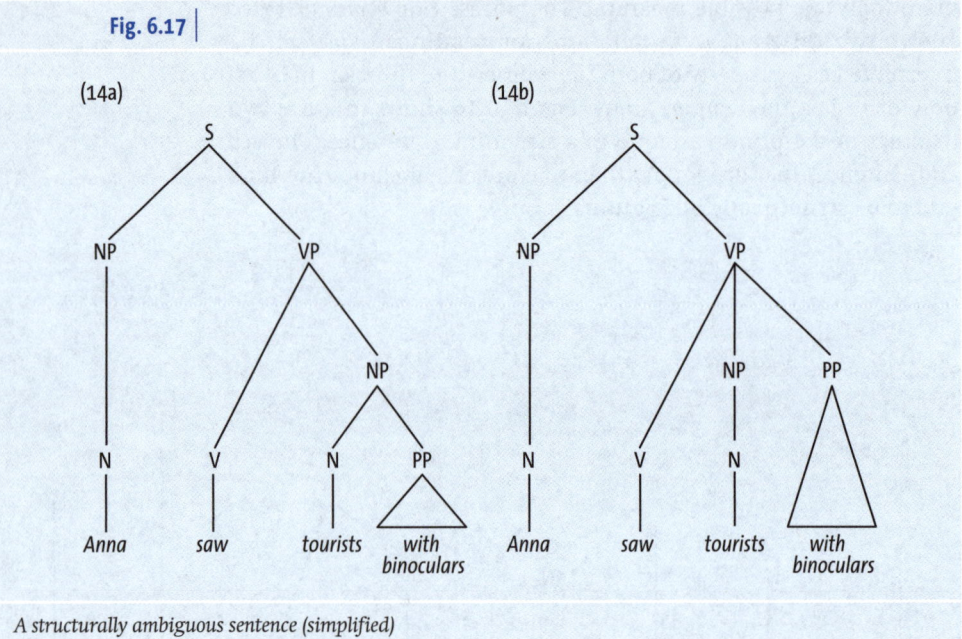

A structurally ambiguous sentence (simplified)

Limits of Compositionality

The Principle of Compositionality, however, does have its limits. When we say that Kenny from example (11) above *passes away* or *bites the dust*, it means nothing else than that he dies. We have no difficulty understanding the words *pass*, *away*, *bite*, *the*, and *dust*, but we can still not immediately infer the meaning of the whole phrases from this knowledge of the individual meanings of the words. Fixed phrases of this kind are called **idioms** (or **idiomatic phrases**). As the meaning of idiomatic phrases cannot be predicted from the words they are made up of, they have to be learned just like individual words. The same holds true for exocentric compounds such as *blackbird* and *redneck*, which have meanings that cannot be inferred from the meaning of their components, as we have seen in the section on word formation (cf. 4.3.2).

We have seen that our knowledge of word meanings and syn- *Presuppositions* tactic structures is important in interpreting sentences, but there are even more factors involved in sentence interpretation. When we utter a sentence, in many cases our attitudes and beliefs as well as the attitudes and beliefs of the addressee play an important role for the way the sentence is interpreted. The sentence *The mayor of Boston is in town today* implies the belief or assumption of the speaker that there is a mayor of Boston. Such an assumption is called a **presupposition**. The sentence *The mayor of Boston is in town today* is said to **presuppose** the sentence *There is a mayor of Boston*.

Presuppositions are different from entailment, among other things, in that presuppositions also hold true when the presupposing sentence is negated (cf. 6.3.1). This is illustrated in the following examples:

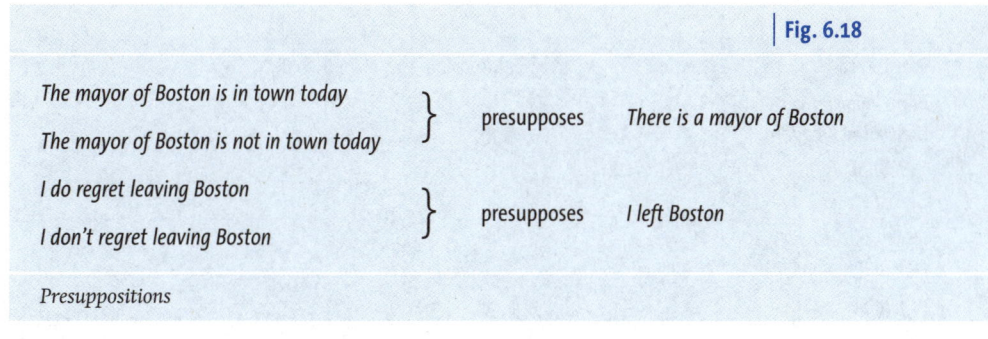

| Fig. 6.18

Presuppositions

Presuppositions also hold true in questions. The question *Is the mayor of Boston in town today?* also presupposes the sentence *There is a mayor of Boston*.

In the sentence *She managed to open the door*, the verb *manage* implies that she both tried and succeeded to open the door. The presupposed sentence would be *She tried to open the door*. There are a number of words like *manage* that are regularly associated with, i.e. they trigger, certain assumptions. Such words are called **presupposition-triggers**. As presuppositions play an important role in the interpretation of meaning in context, they are on the boundary between semantics and pragmatics, which will be discussed in the next chapter.

6.4 | Exercises

1. Identify the meaning relation of the words for each of the following pairs:
   a) *leave ~ return*
   b) *door ~ house*
   c) *young ~ old*
   d) *bright ~ intelligent*
   e) *flower ~ rose*
   f) *examiner ~ examinee*
   g) *freedom ~ liberty*

2. Explain the phenomenon called lexical ambiguity.

3. When discussing the nature of meaning, we distinguished between extension and intension. Give the extension and intension of each of these words/phrases.

Word/Phrase	Extension	Intension
Prime Minister of the United Kingdom		
capital of United States		
Queen of the United Kingdom		
vegetable		

4. Fuzziness
   a) Explain why the words *rich* and *clean* represent fuzzy concepts.
   b) Are all concepts fuzzy?

5. Which meaning relation can you identify for each of the following pairs of sentences? Provide the truth conditions for each pair.
   a) *William is single ~ William is married*
   b) *Planes are very loud ~ Planes are very noisy*

c) *James is Mary's husband ~ Mary is married*

d) *I am rather exhausted ~ I am pretty tired*

e) *Christina and Mat are workaholics ~ Mat and Christina are lazy*

f) *My car is red ~ My car is not white*

6. Explain the structural ambiguity in the following sentences:
   a) *The student hit the teacher with the book*
   b) *A lady watched an actor with opera glasses*

7. Identify the presupposition in each of the following sentences:
   a) *Some books written by Chomsky are not very expensive*
   b) *The present pope is German*
   c) *I am glad that my colleague sent me an e-mail*
   d) *They intend to close more libraries*

8. One of the two sentences in each of the following pairs of sentences contains a presupposition. Decide for each pair which sentence contains the presupposition and identify the presupposition-trigger:

   1a) *Anna thought she was in debt*

   1b) *Anna realised she was in debt*

   2a) *Have you stopped running marathons?*

   2b) *Have you tried running a marathon?*

Bibliography | 6.5

Aitchison, Jean. 2003. *Words in the Mind. An Introduction to the Mental Lexicon.* 3rd edition. Malden: Blackwell. *(A readable up-to-date introduction to mental lexicon issues)*

Cruse, Alan. 2004. *Meaning in Language. An Introduction to Semantics and Pragmatics.* Oxford: Oxford University Press. *(Accessible and thorough, mostly devoted to semantics)*

Davidson, George. 2006. *Roget's Thesaurus of English Words and Phrases: 150th Anniversary Edition.* London: Penguin. *(A new edition of the most famous English thesaurus)*

Gregory, Howard. 2000. *Semantics.* London: Routledge. *(Rich in useful exercises)*

Hitchings, Henry. 2005. *Dr Johnson's Dictionary. The Extraordinary Story of the Book that Defined the World.* London: Murray. *(An excellent portrait)*

Hüllen, Werner. 2004. *A History of Roget's Thesaurus. Origins, Development, and Design.* Oxford: Oxford University Press. *(Another excellent portrait)*

Hurford, James R. et al. 2007. *Semantics: A Coursebook.* 2nd edition. Cambridge: Cambridge University Press. *(An introductory coursebook with exercises)*

Jackson, Howard & **Etienne Zé Amvela**. 2007. *Words, Meaning and Vocabulary. An Introduction to Modern English Lexicology.* 2nd edition. London: Continuum. *(A beginner-friendly survey)*

Jaszczolt, Katarzyna M. 2002. *Semantics and Pragmatics. Meaning in Language and Discourse.* London: Longman. *(Broad in scope, highly recommended)*

Johnson, Samuel. 1765. *A Dictionary of the English Language: in which the Words are Deduced from their Originals, and Illustrated in their Different Significations by Examples from the Best Writers, to which are Prefixed a History of the Language, and an English Grammar.* 3rd edition. London: Strahan. *(One of the most influential English dictionaries of all times)*

Lakoff, George & **Mark Johnson**. 2003 [1980]. *Metaphors We Live by.* Reprint with a new afterword. Chicago: University of Chicago Press. *(One of the most influential texts on the cognitive theory of metaphor)*

Löbner, Sebastian. 2002. *Understanding Semantics.* London: Arnold. *(Rich in useful exercises)*

Lyons, John. 1995. *Linguistic Semantics. An Introduction.* Cambridge: Cambridge University Press. *(One of the classic introductory texts)*

Oxford English Dictionary online (*OED online*) <http://www.oed.com>

Portner, Paul. 2005. *What is Meaning? Fundamentals of Formal Semantics.* Malden, MA: Blackwell. *(Beginner-friendly)*

Saeed, John I. 2003. *Semantics.* 2nd edition. Malden, MA: Blackwell. *(A comprehensive introduction)*

The Oxford Advanced Learner's Dictionary. 2005. 7th edition. Oxford: Oxford University Press.

Pragmatics

Contents

Abstract

Pragmatics examines how speakers understand and communicate more than the literal meaning of words or sentences. The type of meaning studied in pragmatics is known as utterance meaning, meaning in context or meaning in interaction. In short, pragmatics is about getting from what is said to what is meant.

7.1 | What Does Pragmatics Do?

Pragmatics and Meaning

Pragmatics is the systematic study of how people understand and communicate more than the literal meaning of words or sentences when they speak, write or gesture, or, in more general terms, when they interpret and produce what linguists call **utterances**. Utterances are spoken, written or gestured contributions within a particular social context that derive their meaning partly from that context. Therefore, pragmatics is also called the study of **utterance meaning**, or **meaning in context**, or **meaning in interaction**. These terms take into account that contexts develop and redevelop dynamically, most markedly when we engage in live encounters with others. Our utterances are not only shaped by the contexts in which they occur but also create new contexts for what can follow. In other words, they are not only **context shaped** but also **context renewing**. Such relationships between speakers, texts and contexts are also explored within **discourse analysis** and **text linguistics**. This chapter focuses mainly on a selection of central pragmatic principles and processes that enable us to create and interpret meaning in context.

Pragmatics and Culture

Why do we very often not spell out explicitly what we mean? On the one hand, this has to do with saving effort by leaving many things unsaid. On the other hand, it has to do with social and cultural norms, which may vary strongly across cultures. Linguists approach these differences from various perspectives. **Cross-cultural** analysis compares linguistic practices across cultures, for example differences between interviewers' questions in British and German television interviews. Recently, linguists have also started to explore pragmatic variation across varieties of the same language (cf. Chapter 8), for example comparing English English usage with other varieties such as American English or Irish English. **Intercultural** research analyses linguistic interaction between members of different cultures, for example misunderstandings between American and German students. In the age of globalisation, studies of this kind are rapidly gaining importance.

Pragmatic Competence

Students of a foreign language will know from their own experience, for example as exchange students or from traveling, that the best theoretical knowledge of a language is not sufficient as soon as it comes to communicating with real people. As you know from the chapters on syntax and semantics, our general linguistic competence provides us with rules that tell us how to judge whether a sentence is grammatical, and how to make sense of single words or single sentences. But as indicated above, this may not be sufficient when you try to communicate with other people. What you need to successfully communicate in face-to-face conversation, on the telephone, or when writing letters, e-mails or text messages, is **pragmatic competence**. Pragmatic competence is the ability to use language appropriately within social contexts. The following sections will give you a brief overview of some core notions of pragmatics, starting with **deixis**.

Deixis

| 7.2

The term **deixis** corresponds to the Greek verb *deiknynai* meaning 'to point' or 'to show'. Deixis refers to all linguistic means that have mainly to do with pointing at extralinguistic contexts. Imagine finding the room of your linguistics class empty with the following notice on the door:

Deixis and Context

Introduction to Linguistics
We are here today:
Guest Lecture Professor XY
Room Z

| **Fig. 7.1**

Deixis and context

You will know how to interpret this notice, although you are not in the same physical context as its authors who are obviously not present. Instead, their absence tells you that the *here* refers to room Z because *here* is an expression which is normally used for locations close to a speaker.

All linguistic expressions that are used to point at someone or something, such as *me* and *you*, or *here* and *there,* are called **deictic expressions** (or **deictics**). Occasionally, deictic expressions are also called **indexicals**, corresponding to the Latin verb *indicare*, which also means 'to point' or 'to show'. We use deictic expressions to point at persons (**person deixis**), at places (**place deixis**), or at particular points of time (**time deixis**). Some authors also describe further dimensions of deixis, such as social relationships that are reflected in language (**social deixis**) or pointing activities within a

Deictic Expressions

text (**discourse deixis**), such as *in the next paragraph* or *as outlined above*. (cf. Fig. 7.2)

Fig. 7.2 |

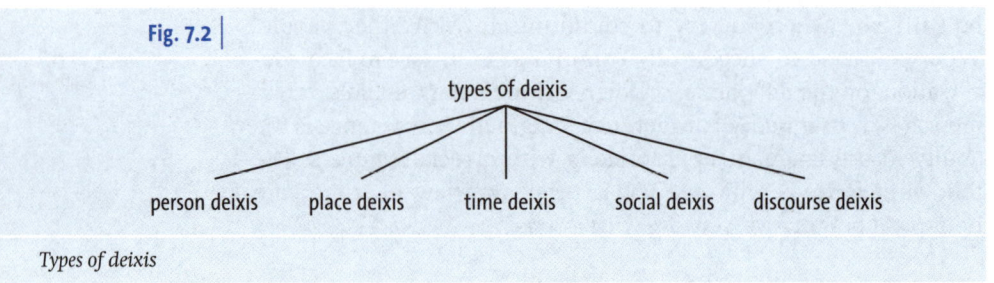

Types of deixis

The Deictic Centre

As indicated above, all dimensions of deixis have in common that they cannot be understood out of their context. Therefore, understanding deixis has a lot to do with finding out from which perspective something is being communicated. This perspective is called the **deictic centre**. The deictic centre is easiest to identify in face-to-face interactions in which all participants of a conversation are present. When speakers use deictic expressions in such a context, we usually take their perspective to be the deictic centre of their utterances. Additionally, they may accompany and support deictic expressions with nonverbal signals such as gestures or gaze.

Deictic Projection

However, we may also shift the deictic centre and still be understood. For instance, in the example in Fig. 7.1, the deictic centre has been moved from the classroom to room Z, together with the authors of the notice. Whereas the deictic expressions *we* and *today* still refer to the same group and to the same time, the deictic expression *here* in the notice does not refer to the empty classroom where you are reading the notice. In this case, *here* refers to the room where the guest lecture is taking place. Such a shift is also called **deictic projection**. Identifying the deictic centre is relevant for all types of deixis. This will become more apparent as we take a closer look at the three main types of deixis.

7.2.1 | Person Deixis

Pointing at Persons

Person deixis is about **pointing at persons**. Consider the following extract from the British play *Feelgood*, a political satire by Alistair Beaton (2001). The beginning of Act One shows two men, one of them busy at a laptop, the other watching him. Paul is a young professional speechwriter, and Eddie is the Press Secretary of the present government. Now try to list all expressions pointing at individuals in the opening dialogue of *Feelgood*. Whom are they referring to?

Paul   *(reading from the laptop screen)* 'There will be other challenges facing us in the twenty-first century. But I can tell you now: the greatest challenge of all will be the challenge of change. And to those who –'
Eddie   Ch. Ch.
Paul   Sorry?
Eddie   Ch. Ch.
Paul   Ch. Ch?
Eddie   Ch. Ch. Challenge of change. Don't like it.
Paul   It's alliteration.
Eddie   Yeah, bad alliteration. Challenge of change. Awful. It'll make him sound like he needs dentures.
        (Beaton 2001:1-2)

If you do not know the play, you may think at first that Paul is the first person singular *I* in *But I can tell you now*. This is what person deixis via the first person singular personal pronoun would normally suggest, because we usually assume speakers to be the deictic centre of their utterances. Only Eddie's utterance *It'll make **him** sound like **he** needs dentures* reveals that Paul's text is obviously not going to be read out by Paul but by another male person. We are told so by the masculine third person singular pronoun *him*. But who is that person? To create suspense, it is revealed only gradually in the course of Paul's and Eddie's conversation that *he* is the current British Prime Minister and that Paul and Eddie are spin doctors working on a speech for him. That is, in the utterances *There will be other challenges facing us in the twenty-first century* and *But I can tell you now*, which Paul quotes from the Prime Minister's future speech, it is not Paul who is going to be the deictic centre of these utterances but the Prime Minister.

Another important dimension of person deixis can be observed in the so-called **T/V distinction** which derives its name from the initial letters of the distinct familiar and polite forms of personal pronouns in many Romance languages, as in French *tu* (singular) and *vous* (singular and plural). These forms ultimately go back to the Latin singular pronoun *tu* and the plural pronoun *vos*. The T/V

The T/V Distinction

distinction also plays an important role in the choice of forms of address such as first name, surname or title, or in different choices of style and register (cf. Chapter 8), especially in languages such as English that do not have distinct pronouns for representing familiarity or distance. This aspect of person deixis is also called **social deixis**, because it reflects how we represent, establish and change social distance and, accordingly, social relationships. As the rules of social deixis are observed differently across cultures, they may cause considerable trouble for second language learners.

7.2.2 | Place Deixis

Pointing at Locations

Place deixis is about **pointing at the location** of individuals or things. To give you an example: Imagine buying cheese at the market. What do you do if you do not know the name of a particular cheese you would like to try? Most people would simply point at the cheese in question and ask for a piece of it, saying: "Could I try a piece of this one, please?" Usually, this straightforward practice of place deixis works quite well. But what if the person serving you picks out the wrong cheese? You would probably say: "No, not that one, this one!" If this fails, too, you would either have to physically point at your desired cheese in an unmistakable manner, or, if you find that embarrassing or unhygienic, you would have to use further linguistic means, for example to precisely describe the location of the cheese relative to some prominent object, e.g. "next to the stuffed green peppers".

Closeness and Distance

Generally, the English language distinguishes between referring to individuals or things close to the deictic centre, and referring to individuals or things away from the deictic centre. We use **proximal terms** like *this* or *here* to refer to individuals or objects relatively close to the speaker, and **distal terms** like *that* and *there* for relatively remote individuals or objects. This is even the case when the reference of these expressions changes. For instance, when one of your friends is travelling through the world and sends you an e-mail each time she comes across an Internet cafe, you might not know where exactly the *here* is which she praises so enthusiastically in her messages. The only thing you can say for sure is that it refers to the place where she is at the time of writing. This example shows that there is a temporal dimension to place deixis, too. Interestingly, distal terms such as *that* are often also used to express psychological distance or even dislike (*that boring book*, *that awful lesson*). When such deictic terms are used to refer to humans (*that silly cow*, *that stupid guy*), this may also be interpreted as social deixis because they are used to indicate social distance.

Time Deixis

7.2.3

Like place deixis, **time deixis** also distinguishes between **close to the deictic centre** and **away from the deictic centre**. This is reflected in expressions like *now*, *today* or *this week* for a time close to the moment of speaking (= proximal), and *then*, *yesterday* or *next month* for a time remote from the moment of speaking (= distal), i.e. either in the past or in the future. Expressions like *soon, ten minutes later* or *two weeks ago* also mark points or periods of time relative to a speaker's current situation. Many literary texts make extensive use of time deixis. For instance, fairy tales usually begin with "Once upon a time, there was …". As this fairy tale beginning also shows, another important device for establishing temporal reference is the choice of **verb tense**. Consider the following examples:

Time and Distance

(1) *I live here now.*
(2) *I lived there then.*
(3) *I could swim (when I was a child).*
    (Yule 1996:15)

The choice of verb tense depends on the options a language provides: "Whereas other languages have many different forms of the verb as different tenses, English has only two basic forms, the present and the past. [...] The present tense is the proximal form and the past tense is the distal form." (Yule 1996:14-15)

Additionally, time deixis may serve to mark events as distant from the speaker's current situation in a hypothetical sense, i.e. away from the reality of the present. This can be seen in the use of past verb forms for the subjunctive mood or in certain types of if-clauses, as in examples (4) and (5):

(4) *I could be in Hawaii (if I had a lot of money).*
(5) *If I was rich ...*
    (Yule 1996:15)

All in all, we can say that deixis is a very efficient tool for saving communicative effort. However, this tool only works if the deictic centre is clear. The following sections will discuss further pragmatic aspects of face-to-face communication.

7.3 | The Cooperative Principle

Unrelated Utterances?

Human face-to-face communication is full of exchanges that may appear, at first sight, rather unrelated, such as the following three examples:

(6)   A   *Can you tell me the time?*
       B   *Well, the milkman has come.*
         (Levinson 1994:83)

(7)   A   *I do think Mrs. Jenkins is an old windbag, don't you?*
       B   *Huh, lovely weather for March, isn't it?*
         (Levinson 1994:111)

(8)   A   *Where's Bill?*
       B   *There's a yellow VW outside Sue's house.*
         (Levinson 1994:102)

How can we interpret these exchanges? In his ground-breaking lecture "Logic and Conversation" (1975), H. Paul Grice presents a basic principle that governs human interaction: the so-called **Cooperative Principle (CP)**:

Fig. 7.3 *The Cooperative Principle (CP)*	Make your conversational contribution such as is required, at the stage at which it occurs, by the accepted purpose or direction of the talk exchange in which you are engaged. (Grice 1975:45)

Grice's Maxims

From this principle, four maxims are derived:

Fig. 7.4 *Maxims of Conversation*	**The Maxim of Quantity** 1. Make your contribution as informative as is required for the current purpose of the exchange. 2. Do not make your contribution more informative than is required.

The Maxim of Quality
Try to make your contribution one that is true, specifically:
1. Do not say anything that you believe to be false.
2. Do not say anything for which you lack adequate evidence.

The Maxim of Relation (or **The Maxim of Relevance**)
Make your contribution relevant.

The Maxim of Manner
Be perspicuous (= be clear). More specifically:
1. Avoid obscurity.
2. Avoid ambiguity.
3. Be brief.
4. Be orderly.

(adapted from Grice 1975:45-46)

When one or more of these maxims are not being observed, as it is the case in examples (6) to (8) above, this gives rise to **conversational implicatures**. Conversational implicatures are not part of the conventional meaning of what is said. Their interpretation is context-dependent. If somebody **violates** (or **flouts**) one or more of the Maxims of Conversation, we are alerted to look for additional information that might help to make the utterance in question meaningful, provided that we have reason to believe that the person who is uttering it is acting rationally and intentionally. Finding such additional information is also known as **inferring**.

For instance, in example (6), B does not observe the Maxim of Relation. *Well, the milkman has come* is, at first sight, not a relevant answer to the question *Can you tell me the time?* However, we are able to bridge the gap between what is said and what is meant by interpreting B's answer as a cooperative attempt of giving A at least some helpful hint if not the exact time. Apparently, B does not know the exact time but knows that A knows the time at which the milkman usually comes and will interpret B's utterance accordingly. This is what we can infer from B's reply.

Example (7) is another example for the violation of the Maxim of Relation. B's reply *Huh, lovely weather for March, isn't it?* bears no obvious relevance to A's remark *I do think Mrs. Jenkins is an old windbag, don't you?* But it may implicate a warning for A, who is backbiting Mrs Jenkins and possibly about to go on with it.

Conversational
Implicature

Alarmed by B's irrelevant remark, A can infer that B's utterance might mean something like *Watch out, her nephew's standing right behind you.*

Occasionally, more than one maxim is violated at the same time. This is the case in example (8). When B answers *There's a yellow VW outside Sue's house* to A's question *Where's Bill?*, he or she flouts both the Maxim of Quantity and the Maxim of Relation. But his or her answer is at the same time co-operative and effort-saving. Obviously, B knows that A knows that Bill owns a yellow VW. If the yellow VW outside Sue's house is his, Bill may well be in Sue's house. But B avoids such a lengthy reply by simply producing an utterance that enables A to infer what B does not say explicitly.

All in all, these examples show that finding out about speakers' communicative intentions plays an important role for our interpretation of utterances. At the same time, human communication is also about making things happen in the real world. Such aspects of meaning in interaction are discussed in **speech act theory**.

7.4 | Speech Acts

Utterances as Actions

Take the simple utterance *It's cold in here*. What does it mean? Who could say it to whom in what situation? At first sight, this is a statement about the temperature in a particular room. However, this is not always the communicative intention with which this declarative sentence is uttered. Most people who say *It's cold in here* to another person will want this person to do something about the cold. In this case *It's cold in here* may mean *Could you please close the window?* or *Could you please turn on the heating?* or *Could you please lend me one of your famous hand-knitted sweaters?* In short, the utterance may serve as a polite request for some appropriate action in order to make the speaker more comfortable. Depending on the relationship between the participants of the conversation, it could also be used as a command.

Speech Acts and Speech Act Theory

As we have seen, utterances can be used to perform actions. **Actions performed via utterances**, such as requesting, threatening, or thanking, are based on **speech acts**. The systematic study of speech acts is based on **speech act theory**. Speech act theory has its roots in thoughts formulated by John L. Austin in *How to Do*

Things with Words (1962) and John R. Searle in *Speech Acts. An Essay in the Philosophy of Language* (1969).

All actions performed by utterances can be divided into three related acts: the **locutionary act**, the **illocutionary act**, and the **perlocutionary act**. The **locutionary act** is the physical act of producing understandable language that may be regarded as meaningful within a given context. Consider the indirect request *Do you know where I left my textbook?*

Locutionary, Illocutionary, and Perlocutionary Acts

Fig. 7.5

Locutionary act

What we intend to do by producing an utterance is called the **illocutionary act**, i.e. in this case the intention of asking for information.

Fig. 7.6

Illocutionary act

The cognitive or emotional effect an illocutionary act has on an addressee or addressees in reality is called the **perlocutionary act** (or **perlocutionary effect**).

Fig. 7.7

Perlocutionary effect

Illocutionary Force

As you can see in Fig. 7.5 – 7.7, the locutionary and the illocutionary act are within our control, whereas the perlocutionary act is not. In these examples, the first speaker's illocutionary act of requesting succeeds because the speaker has managed to produce an utterance that is suitable to convey her communicative intention, even though the perlocutionary effect is negative. This communicative intention is often called the **illocutionary force**.

Speech Act Types

Generally, linguists distinguish between several main types of speech acts, to describe what humans may do by performing these acts. We use **representatives** (or **assertives**) to make statements about the world (*Germany is a country in Europe*); **directives** like requests or commands to get others to perform certain actions, e.g. to do us a favour, or to answer our questions (*Please send me an e-mail*); **commissives** like promises or threats to inform others about our future actions (*I will write to you every day*); **expressives** like greetings, thanks and congratulations to express our feelings (*Hi!*, *Thank you!* or *Happy birthday!*); and **declarations** for actions that are performed by pronouncing the appropriate formula, e.g. marrying a couple or baptising somebody.

Fig. 7.8

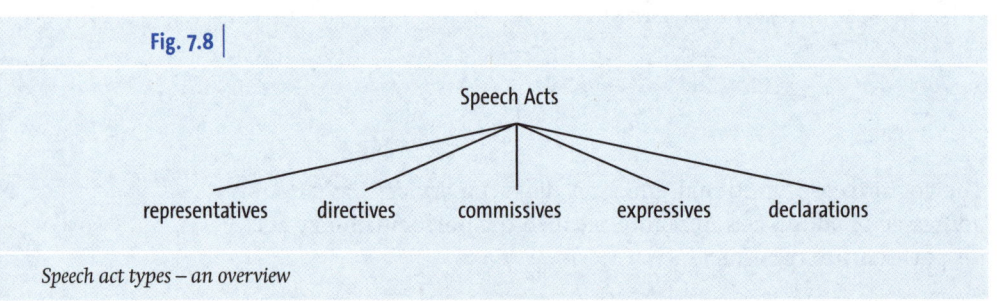

Speech act types – an overview

Felicity Conditions

There are certain preconditions that need to be fulfilled if a speech act is to succeed. These preconditions are called **felicity conditions**. Accordingly, speech acts can be **felicitous** or **infelicitous**. For instance, for a felicitous request, the following criteria must be fulfilled:

	Fig. 7.9
Content	*Felicity conditions for requests*
Future act (A) to be performed by the hearer (H).	
Preparatory conditions	
H is able to do A.	
The speaker (S) believes that H is able to do A.	
It is not obvious to both S and H that H will do A in the normal course of events of her or his own accord.	
Sincerity condition	
S wants H to do A.	
Essential condition	
Counts as an attempt to get H to do A.	
(based on Searle 1969: 66-67)	

The felicity conditions of commands are similar to those of requests. Additionally, commands have the preparatory condition that the speaker must be in a position of authority over the hearer. In this case, the preparatory condition of non-obviousness becomes less relevant.

Declarations are only felicitous if the speaker is actually in a position that entitles her or him to perform the desired action, and that the formula used actually counts as performing the action within a particular culture. For instance, you cannot baptise or marry others unless you have the authority to do so because of your profession. Additionally, you have to utter the relevant formula for baptising or marrying. Jenny Thomas (1995:43) cites a newspaper report about a Muslim actor in Pakistan who unintentionally divorced his wife while playing a movie character who divorced his movie wife by pronouncing the corresponding phrase *Talaq* 'I divorce you' the ritual three times required for a divorce. As his real spouse played the movie wife and the religious authorities insisted that the actor's words could not be withdrawn, even though they were uttered in a work of art, the divorce became valid.

Linguists distinguish between **direct speech acts** and **indirect speech acts**. Direct speech acts are associated with corresponding basic sentence types (cf. section 5.2). For instance, **declarative sentences** are commonly used for representative (or assertive) speech acts. **Interrogative sentences** are commonly used for questions (which are often interpreted as subtypes of directive speech acts, because they can be seen as requests for information). **Imperative sentences** are associated with directive speech acts, and **exclamative sentences** are used for expressive speech acts:

Direct Speech Acts

Fig. 7.10

	Sentence Type	Direct Speech Act
(9) *Anna is singing.*	declarative	representative (or assertive)
(10) *Is Anna singing?*	interrogative	question (= subtype of directive speech act)
(11) *Sing!*	imperative	directive
(12) *How beautifully she is singing!*	exclamative	expressive

Sentence types and direct speech acts

Indirect Speech Acts

Indirect speech acts are speech acts that depart from this pattern. For instance, declarative sentences may be used as indirect directives, either in order to avoid giving orders, as in the above-mentioned utterance *It's cold in here* for *Close the window*, or, in some social contexts, to intensify the force of a command, as in the following example from *Feelgood*:

Fig. 7.11

An indirect speech act

Asha	You don't switch off your bleeper. Ever. All right?
Paul	*(cowed)* Okay okay. *(Mutters.)* Sorry. *(Leans down, fumbles with the pager on his belt.)*
	(Beaton 2001:7-8)

As you have seen in Sections 7.1 to 7.4, pragmatics examines how we can interpret and produce utterances to identify and create meaning in social contexts. However, most of the examples used so far were made up by linguists or playwrights. If that makes you suspicious because you wonder whether people really talk and act this way, you may benefit from the methods of **conversation analysis**.

7.5 | Conversation Analysis

Working with Authentic Data

At the end of the 1960s, a group of sociologists developed a growing interest in gathering and analyzing authentic language data. This led to a new discipline called **Conversation Analysis (CA)**. CA concentrates on data from everyday life, such as face-to-face talk or telephone conversations, or from institutional backgrounds, for example courtroom proceedings or news interviews. Data are recorded and closely transcribed, as in the following example taken from the transcription course on the homepage of Emanuel Schegloff, one of the founding fathers of CA:

| Ava | I 'av [a lotta t]ough cou:rses. |
| Bee | [Uh really?] |

Fig. 7.12

A close transcript

Close transcripts include features like hesitations, pauses, interruptions, and simultaneous speech. Nowadays, there is a lot of interdisciplinary exchange between conversation analysis and various subdisciplines of linguistics, such as pragmatics.

One important area of research within CA is the analysis of **turns**, the smallest units from which conversations are built. Researchers observed that conversations usually consist of a more or less smooth sequence of turns. For instance, each of the utterances by Asha and Paul in Fig. 7.11 and by Ava and Bee in Fig. 7.12 is one turn. Accordingly, the systematic organisation of the way the participants of an interaction take turns at speaking is called **turn-taking**. Turns consist of so-called **turn constructional units** (TCUs). Such units correspond closely to syntactic units such as sentences, clauses, or noun phrases. Additionally, speakers may employ prosodic or intonational means for signalling whether a turn-constructional unit is completed and another speaker may start talking. Ends of turn-constructional units are called **transition relevance places** (TRPs). The right to speak is called the **floor**.

Turn-Taking

Utterances that usually appear in pairs in dialogue are called **adjacency pairs**. All first parts are associated with **preferred** or **dispreferred** second parts. The following table shows some typical adjacency pairs with preferred second parts:

Adjacency Pairs

greeting	–	greeting
self-identification	–	self-identification
question	–	answer
request	–	acceptance
assessment	–	agreement

Fig. 7.13

Adjacency pairs

Preference Structure

Preference and **dispreference** are usually associated with characteristic verbal and nonverbal features. Whereas preferred second parts of adjacency pairs are usually delivered immediately, fluently and in a brief form, dispreferred second parts are often preceded by a pause and accompanied by so-called **dispreference markers**, for example:

Fig. 7.14

Dispreference markers

- silence, delays and hesitations such as pauses or *er, em*
- prefaces like *well* or *oh*
- token *yes*, often followed by *but*
- expressing doubt or uncertainty
- apologies, accounts, referring to obligations
- appeals for understanding, generalisations

For instance, imagine asking a colleague whether they would like to have a cup of coffee with you. A preferred second part to the request would be *Yes, I'd love to!*, uttered spontaneously, whereas a dispreferred second part would be some initial silence, followed by an utterance like *Well … er … I'm awfully sorry, but … you know … I've got to finish this essay today ….* Some linguists assume that there is a direct relationship between the amount of communicative effort employed and the relative weight of the dispreferred response within a particular social context. This is explored in theories on **politeness**, a topic we cannot even attempt to address in this introductory textbook because of its extremely wide scope. Many politeness theories combine insights from both pragmatics and **sociolinguistics**.

7.6 | Exercises

1. Identify the deictic expressions and devices in the following sentences and decide for each expression which type of deixis it represents:
   a) *I like this shirt better than that one.*
   b) *I saw him there.*
   c) *I will meet her here.*
   d) *I will visit them then.*

2. a) Identify the deictic expressions and devices in the following extract from a British political novel:

> Frank Rist was in the next room. Joseph could even hear that familiar voice, its staccato syllables drawn from deep in the larynx.
> (McSmith 2001:80)

b) Identify the deictic centre.
c) What does this extract reveal about the relationship between the two men? Consider the deictic expressions and give reasons.

3. Which conversational maxims are violated by B in the following pairs of utterances?
a) A *Are we late for the lesson?*
   B *The teacher is still in the cafeteria.*
b) A *I hate linguistics.*
   B *Oh, you must see the new Harry Potter Film!*
c) A *Did you bring the video and the DVD?*
   B *I brought the DVD.*

4. Imagine the following situation: A family is preparing dinner. The mother is directing the activities of father and daughter, while she is in charge of the roast. The following dialogue occurs:

Daughter *(cleaning brussel sprouts)*	*How many people will be eating brussel sprouts?*
Mother *(busy with the roast)*	*We will clean all the sprouts.*
Daughter *(sighing)*	*O.K.*

a) Does the mother observe the Cooperative Principle? Give reasons.
b) Does she violate any Gricean maxims? If so, which one(s)?

5. Identify the direct speech acts performed by uttering the following sentences:
a) *Berlin is the capital of Germany.*
b) *I hereby name this ship Mary Anne.*
c) *Pass the salt, please.*

d) I promise you to be on time.

e) What a lovely morning!

6. This cartoon was published during a time of massive cuts in the British National Health System initiated by the former Labour government under Prime Minister Tony Blair:

Fig. 7.15

Take up thy bed and … work!

The Independent Online Edition, Feb 2, 2005, <http://comment.independent.co.uk>

a) Which sentence type does Tony Blair use in this cartoon?

b) Which speech act does he perform?

c) Are the felicity conditions for this speech act satisfied here?

7. Which types of speech acts are performed by the expressions in bold type in the following extract from the *MediaGuardian*?

Guardian forces government u-turn on freedom of information
The Guardian today won a landmark victory in its campaign for freedom of information after the government **admitted** it had been wrong to impose a blanket gagging order on the parliamentary ombudsman preventing disclosure of information **requested** by the paper. (…) The order, also signed by Douglas Alexander, the minister for the cabinet office, **forbade** the parliamentary ombudsman, Ann Abraham, from releasing information about potential conflicts of ministerial interest. (…) "For the last four years the Guardian has been campaigning for freedom of information and arguing that the government was being unnecessarily secretive," **said** the Guardian editor, Alan Rusbridger. "The attempt to gag the ombudsman was disgraceful, and we hope this landmark judgment will encourage the government to be more open in future, and allow the ombudsman to do her job." (*MediaGuardian*, March 18, 2004)

8. The following dialogue is an extract from the British play *Feel-good*:

   (1) Eddie   *There's more?*
   (2) George *It gets worse.*
   (3) Eddie   *I find that hard to imagine, George.*
   (4) George *Well, it ... Right. The thing is ... the hops ... well, I mean, drinking the beer seems to have ... some ... side effects.*
            (Beaton 2001:47)

a) Identify the direct and indirect speech acts in this extract.
b) Identify the adjacency pairs.
c) Does George's final turn in this extract resemble a preferred or a dispreferred response? Give reasons.

Bibliography

| 7.7

Austin, John L. 1962. *How to Do Things with Words*. Oxford: Clarendon. *(Foundations for the development of speech act theory)*

Cutting, Joan. 2008. *Pragmatics and Discourse: A Resource Book for Students*. 2nd edition. New York: Routledge. *(Beginner-friendly, with key readings and suggestions for activities)*

Fillmore, Charles. 1997 (1971). *Lectures on Deixis*. Stanford: CSLI Publications. *(A collection of central observations on deixis)*

Grice, H. Paul. 1975. "Logic and conversation." In: Cole, Peter & Jerry L. Morgan, eds., *Syntax and Semantics 3: Speech Acts*. New York: Academic Press, 41-58. *(Groundbreaking text)*

Grundy, Peter. 2008. *Doing Pragmatics*. 3rd edition. London: Arnold. *(Applied perspective, with lively examples and exercises)*

Horn, Lawrence & **Gregory Ward**, eds. 2004. *The Handbook of Pragmatics*. Oxford: Blackwell. *(Excellent survey over the core areas of pragmatics, with contributions by leading scholars)*

Huang, Yan. 2007. *Pragmatics*. Oxford: Oxford University Press. *(An advanced students' textbook focussing on theoretical issues in pragmatics, with exercises)*

Jaworski, Adam & **Nikolas Coupland**, eds. 2006. *The Discourse Reader*. 2nd edition. London: Routledge. *(Contains a wealth of seminal texts)*

Kasper, Gabriele & **Kenneth Rose**. 2002. *Pragmatic Development in a Second Language*. Malden, MA: Blackwell. *(Examines the acquisition of pragmatics by second language learners)*

Levinson, Stephen C. 1983. *Pragmatics*. Cambridge: Cambridge University Press. *(Still an important standard reference book)*

LoCastro, Virginia. 2003. *An Introduction to Pragmatics. Social Action for Language Teachers*. Ann Arbor: University of Michigan Press. *(Accessible introduction with applied orientation)*

Mey, Jacob L. 2001. *Pragmatics. An Introduction*. 2nd edition. Malden, MA: Blackwell. *(Focuses on social aspects of pragmatics)*

Östman, Jan-Ola et al., eds. 1995-2002. *Handbook of Pragmatics. Manual and Installments*. Amsterdam: Benjamins. *(Excellent survey over pragmatics and adjoining fields of research, written by prominent scholars and constantly updated between 1995 and 2002)*

Östman, Jan-Ola et al., eds. 2003. *Handbook of Pragmatics Online*. Amsterdam: Benjamins. <www.benjamins.com/online/hop/> *(Online successor of Östman, Jan-Ola et al., eds. 1995-2002)*

Renkema, Jan. 2004. *Introduction to Discourse Studies*. Amsterdam: Benjamins. *(Comprehensive and accessible)*

Sacks, Harvey. 1992. *Lectures on Conversation*. Edited by Gail Jefferson. Oxford: Blackwell. *(A collection of central texts in Conversation Analysis)*

Schegloff, Emanuel (n.d.) *Emanuel Schegloff's Home Page*. <http://www.sscnet.ucla.edu/soc/faculty/schegloff/> *(Extensive online material on conversation analysis)*

Schneider, Klaus P. & **Anne Barron**, eds. 2008. *Variational Pragmatics: A Focus on Regional Varieties in Pluricentric Languages*. Amsterdam: Benjamins. *(One of the cornerstones of variational pragmatics)*

Searle, John R. 1969. *Speech Acts. An Essay in the Philosophy of Language*. Cambridge: Cambridge University Press. *(Important text for the development of speech act theory)*

Searle, John R. 1979. *Expression and Meaning. Studies in the Theory of Speech Acts*. Cambridge: Cambridge University Press. *(Further central texts for the development of speech act theory)*

Thomas, Jenny. 1995. *Meaning in Interaction: An Introduction to Pragmatics*. London: Longman. *(Brief but profound, with excellent examples)*

Verschueren, Jef. 1999. *Understanding Pragmatics*. London: Arnold. *(Accessible introduction, focuses on pragmatics as a perspective)*

Wooffitt, Robin. 2005. *Conversation Analysis and Discourse Analysis. A Comparative and Critical Introduction*. London: Sage. *(Inspiring and accessible)*

Yule, George. 1996. *Pragmatics*. Oxford: Oxford University Press. *(Brief and beginner-friendly, with well-chosen readings to incite discussion)*

Selected Journals

Intercultural Pragmatics
Journal of Pragmatics
Pragmatics

Further References

Beaton, Alistair. 2001. *Feelgood*. London: Methuen. *(A satirical political play)*

McSmith, Andy. 2001. *Innocent in the House*. London: Verso. *(A satirical political novel)*

Sociolinguistics | 8

Contents

Abstract

Sociolinguistics is the scientific study of the relationship between language and society. The primary concern of sociolinguistic research is to investigate linguistic variation and the influence of social factors on language use und language structure. Sociolinguistics is a young and rapidly evolving discipline that is characterised by diverse research interests and increasing heterogeneity.

8.1 | The Subject Matter

What is Sociolinguistics?

There are no two individuals in the world who speak exactly alike. The language of the individual members of a **speech community**, i.e. of people who can communicate with each other, may be more or less similar. Each speaker's language use shows its unique characteristics and is referred to as her or his **idiolect**. When we communicate, we consciously or unconsciously choose between different forms of language known as **varieties** (or **speech varieties**, or **lects**). **Sociolinguistics**, as the **scientific study of the relationship between language and society**, investigates the effects of extralinguistic factors on the linguistic choices we make. These choices immediately convey information about the social and geographical background of a speaker. Speakers who make similar choices are said to speak the same **variety**. Similarity in linguistic choices is also one of the main elements constituting **group identity**. Listeners draw conclusions about the background of speakers on the basis of their language, for example about their education, socioeconomic status or occupation. As a result, speakers can even deliberately use language to signal that they are, or would like to be, members of a certain group.

Sociolinguistics has only been around for about half a century. Since the first use of the term *sociolinguistics* in the 1950s, the field has become a recognised core branch of linguistics. The discipline in its contemporary definition does, however, include some older subbranches of linguistics, such as **dialectology**, which was already popular in the 19th century and is partly continued by so-called **geographical sociolinguistics**.

But sociolinguistics is not the only discipline that studies the relationship between language and society. Many linguists distinguish between **sociolinguistics in the narrow sense** (or **microsociolinguistics**) and the **sociology of language** (or **macro-sociolinguistics**), which look at the subject matter from different perspectives. Sociolinguistics is concerned with the influence of social factors on language use and language structure, whereas the sociology of language investigates language with the aim of better understanding the structure and organisation of society. There are, however, neither sharp dividing lines between sociolinguistics and the sociology of language, nor between sociolinguistics and its neighbouring disciplines such as psycholinguistics, social psychology, ethnology, anthropology or human geography, to name just a few.

Sociolinguistics is thus a relatively young, multifaceted, and rapidly evolving discipline with diverse research interests. There is a considerable amount of overlap with many related fields. Contemporary sociolinguistics incorporates a number of other research areas that cannot be covered here in detail. This includes the enormous range of phenomena brought about by language change, multilingualism, language planning and all kinds of language contact situations. For example, **pidgins** and **creoles**, i.e. contact languages that developed for the most part in the context of colonialism, have been receiving considerable attention by sociolinguists in recent decades.

Language Variation | 8.2

The observation, description and explanation of **linguistic variation** is one of the main concerns of sociolinguistics. Such variation shows in different language use at **all levels of linguistic analysis**, including pronunciation, vocabulary, morphology, syntax, semantics and pragmatics. For example, a speaker from America who takes the *elevator* to the *second floor* usually does exactly the same as an English person who takes the *lift* to the *first floor*. In this case, it is obviously lexical variation that could lead to a misunderstanding between these two speakers. At the same time, most Americans would articulate the word-final /r/ suggested by the spelling in *floor*, thus pronouncing the word as /flɔːr/, whereas most speakers from England would pronounce the word as /flɔː/. We say "most speakers", because it is important to keep in mind that not all speakers of a certain variety use all linguistic features associated with this variety 100 per cent of the time and in all contexts. This means that although the pronunciation /flɔː/ is very common in England, there are also speakers who sometimes or always do pronounce the /r/ at the end of the word. When we speak about variation we are thus usually concerned with tendencies rather than exclusive differences.

> "Sociolinguists aim to describe sociolinguistic variation and, if possible, explain why it happens."
> (Holmes 2001:11)

Types of Varieties

According to the extralinguistic factors that motivate the use of a variety, we distinguish **three major types of varieties**: **geographical varieties** (traditionally called **regional dialects** or simply **dialects**, cf. 8.2.1), **sociolects** (or **social dialects**, cf. 8.2.2) that are motivated by social factors such as socio-economic status, occupation, ethnic group, gender, age and religion, and **functional varieties** that depend on the particular communicative situation. Additionally, in most societies there is another variety, the so-called **standard**, which has a special position and does not fit into any of the other types of varieties.

Fig. 8.1

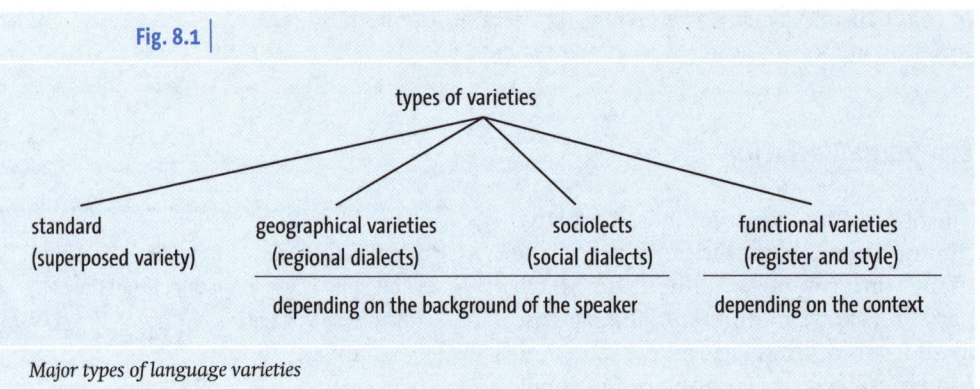

types of varieties

| standard | geographical varieties | sociolects | functional varieties |
| (superposed variety) | (regional dialects) | (social dialects) | (register and style) |

depending on the background of the speaker — depending on the context

Major types of language varieties

Variety, Dialect and Accent

Unfortunately, the linguistic usage of the terms **variety**, **dialect** and **accent** is not identical with the popular usage of these designations. In linguistics, both *dialect* and *accent* do not have the negative undertone associated with them in everyday speech and are clearly distinguished from each other. The term *dialect* refers to differences between "kinds of language" in pronunciation, vocabulary and grammar, whereas *accent* applies exclusively to differences in pronunciation. *Variety* is usually employed as a neutral term to refer to any "kind of language" without being specific.

To complicate the matter even further, the terms are not always used consistently in linguistics either. *Dialect* is either used for geographical varieties only, or in a broader sense in expressions such as *social dialect* or *standard dialect*. What seems to be clear is that all these terms refer to subdivisions of *one language*.

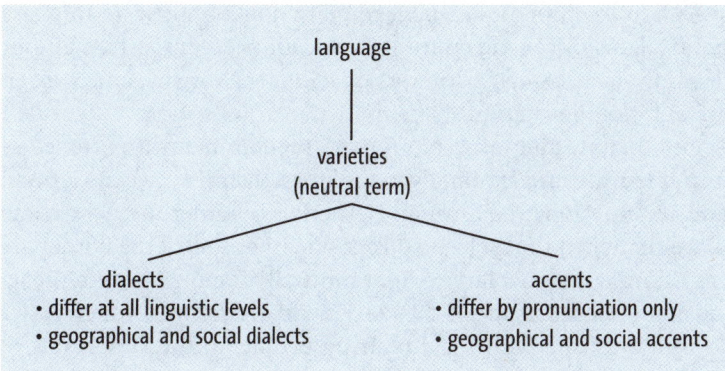

| Fig. 8.2

The terms language, variety, dialect and accent

We have so far assumed that dialects are subdivisions of a language. To non-linguists, the term **language** may seem to be a clear-cut concept, but at a second glance its linguistic definition and distinction from dialect cause some rather fundamental problems.

Concerning the dialect situation in England, for example, we frequently speak of a "Norfolk dialect" and a "Suffolk dialect". Studies have shown, however, that the rural dialects in the area change gradually from place to place and that there is no clear linguistic break between the two areas. The distinction between Norfolk dialect and Suffolk dialect is thus based on social, namely the county boundary as an administrative dividing line, rather than linguistic facts. From a purely linguistic point of view we are concerned with a so-called **dialect continuum** (or **dialect chain**), in which greater geographical distance generally means greater linguistic differences as well. Some dialects in the southern part of Norfolk may in fact be linguistically closer to dialects in northern Suffolk, than to other "Norfolk dialects" in the north of the county.

Language vs. Dialect

When we attempt to find a purely linguistic definition of *language*, we encounter the same problem. We usually feel that people who can communicate with each other speak the same language and thus consider **mutual intelligibility** the crucial defining factor. But why is it

> "The criterion of 'mutual intelligibility', and other purely linguistic criteria, are, therefore, of less importance in the use of the terms language and dialect, than are political and cultural factors, [...]."
> (Trudgill 2000:4)

then that educated speakers of Danish, Norwegian and Swedish can communicate well with each other and we still consider their speech to be different languages? Again non-linguistic, in this case political, historical and cultural factors are more important for our decision than linguistic criteria, as Denmark, Norway, and Sweden are autonomous nation states.

Another striking example for the predominant importance of non-linguistic criteria involves the relationship between German and Dutch. Along the German-Netherlands border there are some places in which the dialects spoken on either side of the border are very similar and to a large extent mutually intelligible. The speakers on the German side of the border will often find it much easier to communicate with neighbouring people on the Dutch side of the border than with speakers of other German dialects from distant parts of southern Germany, Austria or German-speaking Switzerland. Still we would not hesitate to say that people on one side of the border speak Dutch and those on the other side German, although there is no linguistic justification for our decision. This situation is the result of a West Germanic dialect continuum (cf. Fig. 2.3: *The Indo-European language family*) which links the dialects of Flemish, Dutch and German from Belgium through the Netherlands and Germany to Austria and Switzerland.

Standard

The notion of **standard** deserves individual consideration, as it is special in a number of respects. Standard English is the variety of English that is usually used in print, broadcasting and administration, normally taught in schools and to non-native learners, and used by most educated speakers of English most of the time. On the basis of these functions it is imposed over all other dialects and can thus be called a **superposed variety**.

It is important to note that Standard English is a dialect as well and, just like Standard German and other standard varieties, linguistically no better or worse than any other dialect. Dialects, in the linguistic sense of the term, are thus not deviations from the standard, or deficient in any respect. To be precise, from a diachronic point of view, it is absolutely impossible for dialects to be deviations from the standard, as the dialects of English existed long before Standard English ever came into existence (cf. 2.1.1). In fact, there are no languages or dialects that are inferior to any others as linguistic systems. The definition of the standard as well as its prestige and its important position in society depend solely on social and functional considerations. Along the same lines, all pronunciation varieties, even the most prestigious, are referred to as accents and, from a linguistic point of view, no accent is superior to any other.

The difference between Standard English and other dialects is that Standard English is only defined by grammar and vocabulary, whereas all other dialects differ at all levels of language including pronunciation. Standard English can for this reason be spoken with any accent, not just prestige accents such as RP or GenAm (cf. 3.1.3). For example, the sentence *Linguistics is fun* uses both mainstream grammar and vocabulary and is considered Standard English, no matter whether you say it with an RP, a GenAm, a Scottish, a working class or a French accent.

Styles and **registers** are so-called **functional varieties**, as they depend on the context of a communicative situation. Styles and registers are characterised by the function of language in a particular situation and the consideration of such factors as addressee, topic, location and interactional goal rather than the background of the speaker. The exact definition of style and register is difficult. Both terms are used in a number of different and often overlapping ways, even by linguists. A common distinction is that style refers to the level of formality of an utterance or a text, whereas register refers to the choice of vocabulary in a specific communicative situation.

Functional Varieties

(1) *A not as such inexpensive domicile has recently been purchased by our family.*

(2) *We have just bought a pretty pricey house.*

Most people would agree that the above sentences mean more or less the same. The difference between the sentences is essentially a stylistic one: they differ by their level of formality. Sentence (1) is written in a formal style, whereas sentence (2) is relatively informal. Most speakers of English would agree that the sentence *We have just bought a fairly expensive house* fits stylistically somewhere in between sentence (1) and sentence (2). Styles are organised along a continuum that ranges from very informal to extremely formal. Among others, the pairs *not inexpensive ~ pricey, domicile ~ house* and *purchase ~ buy* in the example sentences indicate that styles in English are mainly characterised by vocabulary differences. Stylistic differences, however, can also show in the frequency of certain syntactic structures: in English, the passive voice, used in sentence (1), is more frequent in formal styles.

Styles

Registers

Registers, on the other hand, are usually characterised by a set of specialised vocabulary or specialised meaning of words that certain groups of people use in certain situations. Registers are often associated with occupational groups. For instance, lawyers use words such as *felony*, *tort* or *vagrant*, in their register also referred to as "legalese". Pilots and aviation enthusiasts use the word *fuselage* whereas laypeople would more likely call the same "thing" the *body* of an aircraft.

The sternum requires great force to fracture.

As the above example sentence from a conversation between doctors shows, doctors and other medically trained people usually refer to the long, flat vertical bone in the centre of our chest as the *sternum* and normally use *fracture* instead of *break* when they talk among themselves. They would, however, probably use the word *breastbone* when they explain a diagnosis to a medically untrained patient. Other registers are associated with criminals, politicians, sports commentators and journalists ("journalese"), to name just a few.

Accommodation

We have said above that speakers often signal that they belong to a certain group by making their language more similar to that of the other group members (cf. 8.1). Depending on the communicative situation we thus adapt our language, dialect, accent, style and/or register to that of our addressee or addressees. This process is called **speech accommodation**. Among the reasons for accommodation may be our desire to identify more closely with the addressee(s), to achieve social acceptance or simply to increase the efficiency of the communication. Accommodation theory also provides explanations for the opposite process, namely the deliberate distancing from another person or a group of people by making our speech less like theirs.

8.2.1 | Geographical Differentiation of Language

In the traditional sociolinguistic view, language variation that is caused by the background of speakers develops when people are separated geographically or socially. Linguistic innovations such as new words or new pronunciations that occur in the language spoken in one geographical area or by one social group may not necessarily spread to the other areas or groups. Social and geographical **distance** slows down the spread to more distant

varieties and **barriers** may even stop the spread of linguistic innovations altogether. This then is also known as **communicative
isolation**. As a result, the boundaries of geographical dialect areas
frequently coincide with geographical barriers like mountain
ranges, oceans or rivers. Geographical variation is also referred to
as **horizontal variation**.

The study of geographical differentiation of language, which is   Traditional Dialectology
now an integral part of sociolinguistics, is rooted in the field of
traditional dialectology. Traditional dialectology has been popular since the middle of the 19th century and focuses on phonological and lexical variation in the speech of predominantly rural
dialect speakers. The methodology of dialectology for data collection has usually included the transcription and analysis of aspects
of speech by interviewers and the use of questionnaires. For several decades now, dialectologists have additionally employed tape-
recorded interviews to lend greater accuracy to their work.

This kind of investigation studies geographical differences concerning individual linguistic features. For example, linguists have
studied the pronunciation of the vowel in words such as *but* in England. The North of England is characterised by the older pronunciation /bʊt/, whereas the newer pronunciation /bʌt/ is the common
form in the South of England. Dialectology indicates the boundary
between the two usage areas on maps by means of a line, the so-
called **isogloss**. The /ʊ/ ~ /ʌ/ isogloss in England runs roughly south
of the East Midlands and West Midlands dialect areas (see Fig. 8.3).
Isoglosses separating other features run through England roughly
along the same line. Bundles of isoglosses form significant **dialect
boundaries**, which are the basis of so-called dialect atlases.

Geographical variation takes time to develop. In the English-
speaking world, dialect diversity is greatest within Britain, where
English has been spoken longest. America takes an intermediate
position, while there is relatively little geographical variation in
Australia and New Zealand, where English has been introduced
more recently.

There are, however, more or less considerable differences at all   National Varieties
linguistic levels between these so-called **national varieties** of English, such as British English, American English, Canadian English,
Australian English and New Zealand English (cf. 2.2). These differences are mainly due to a longstanding communicative isolation
of the separate national varieties, particularly before the advent of

Fig. 8.3

Dialect areas in England and the /ʊ/ ~ /ʌ/ isogloss (adapted from Trudgill 2000:152)

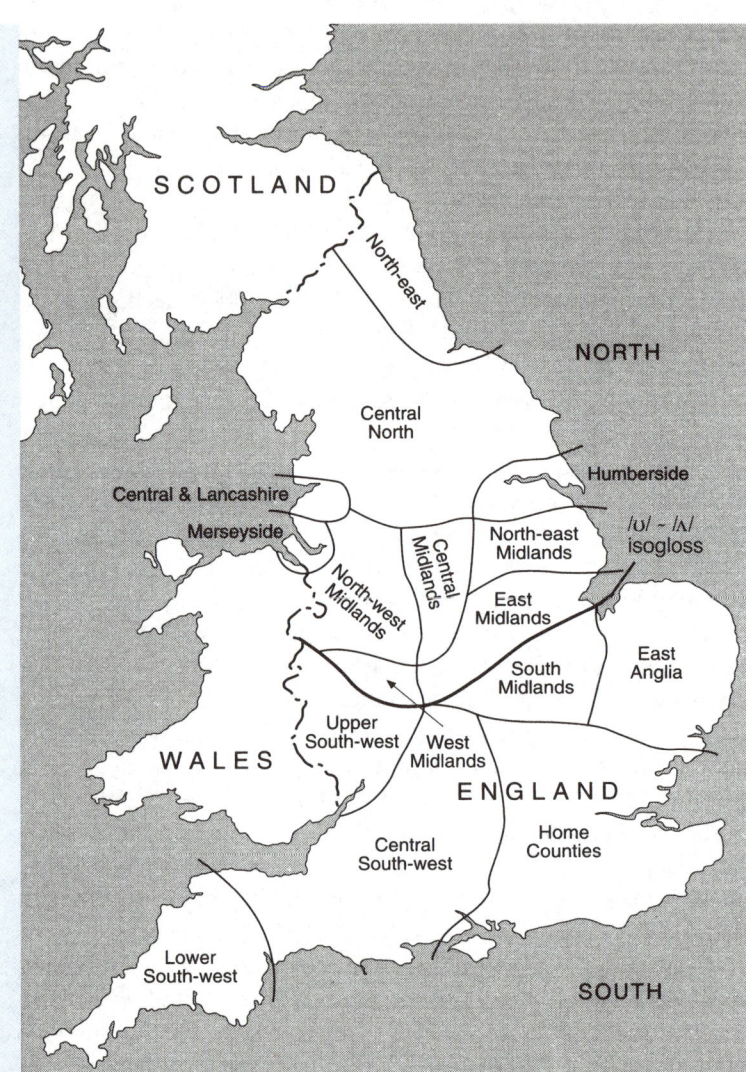

international mass communication and affordable air travel. We have seen earlier in this section that speakers from America are more likely to pronounce the /r/ in *car* than speakers from England. Like most speakers from England, the majority of Australians would not pronounce the /r/ in this environment either. On the other hand, there are numerous jokes and stories based on the fact that the Australian pronunciation of the sentence *I have come here today* sounds like *I have come here to die* to most non-Australian ears. As far as vocabulary is concerned, most foreign learners of English are taught that the American *subway* is referred to as *underground* in Britain, but not many know that South African speakers of English use *robot* for the shared British and American term *traffic light*. Vocabulary differences can even cause embarrassment. Just think of the usage of the term *pants* meaning 'a pair of trousers' in America but 'men's underpants' in Britain. Grammatical differences are usually less salient, but do also exist. American English allows the simple past tense in sentences such as *I just came here* while most speakers of British English would prefer *I have just come here*, i.e. the use of the present perfect.

Although traditional dialectology, with its focus on predominantly rural dialects, has not ceased to exist, the field of **modern dialectology** is increasingly concerned with the study of urban dialects, frequently combining aspects of geographical and social variation (cf. 8.2.2). Modern dialectology still makes use of questionnaires and observations by interviewers but also employs statistical analysis of so-called language corpora, i.e. large databases of speech samples.

Modern Dialectology

Social Differentiation of Language

8.2.2

Similarly to the geographical differentiation of language, social variation depends on a speaker's membership in various social groups and is at least to some extent due to **social barriers** and **social distance** (cf. 8.2.1). Socio-economic status, ethnic group membership, gender (cf. 8.3) and age are just some of the social factors that can act as linguistic barriers and may prevent innovations from spreading. More frequently, the social distance between groups such as young and old speakers or upper class and lower class speakers slows down the spread of innovations from one group to the other just as geographical distance does. Social variation is a very complex phenomenon, as speakers usually have only one main geographical background, but belong to a multitude of social groups. For example, a speaker can be upper class, African American, female and old at the same time. Language **attitudes** are another crucial factor that contributes to the development of social variation. Social differentiation of language is also referred to as **vertical differentiation**.

Fig. 8.4

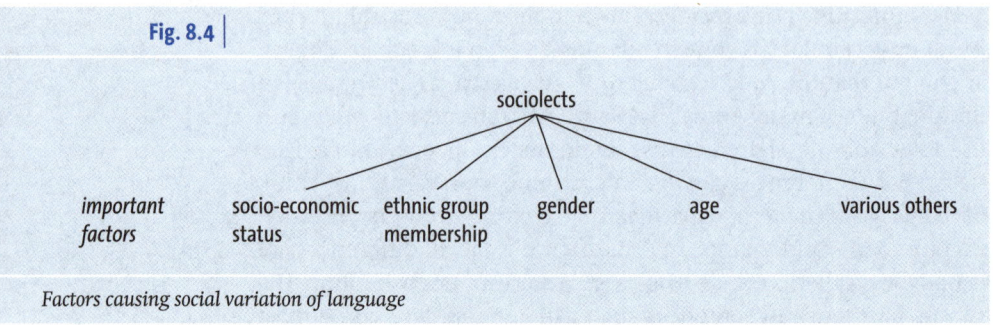

Factors causing social variation of language

Socio-Economic Status   One of the earliest and most striking discoveries of sociolinguistics was an observable pattern in the relationship between social and geographical variation. Studies found that the **socio-economic status** (or **social class**) of a speaker influences her or his use of regional dialect forms. Socio-economic status is associated with a speaker's education, occupation, income level and similar characteristics. According to these studies, British speakers of the highest socio-economic status usually speak the dialect called Standard British English (cf. 8.2), which does show some differences in different parts of the country but allows for comparatively little geographical variation. In contrast, regional variation was found to be far more extensive among speakers of the lowest social class, who use a wide variety of non-standard linguistic features. Fig. 8.5 illustrates the different range of regional variation in the speech of speakers from different socio-economic backgrounds.

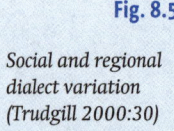

Fig. 8.5

Social and regional dialect variation (Trudgill 2000:30)

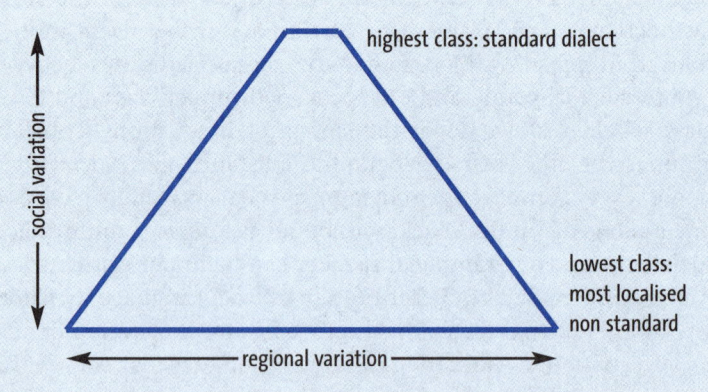

The analysis of the correlation of language and socio-economic status is inseparably connected with the American linguist **William Labov** (*1927), who pioneered the quantitative study of language variation in the early 1960s and is by many considered the founder of modern sociolinguistics. Labov conducted a number of studies concerning the social variation of individual linguistic features. For example, one of the studies looked into the realisation of non-prevocalic /r/ in New York City, i.e. the frequency with which speakers with different socio-economic backgrounds articulate the r suggested by the spelling of words like *cart* and *car* before a consonant or silence. In this example, rhoticity is what Labov refers to as the **linguistic variable**, while he calls the possible realisations of this variable as [ɹ] and Ø (= zero) its **linguistic variants**.

William Labov

Like most accents of English in the North-East of the United States, the New York accent is traditionally non-rhotic (or r-less), whereas the prestige pronunciation referred to as GenAm is generally rhotic (cf. 3.1.3). Probably due to the prestige of GenAm, the New York accent has become increasingly rhotic for quite some time, particularly since World War II. Labov tested his hypothesis that non-prevocalic /r/ usage would be correlated with socio-economic status in an experiment. He asked a number of shop assistants in a high, a medium and a low status New York City department store questions like *Excuse me, where are the women's shoes?* that made them say *fourth floor*, which has two occurrences of the linguistic variable non-prevocalic /r/. 83 per cent of the low-ranking shop assistants, 49 per cent in the medium-ranking store and only 38 per cent in the high-ranking store used the less prestigious r-less variant. Labov showed that the lower the status of the store, the more likely it is that shop assistants use the less prestigious variant.

Example: The First Study

At least equally important as the intriguing results of Labov's early studies are the innovative sampling methods Labov has developed himself or introduced into linguistics from other fields, which is why he has been described as a "methodological genius" by other sociolinguists. For example, the shop assistants in New York did not know that they were being interviewed by a linguist. This is just one of the techniques Labov has employed to overcome what he called the **observer's paradox**, i.e. the fact that people behave differently when they know that they are being systematically observed. Labov has developed a variety of other methods that elicit natural speech from informants despite the interview situation. He has shown, for instance, that interviewees tend to forget the unnaturalness of the situation when they are asked to talk about life-threatening situations they have been in. Additionally, Labov was among the first scholars to bring sociological methods like random sampling to linguistics, while most earlier studies were conducted among friends or personal contacts of the linguists involved. Random sampling ensures that though not every member of a linguistic group can be interviewed, each member has an equal chance of being selected for an interview. This way, the studies can claim to be truly representative of the linguistic group investigated.

An ethnic group is a "[s]ocial group or category of the population that, in a larger society, is set apart and bound together by common ties of language, nationality, or culture."
(Encyclopedia Britannica)

Ethnic Group Membership

When we communicate, we often consciously or unconsciously signal our **ethnic identity** by the way we speak. Listeners, on the other hand, draw conclusions about the ethnic background of a speaker from the language she or he uses, particularly when there is no visual contact between the people taking part in a conversation. The linguistic choices we make are thus an important ethnic group marker.

African American Vernacular English

One of the most-researched ethnic varieties is so-called **African American Vernacular English** (AAVE, formerly also called Black English), which is an important identifying characteristic of the group of African Americans in the United States. AAVE is heard especially in the northern cities of the United States and has a number of linguistic features that do not or only much less frequently occur in Standard American English (SAE).

The **grammatical properties** of AAVE include the frequent use of multiple negation, as in *I ain't owe you nothing*, and the omission of the 3rd person singular present indicative *-s*, as in *she say* or *he kiss*. Another important grammatical characteristic of AAVE is the absence of the copula verb *be* in linguistic contexts in which speakers of SAE would often use reduced forms: SAE *she's happy* corresponds to AAVE *she happy*. To indicate habitual aspect, i.e. when an event is repeated and not continuous, AAVE employs the uninflected so-called invariant *be*. Together with the omission of the copula *be*, this results in a contrast between *she tired* 'she is tired (now)' and *she be tired* 'she is (always) tired', which can only be achieved by lexical means, i.e. the addition of *now* and *always*, in SAE.

The **phonological characteristics** of AAVE include the frequent deletion of /l/ at the end of words or before consonants, as in *cool* /kuː/ or *help* /hɛp/, creating homophonic pairs such as *toll* and *toe*. AAVE is non-rhotic and thus regularly deletes /r/ in all positions except before a vowel. Another phonological property is the simplification of so-called consonant clusters. Particularly at the end of words, the last consonant is frequently deleted, especially when one of the two consonants is an alveolar (cf. IPA chart inside the front cover). This process can create homophones, as both *meant* and *mend* are then frequently pronounced the same as *men* /mɛn/.

Talking about AAVE, it is, however, important to keep in mind that not all African Americans speak AAVE and that we are more likely to encounter non-standard AAVE features in the speech of speakers of lower socio-economic status. In fact, experiments have shown that African American children raised in SAE-speaking households will, of course, speak SAE, while white children who grow up in an AAVE-speaking environment will speak AAVE, because speakers always acquire the linguistic characteristics of those they live in close contact with. This shows that linguistic differences are entirely the result of learned behavior.

Language and Gender | 8.3

The study of issues concerning language and gender is one of the most dynamic fields of current research and has led to two main areas of investigation. On the one hand, linguists have long studied linguistic features of women's and men's ways of communicating, i.e. so-called **gender varieties** (or **genderlects**). On the other hand, feminist linguistics is primarily concerned with **linguistic sexism**, i.e. the linguistic discrimination of women, and the suggestion of non-discriminatory forms of language use. In the study of language and gender, most scholars view gender as a **social category** that is connected to the roles of women and men in society and distinguished from the biological concept of sex, although the two are to some extent interwoven. Gender as a social category refers to individuals and is differentiated from grammatical gender as a linguistic category (cf. section 2.1.1).

There is no community that we know of in which women and men speak in exactly the same way. It has been suggested that **gen-**

Gender-Specific
Language Use

der-specific language use reflects the basic structure of societies. It has been claimed that, in some non-Western communities, women and men speak entirely different languages or one gender generally does not use specific linguistic forms that the other gender does. There are, however, no attested examples for this claim. Differences like that would be called **gender-exclusive speech differences**. In most societies, including all Western communities, women's and men's roles in society overlap to a certain extent and thus the speech forms used also overlap. As a result, women and men do not use entirely different linguistic forms, it is rather the frequency of usage of certain linguistic features that may differ. These differences in frequency and proportion are called **gender-preferential speech features**. We will now focus on one such example.

Gender-Preferential
Speech

Numerous studies investigating gender-preferential speech features in English have shown that there is a clear difference concerning the **frequency of standard features** used by women and men of the same social class. For example, the pronunciation of the variable -ng at the end of words like *swimming* and *walking* has been studied in several cities in the English-speaking world. For Norwich, Fig. 8.6 shows that men used the non-standard variant [-n] instead of the standard variant [-ŋ] more often than women in each of the five social classes under investigation:

Fig. 8.6

Pronunciation of [-n] by sex and social class in Norwich (Holmes 2008:161)

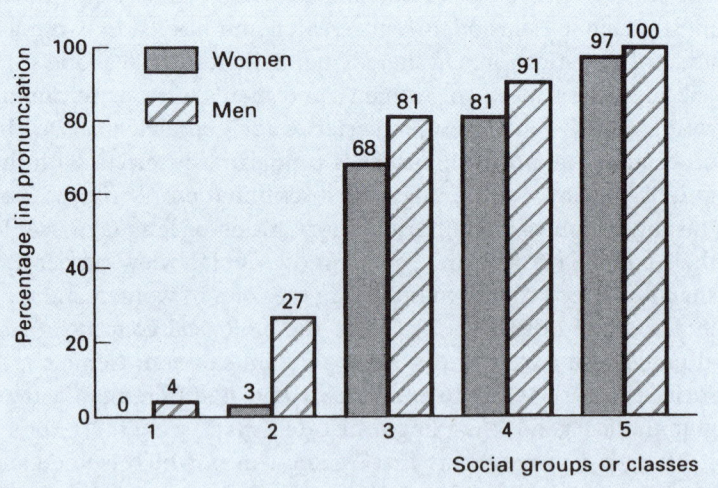

The results from Norwich have been confirmed by other studies conducted in different places. In the speech data of all of the cities investigated, women have been found to use more standard pronunciations [-ŋ] and fewer non-standard [-n] pronunciations than their male counterparts of the same socio-economic status. The pattern that women use more standard forms than men also holds true for other variables at all linguistic levels, for example, the frequency of use of multiple negation in the speech of female and male African American speakers in Detroit. In fact, the correlation of gender and the usage of standard forms can be generalised to most Western speech communities. The sociolinguist Peter Trudgill (2000:73) describes this pattern as "the single most consistent finding to emerge from sociolinguistic work around the world in the past thirty years".

We have seen that the pattern is clear and widespread in the languages investigated so far, but we do not know exactly why women use more standard forms than men. Linguists have suggested at least four possible explanations: Firstly, it has been claimed that societies seem to expect a higher level of adherence to social norms from women than from men. Secondly, it has been proposed that women are a subordinate group in society and thus have to speak more carefully and more politely in order to avoid offending men. Thirdly, linguists have suggested that women use more standard forms than men because they are more status-conscious than men and try to signal higher social status by the way they speak. A fourth approach inverts the question and asks why men do not use more standard forms than they do. The explanation seems to lie in the fact that numerous non-standard forms carry connotations of masculinity and toughness that are viewed positively by many men. While women more frequently choose standard forms, which are models of correctness and have obvious prestige which Labov calls **overt prestige**, it is probably because of these masculine connotations that men frequently use non-standard vernacular forms. The vernacular forms are said to carry a different type of "hidden" prestige which Labov calls **covert prestige**. Language choice can thus be said to be equally important for signalling one's gender identity, as it is for indicating socio-economic status and ethnic group membership (cf. 8.2.2).

Sentences like *Doctors and their wives* used to be frequently encountered on invitations. This shows that inequality and the asymmetrical roles of women and men in society do not only

Linguistic Sexism

influence women's and men's ways of communicating, but also the way women and men are represented in language structure and language use. Linguistic discrimination by means of the asymmetrical representation of women and men in language is referred to as **linguistic sexism**, **sexism in language** or **gender-biased language use**. It is usually women who are excluded, trivialised or insulted by **sexist language use**.

The awareness and documentation of sexist practices in language use has led to a lively discussion and the development of many guidelines for **non-sexist usage** in a variety of languages since the 1970s. There are a number of other terms referring to the same or similar concepts including **gender-fair**, **non-discriminatory**, **gender-neutral** and **gender-inclusive language**. We will now take a look at the most important mechanisms of linguistic discrimination of women, namely **female invisibility**, **stereotyping** and **asymmetrical gender marking**, and briefly discuss proposals for the elimination of sexist language.

Female Invisibility

English has been accused of being a patriarchal (= 'male dominated') and sexist language, partly on the grounds that women are frequently invisible in language. So-called personal nouns (or human nouns) referring to individuals and pronouns play the central role in the debate. Traditionally, male-biased nouns like *chairman* and *mankind* are used in a so-called generic sense to refer to both female and male referents. Similarly, traditional prescription requires the use of the so-called "generic *he*" in contexts in which the gender of the referent is unspecified or unimportant, as in *If a student works hard, he will be successful*. In both cases, women are allegedly included but not visible. These usages of male-biased nouns and pronouns are called **androcentric** (= 'male dominated') and follow the traditional *MAN* (= 'male as norm') principle. Psycholinguistic studies have shown that *he* and *man* are associated with male images, even when they are employed generically. The result is that *man* cannot be used in a completely generic sense and that English does not have a truly gender-neutral third person singular pronoun, except the recent usage of *they* with a singular meaning. This is why the androcentric "generics" have also been called **pseudo-generics** or **false generics**. For the same reason, it has also proven totally unsuitable to add a footnote to a text explaining that all male pronouns used in the text are meant to include women as well.

The meaning of some personal nouns includes the notion of so-called **lexical gender**. For example, personal nouns such as *mother* and *father* are gender-specific as they are lexically specified as [+female] and [+male] respectively. However, most English personal nouns such as *student* or *passenger* are considered gender-neutral (or gender-indefinite). In contrast to German, where personal feminines are usually marked by means of the productive suffix *-in* as in *Studentin* 'female student', the majority of English personal nouns are not formally marked for lexical gender, with exceptions such as *princess* or *widower*. In English, gender thus shows mainly in the pronouns accompanying a personal noun.

If the choice of an associated pronoun cannot be explained by grammatical gender or lexical gender, as in *A pilot must love his plane*, the noun has so-called **social gender** (or covert gender). Social gender depends on stereotypical assumptions about the "appropriate" roles for women and men in society. This is why personal nouns like *nurse* or *typist* are frequently pronominalised by *she*, whereas many high-status occupational terms like *pilot*, *doctor* or *scientist* will often be pronominalised by *he* in situations where the person's gender is unknown or irrelevant.

Linguistic **stereotyping** and **asymmetrical gender marking** are the result of these allegedly stereotypical roles of women and men in society. The initial example sentence *Doctors and their wives* shows so-called stereotyping based on an underlying gender-bias and an asymmetrical structure of society. Similarly, asymmetrical gender marking — as in the increasingly rare terms *woman doctor*, *lady scientist* or *male nurse* — refers to the combination of a lexically gender-neutral noun with a gender-specific element when the referent does not have the stereotypically assumed gender. Even morphologically symmetrical pairs of terms can be semantically highly asymmetrical, often with the female representing the lesser category. This process is called **semantic derogation** and can be encountered in pairs like *governor* 'the official head of a state or region' and *governess* 'a woman who lives with a family, and takes care of and teaches the children'. Semantic derogation applies to many terms for women with originally positive or neutral associations, which have undergone a process of derogation. For example, *mistress* simply used to be the female equivalent of *master* and now refers to a woman who has a sexual relationship with a man married to another woman.

Stereotyping and
Asymmetrical Gender
Marking

Another asymmetry shows in the terms of address for men and women. In English and German, women were traditionally identified in terms of their relationship to men as either being married or unmarried. The disappearance of *Fräulein* 'Miss' as a term of address for unmarried female adults in German has created a truly symmetrical pair of address terms (*Frau/Herr*). The strategy to introduce a new neutral term *Ms* [mɪz] in English has been less successful. *Ms* is on the increase but has not yet replaced *Mrs* and *Miss* completely and transports a number of unintended meanings such as 'separated/divorced' or 'living in a de facto relationship'.

Non-Sexist Language Reform

Particularly since the 1970s, feminist linguistics has been making proposals how to avoid sexist language. **Two major strategies of non-sexist language reform** have been proposed:

One approach claims that linguistic equality can be achieved by **gender-neutralisation**, i.e. the elimination of gender-specific forms in generic contexts. The replacement of generic *he* by the pronoun *they* in the singular, as in *everyone should wash their hands now*, is probably the most frequently used form of gender-neutralisation in English. Interestingly enough, this usage was widespread for most of the history of English, before eighteenth century grammarians created the rule which calls for the generic usage of the male pronouns. Generically used *man* can also be rendered in a gender-neutral way, for example by the use of *chairperson* or simply *chair* instead of *chairman*, and *humankind* instead of *mankind*. Similar proposals have been made concerning gender-neutral job titles, such as the introduction of *flight attendant*, *firefighter* or *police officer*.

The second approach proposes to achieve linguistic equality by so-called **gender-specification** (or **feminisation**), i.e. by making the woman/female visible through the explicit naming or inclusion of both genders. For example, it is now common to explicitly mention both genders in constructions like *she or he* or *he or she*, replacing traditional generic *he*. In writing the same effect can be achieved by the frequently encountered spelling *s/he*. Feminisation can also be applied to avoid generic *-man* through the use of so-called "**gender-splitting**", as in *chairwoman or chairman*, in contexts in which we do not know the gender of the referent. Splitting is now also a frequently encountered strategy when addressing an unknown recipient in a letter as *Dear Madam or Sir*.

These examples show that both strategies are in widespread use today. The preference for either gender-neutralisation or gender-specification is partly a matter of ideology and other non-linguistic parameters, and partly based on the structural properties of the languages in question. From a linguistic perspective, the feminisation strategy is more effective in languages such as German, which have grammatical gender and regularly mark gender morphologically, than in natural gender languages such as English, in which gender mainly shows in pronoun use. German has the productive feminine suffix *-in* that can be employed to explicitly mention both genders by gender-splitting in phrases such as *jede Studentin und jeder Student* 'every female and male student'. In writing, German-speakers can refer to the generic notion of *student* by spellings like *der/die Student/in* 'the student' or *die StudentInnen* 'students'. Feminisation has thus been favoured by many German feminist linguistic activists, although there are some instances of neutralisation as well, such as the use of *Studierende* 'students' in the plural instead of *Studentinnen* 'female students' or the ambiguous term *Studenten* meaning 'male students' or traditionally also 'male and female students'. In English, on the other hand, it has been more popular to neutralise gender differences by creating terms like *chairperson* or *salesperson* that are not marked for gender at all. The following table gives an overview of the most important guidelines on non-sexist usage in English:

		Fig. 8.7
guideline	**traditional usage**	**non-sexist alternative(s)**
▶ avoid pseudo-generic he/his/him	▶ *Everyone should wash his hands now.*	▶ use singular *they*: *Everyone should wash their hands now.*
	▶ *If a student works hard, he will be successful.*	▶ use *she or he or he or she*: *If a student works hard, she or he will be successful.*
		▶ use singular *they*: *If a student works hard, they will be successful.*
		▶ use graphemic devices (in writing only): *... s/he will be successful.*
		▶ use the plural: *Students who work hard will be successful.*

▶ avoid pseudo-generic *man*	▶ *mankind* or *man* (as in *The history of man*)	▶ use *humankind* instead
	▶ *chairman* or *policeman*	▶ use gender-neutral forms: *chair* or *chairperson* and *police officer*
	▶ *the best man for the task*	▶ use *person* instead: *the best person for the task*
	▶ *man the ticket booth*	▶ use a gender-neutral alternative: *staff the ticket booth*
▶ avoid stereotyping and asymmetrical gender marking	▶ *doctors and their wives*	▶ use a gender-neutral alternative: *doctors and their spouses*
	▶ *woman scientist* ▶ *lady scientist*	▶ do not add gender-specific elements, use *scientist* instead
	▶ *The reading list includes Joyce, Jane Austen, Virginia Woolf and Faulkner.*	▶ use first names for all or none of the people mentioned: *The reading list includes Joyce, Austen, Woolf and Faulkner* (or: *James Joyce, Jane Austen, Virginia Woolf and William Faulkner*).
	▶ *forefathers*	▶ use *ancestors* instead
▶ avoid forms of address that are marked for marital status	▶ *Miss* (unmarried) ▶ *Mrs* (married)	▶ use *Ms* /mɪz/ instead of both terms
	▶ *Mr and Mrs James Smith*	▶ use first names or unmarked forms of address instead: *Emma and James Smith* or *Mr and Ms Smith*
▶ avoid diminutive forms and semantic derogation	▶ *authoress, poetess, stewardess* (on a plane)	▶ avoid *-ess*, use *author, poet* and *flight attendant* instead

Selected guidelines on non-sexist language use in English

To sum up, we can say that today, at least officially, gender equality is one of the primary goals of social development. Many governments, international institutions and private organisations have adopted guidelines for the use of non-sexist language in public speech and documents as part of a **gender mainstreaming** policy. The objective of gender mainstreaming is the explicit consideration of both women and men as well as gender equality in all decision-making processes. From a linguistic point of view, gender mainstreaming is a matter of non-sexist language planning. The first results of such planning and the spread of non-sexist language in society are currently under investigation and evaluation.

Exercises

1. In 1945, the linguist Max Weinreich proposed the following distinction of the terms language and dialect: "A language is a dialect with an army and a navy." If we ignore the fact that it is not languages but the corresponding countries that have an army, this definition works well for the linguistic situation in Scandinavia (Denmark, Sweden and Norway), where we are concerned with three different languages that are to a large extent mutually intelligible. How can you relate the definition to the situation of British English, American English and Australian English?

2. What type of variety are we concerned with in the following sentence? Give reasons.
   Henry scored twice in the first half and once in the second half when he raced on to a pass from Reyes in the 68th minute.

3. Sentence a) is written in a rather formal style, sentence b) in a rather informal style.
   a) Please rewrite the sentence in a less formal style and explain your choices:
      Mother was somewhat fatigued after her lengthy journey.
   b) Please rewrite the utterance in a more formal style and explain your choices:
      I gotta head home and hit the hay. I'm pretty beat.

4. What would you have to change to make the following excerpts gender-neutral:
   a) *We hold these truths to be self-evident, that all men are created equal, that they are endowed by their Creator with certain unalienable Rights, that among these are Life, Liberty and the pursuit of Happiness.* (from the *Declaration of Independence*)
   b) *The English have no respect for their language, [...]. They spell it so abominably that no man can teach himself what it sounds like. [...] German and Spanish are accessible to foreigners: English is not accessible even to Englishmen.* (cf. 3.1.3)
   c) *And the maker of a verse*
      Cannot rhyme his horse with worse? (cf. 3.1.3)
   d) *Miss Power has been named "fireman of the month".*

e) *The poetess Joanna Verse read from her new book on the radio last night.*

f) *An Australian loves his vegemite sandwich.*

5. When Neil Armstrong climbed out of the Lunar Module in 1969 and was the first person ever to set foot on the moon, he said the following sentence containing a small slip of the tongue:

That's one small step for man, one giant leap for mankind.

a) What would be a non-sexist version of this utterance and why does Armstrong's statement, strictly speaking, not make sense?

b) Make an educated guess what he probably wanted to say and give a non-sexist version of his intended sentence.

8.5 | Bibliography

Ammon, Ulrich et al., eds. 2004-2006. *Socio-linguistics/Soziolinguistik: An International Handbook of the Science of Language and Society/Ein internationales Handbuch zur Wissenschaft von Sprache und Gesellschaft.* 3 vols. 2nd edition. Berlin: de Gruyter. *(The authoritative and comprehensive handbook on sociolinguistics)*

Chambers, J. K. 2003. *Sociolinguistic Theory: Linguistic Variation and Its Social Significance.* 2nd edition. Oxford: Blackwell. *(A rather comprehensive treatment of sociolinguistic theory)*

Chambers, J. K. et al., eds. 2002. *The Handbook of Language Variation and Change.* Oxford: Blackwell. *(A collection of articles on issues concerning language variation)*

Coates, Jennifer. 2004. *Women, Men and Language: A Sociolinguistic Account of Gender Differences in Language.* 3rd edition. Harlow: Longman. *(An up-to-date introduction to gender differences in language)*

Coulmas, Florian. 1998. *The Handbook of Sociolinguistics.* Oxford: Blackwell. *(A collection of articles on core sociolinguistic topics)*

Coulmas, Florian. 2005. *Sociolinguistics: The Study of Speakers' Choices.* Cambridge: Cambridge University Press. *(An introductory textbook)*

Coupland, Nick & **Adam Jaworski,** eds. 1997. *Sociolingustics: A Reader and Coursebook.* Basingstoke and London: Macmillan. *(A collection of essays from leading sociolinguists)*

Eckert, Penelope & **Sally McConnell-Ginet.** 2003. *Language and Gender.* Cambridge: Cambridge University Press. *(An overview of the relation between gender and language use)*

Hellinger, Marlis & **Ulrich Ammon,** eds. 1996. *Contrastive Sociolinguistics.* Berlin: Mouton de Gruyter. *(A contrastive approach to basic issues in sociolinguistics)*

Hellinger, Marlis & **Hadumod Bußmann,** eds. 2001-2003. *Gender Across Languages.* 3 vols. Amsterdam: John Benjamins. *(A comprehensive and systematic description of gender issues concerning a variety of different languages)*

Holmes, Janet. 2008. *An Introduction to Sociolinguistics.* 3rd edition. Harlow: Longman. *(An up-to-date introductory textbook on sociolinguistics)*

Holmes, Janet & **Miriam Meyerhoff**, eds. 2003. *The Handbook of Language and Gender*. Oxford: Blackwell. *(A valuable collection of articles addressing issues concerning language and gender)*

Kortmann, Bernd & **Edgar Schneider** in collaboration with Kate Burridge, Rajend Mesthrie & Clive Upton, eds. 2004. *A Handbook of Varieties of English*. 2 vols. + 1 CD-ROM. Berlin: Mouton de Gruyter. *(A comprehensive overview of varieties of English around the world)*

Labov, William. 1966. *The Social Stratification of English in New York City*. Washington D.C.: Center for Applied Linguistics. *(The groundbreaking study for the field of sociolinguistics)*

Labov, William. 2001. *Principles of Linguistic Change. Volume 2: Social Factors*. Malden: Blackwell. *(A detailed account of the social origins and the social motivation of linguistic change)*

Lakoff, Robin Tolmach. 2004. *Language and Woman's Place*. Revised ed. by Mary Bucholtz. Oxford: Oxford University Press. *(Revised edition of one of the classic texts on language and gender with commentaries from a number of leading scholars of the field)*

Mesthrie, Rajend. 2001. *Concise Encyclopedia of Sociolinguistics*. Amsterdam: Elsevier. *(A broad and comprehensive overview of sociolinguistics)*

Miller, Casey & **Katie Swift**. 1995. *The Handbook of Non-Sexist Writing for Writers, Editors and Speakers*. 3rd edition. London: The Woman's Press. *(A pioneering guide to non-sexist language use)*

Romaine, Suzanne. 2000. *Language in Society: An Introduction to Sociolinguistics*. 2nd edition. Oxford: Oxford University Press. *(An introductory textbook to the field of sociolinguistics)*

Stockwell, Peter. 2002. *Sociolinguistics: A Resource Book for Students*. London: Routledge. *(A hands-on introductory textbook)*

Swann, Joan et al., 2004. *A Dictionary of Sociolinguistics*. Tuscaloosa: University of Alabama Press. *(A comprehensive dictionary of sociolinguistic terminology)*

Trudgill, Peter. 2000. *Sociolinguistics: An Introduction to Language and Society*. 4th edition. London: Penguin. *(One of the standard introductory textbooks on sociolinguistics)*

Trudgill, Peter. 2003. *A Glossary of Sociolinguistics*. Edinburgh: Edinburgh University Press. *(A collection of the most important terms used in sociolinguistic analysis)*

Wardhaugh, Ronald. 2005. *An Introduction to Sociolinguistics*. 5th edition. Oxford: Blackwell. *(A comparatively comprehensive introductory textbook)*

Wolfram, Walt & **Natalie Shilling-Estes**. 2005. *American English: Dialects and Variation*. 2nd edition. Oxford: Blackwell. *(An up-to-date description of language variation in American English)*

Selected Journals
Journal of Sociolinguistics
Language and Society
Language Variation and Change
English World-Wide

Appendix |9

Answers |9.1

Chapter 2: A Brief History of English

1. The main aim of historical linguistics is the description and explanation of language change over time.

2. *Kentish*, *West Saxon* and *Anglian* are the three main dialect areas of Old English. *Anglo-Saxon* is used as an alternative term for *Old English*, or to refer to an English person of the period before the Norman Conquest. The term *Cockney* refers to the type of English used by a part of the population of East London or a person who speaks Cockney.

3. a) T   b) F   c) F   d) T   e) F

4. The /uː/ in ModE *moon* goes back to ME long /oː/. It is the result of raising during the Great Vowel Shift. The Modern English spelling does not reflect the sound change, as the spelling of English had largely been fixed before the change took place. — The Modern English pronunciation /aɪ/ of *I* goes back to ME long /iː/, which was diphthongised in the course of the Great Vowel Shift. Again, the spelling has not been adjusted to reflect the sound change.

5. In the countries of the so-called outer circle, such as India, Singapore, Nigeria and South Africa, English is not the native language of the majority of the population, but does have a number of important functions. In India, for example, English is widely used in education, the public administration and as a lingua franca, i.e. for communication between people or groups of people who do not have the same native language.

6. The change that can be observed when looking at the data is part of the so-called High German Consonant Shift (or Second Germanic Consonant Shift). The entire sound change cannot be explained in detail here. What we can observe from the spelling of the words, however, is that ModE *p*- corresponds to ModG *pf*- at the beginning of many historically related words. The change must have taken place after the West Germanic languages had split up into High and Low varieties.

Chapter 3: Phonetics and Phonology

1. a) [b], [k] and [d] represent plosives
   b) [s], [ʃ], [x] and [θ] represent fricatives
   c) [b], [w], [l], [ŋ] and [d] represent voiced consonants; [ʊ] and [ɪ] are vowels, which are always voiced

2.

Place of articulation	Manner of articulation	Examples from English
a) bilabial	plosive	[b], [p]
b) dental	fricative	[θ], [ð]
c) velar	nasal	[ŋ]
d) labiodental	fricative	[f], [v]
e) velar	plosive	[k], [g]
f) bilabial	nasal	[m]

3. Consonants are called homorganic when they share the same place of articulation. There are four groups of homorganic consonants in the data of Exercise 2:
   1) [b], [p] and [m] are all **bilabials**
   2) [k], [g] and [ŋ] are all **velars**
   3) [θ] and [ð] are both **dentals**
   4) [f] and [v] are both **labiodentals**

4. Shared articulatory features are:

phones	*feature(s)*
a) [m], [ŋ], [n]	voiced, nasal
b) [k], [g], [ŋ], [x]	velars
c) [i], [e], [ɛ], [æ]	front vowels
d) [f], [θ], [s], [ʃ]	voiceless, fricative
e) [u], [i]	close (or: high) vowels

f) [d], [n], [r], [l]   voiced, alveolar

5. The phonetic symbols corresponding to the articulatory descriptions are:
a) [z]   b) [ɛ]   c) [u]   d) [ʔ]   e) [ɪ]   f) [ʃ]

6. The following articulatory descriptions correspond to the phonetic symbols provided:
a) mid central unrounded vowel
b) voiced alveolar nasal
c) mid-low low front unrounded vowel
d) voiceless alveolar plosive
e) mid-high high back rounded vowel
f) voiced alveolar approximant

7. Conventional English spelling of the transcribed words and phrases:
a) *cheat*   d) *Old English*   g) *phonetics too / phonetics two*
b) *son / sun*   e) *assimilation*   h) *enough*
c) *bite / byte* f) *linguistics is fun*

8. Examples from the poem for discrepancies between spelling and pronunciation:

type
1) same spelling for different sounds: (*examples from stanzas 1 and 2*)
<ea> represents [eɪ] in *break*, [iː] in *freak*, *speak* and *beard*, and [ɜː] in *heard*
<ew> represents [əʊ] in *sew* and [juː] in *few*
<o> represents [ɔː] in *horse* and *cord*, and [ɜː] in *worse* and *word*
2) different spellings for the same sound: (*examples from stanzas 1 and 2*)
[uː] is represented by <ue> in *true* and <ew> in *few*
[ɜː] is represented by <e> in *verse*, <ea> in *heard*, and <o> in *worse* and *word*
3) silent letters: (*examples from stanzas 4 and 5*)
tom**b**, bom**b**, com**b**, some, home, could, done, gone, lone, **k**nown
4) phantom letter:
[j] in *few*

9. Further examples for discrepancies between spelling and pronunciation:

type   *examples:*

1) <o> represents [ɪ] in *women*, [u:] in *do*, [ɔ:] in *fort*, [ʊ] in *wolf*, RP [ɒ] or GenAm [ɑ:] in *sock*, [ʌ] in *son*, RP [əʊ] or GenAm [oʊ] in *phone*, and [ə] in *oblige* (or similar answers)

2) [i:] is represented by <e> in *we*, <i> in *ski*, <ea> in *meat*, <ee> in *meet*, <eo> in *people*, <ei> in *deceive*, <ey> in *key*, <ae> in *Caesar*, <ay> *quay*, <ie> in *field* and <oe> in *Phoenix* (or similar answers)

3) *debt, handkerchief, name, gnu, hour, knee, half, mnemonic, autumn, psyche, island, glisten, write, grand prix* (or similar answers)

4) [j] in *cute, abuse* and *futile*; in RP also *news, tube* and *deuce* (or similar answers)

10. The explanation is based on the discrepancy between spelling and pronunciation in English. [f] is represented by <gh> in words like *cough* or *laugh*, [ɪ] is represented by <o> in *women* and [ʃ] is represented by <ti> in *nation*. We could theoretically argue that <gh,o,ti> can spell [fɪʃ]. — It should, however, be noted that <gh> does never represent [f] in word-initial position and <ti> does never represent [ʃ] in word-final position in English.

11. The following minimal pairs are suggestions only. There are, of course, many other correct examples of minimal pairs for the pairs of phonemes in question:

phonemes	*minimal pair*
a) /p/ - /b/	*pit - bit* /pɪt/ - /bɪt/
b) /iː/ - /uː/	*reef - roof* /riːf/ - /ruːf/
c) /b/ - /m/	*beat - meet* /biːt/ - /miːt/
d) /n/ - /s/	*knee - sea* /niː/ - /siː/
e) /t/ - /d/	*bat - bad* /bæt/ - /bæd/
f) /ɪ/ - /æ/	*sit - sat* /sɪt/ - /sæt/

12. The distribution of the allophones [f] and [v] of the phoneme /f/ in Old English:

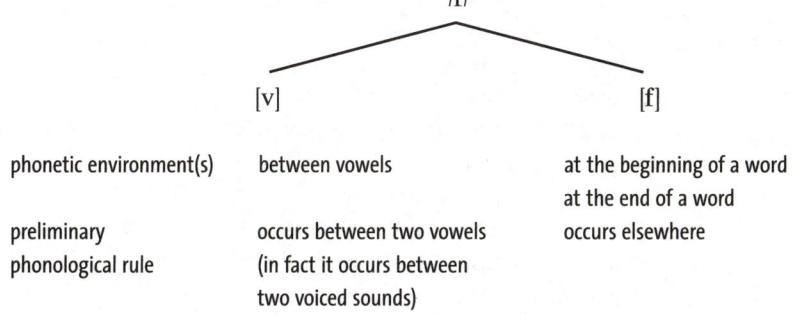

	[v]	[f]
phonetic environment(s)	between vowels	at the beginning of a word at the end of a word
preliminary phonological rule	occurs between two vowels (in fact it occurs between two voiced sounds)	occurs elsewhere

Chapter 4: Morphology

1. Seven word tokens and six word types. Only two word types will be listed in a dictionary in the form in which they appear in this sentence, namely *the* and *and*. The nouns *bird* and *bell* will be listed as singular forms, and the verbs *sing* and *ring* as infinitives.

2. a) *cat*   free
       -s   bound inflectional suffix
     b) *un-*   bound derivational prefix
        happy   free
     c) *mild*   free
        -er   bound inflectional suffix
     d) *bi-*   bound derivational prefix
        cycle   free
     e) *sign*   free
        post   free
     f) *re-*   bound derivational prefix
        join   free
     g) *greed*   free
        -y   bound derivational suffix
     h) *hate*   free
        -ful   bound derivational suffix

3. a) *comfort*   free
        -able   bound derivational suffix

b) *re-*   bound derivational prefix
   condition   free
   -ed   bound inflectional suffix
c) *sense*   free
   -less   bound derivational suffix
d) *ration*   free
   -al   bound derivational suffix
   -is(e)   bound derivational suffix
   -ation   bound derivational suffix
e) *environ*   free
   -ment   bound derivational suffix
   -al   bound derivational suffix
f) *thick*   free
   -en   bound derivational suffix
   -er   bound derivational suffix
   -s   bound inflectional suffix

4. a) base = verb, whole word = noun
    b) base = noun, whole word = adjective
    c) base = adjective, whole word = adjective

5. a) derivational suffix = *-ful*, base = noun, whole word = adjective
    b) derivational prefix = *un-*, base = adjective, whole word = adjective
    c) derivational prefix = *re-*, base = verb, whole word = verb

6. infixation: insertion of infix *-um-* after initial consonant

7. a) compounding (noun *career* and noun *change* and noun *opportunity*)
    b) blending (verb *decrease* and noun *recruitment,* the latter formed by V → N derivation: verb *recruit* + derivational suffix *-ment*)
    c) compounding (preposition *out* and noun *placement,* the latter formed by V → N derivation: verb *place* and derivational suffix *-ment*)

8. *Catfish* and *swordfish* are endocentric compound nouns, whereas *shellfish* is an exocentric compound noun. The adjective *selfish* is the odd one out. It consists of the noun *self* and the bound derivational suffix *-ish*.

9. a) compounding (*air + plane*) and derivation (*talk + -er*);
   compounding (*airplane + talker*)
   b) compounding (*fat + finger*); conversion (N → V)
   c) compounding (*ash + hole*)

Chapter 5: Syntax

1. a) [$_N$ *Bob*] [$_V$ *called*] [$_{Det}$ *a*] [$_N$ *friend*]
   b) [$_{Pro}$ *she*] [$_V$ *called*] [$_{Pro}$ *him*] [$_{Det}$ *a*] [$_N$ *genius*]
   c) [$_{Det}$ *the*] [$_N$ *baby*] [$_V$ *cried*]
   d) [$_{Det}$ *the*] [$_N$ *students*] [$_V$ *sent*] [$_{Det}$ *the*] [$_N$ *teacher*] [$_{Det}$ *some*]
   [$_{Adv}$ *very*] [$_{Adj}$ *interesting*] [$_N$ *suggestions*]

2. *Call* is a verb because it fulfils the criteria for (1) meaning, (2) inflection and (3) distribution: (1) *call* expresses an action; (2) *call* takes verbal inflections (3rd person singular present indicative *-s*, the *-ing*-form, past tense *-ed* (cf. Exercise 1), and past participle *-ed*); (3) *call* may occur as the predicate, usually after the subject and before an object (e.g. *Bob called a friend*), and it may be combined with auxiliaries (*is calling*, *has called*) and modified by an adverb (e.g *she called frequently*).

3. a) imperative
   b) exclamatory
   c) interrogative
   d) declarative

4. Yes, *a book* is a constituent, because it passes several constituency tests: the pronoun *it* can be substituted for *a book* in a sentence (*John read **it** last night*); *a book* can be coordinated with *a newspaper* (*John read a book and a newspaper last night*); *a book* may serve as the answer to a question (*What did John read last night? A book*).

5. a) Simple phrase: *April* (NP)
   Complex phrases: *a cruel month* (NP), *is a cruel month* (VP)
   b) Simple phrase: *midnight* (NP)
   Complex phrases: *the memory* (NP), *shakes the memory* (VP)

c) Simple phrase: *I* (NP)

Complex phrases: *a traveller* (NP), *an antique land* (NP), *from an antique land* (PrepP), *a traveller from an antique land* (NP), *met a traveller from an antique land* (VP)

6. a)

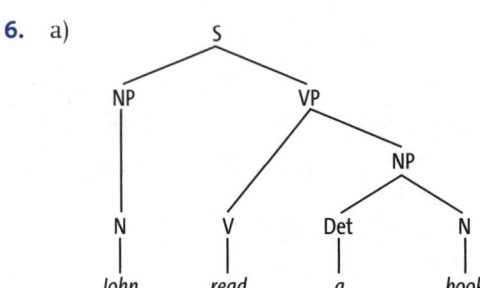

or

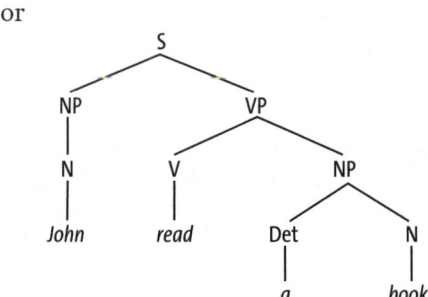

b) [$_S$ [$_{NP}$ [$_N$ *John*]] [$_{VP}$ [$_V$ *read*] [$_{NP}$ [$_{Det}$ *a*] [$_N$ *book*]]]]

7. a)

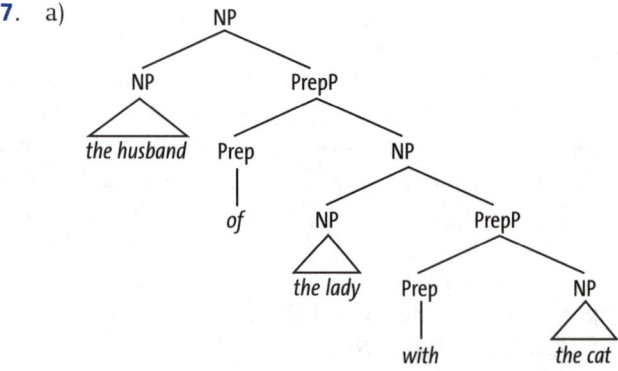

b) [$_{NP}$ *the husband* [$_{PrepP}$ *of* [$_{NP}$ *the lady* [$_{PrepP}$ *with* [$_{NP}$ *the cat*]]]]]

8. a) 1.a) monotransitive; 1.b) complex transitive; 1.c) intransitive; 1.d) ditransitive
    b) 1.a) SPO; 1.b) SPOC; 1.c) SP; 1.d) SPOO
    c) 1.a) divalent; 1.b) trivalent; 1.c) monovalent; 1.d) trivalent

9. Examples b) and c) are grammatical. Example b) follows the SP clause pattern, with a predicate that consists of two simple verb phrases linked by the conjunction *and*. Example c) follows the SPC clause pattern. In example a), the conjunction *and* appears after the two simple verb phrases *rise* and *fall* (instead of between them), and in example d) the word order could be interpreted as an insertion of the subject *we* and the predicate *are* into the complement *the hollow men*. In English (and in many other languages), such patterns are ungrammatical.

Chapter 6: Semantics

1. Identify the meaning relations between the following pairs of words:

    a) *leave ~ return* antonymy (directional opposites)
    b) *door ~ house* meronymy
    c) *young ~ old* antonymy (gradable pair)
    d) *bright ~ intelligent* synonymy
    e) *flower ~ rose* hyponymy (*rose* is the hyponym, *flower* is the hyperonym)
    f) *examiner ~ examinee* antonyms (relational opposites)
    g) *freedom ~ liberty* synonymy

2. Lexical ambiguity occurs when the **same sound sequence** represents **two (or more) different meanings**. Lexical ambiguity is thus either created by the different meanings of **one polysemous word**, or by **two (or more) homophones**.

3.

Word/Phrase	Extension	Intension
Prime Minister of the United Kingdom	David Cameron	leader of the governing party
capital of United States	Washington, D.C.	city which is the seat of the federal government of the United States of America
Queen of the United Kingdom	Queen Elizabeth II	the head of state of the United Kingdom
vegetable	carrots, peas, onions, peppers, cabbage etc.	all words that have the following semantic features: [+plant, +food, -fruit]

4. Fuzziness

a) We say that *rich* and *clean* represent fuzzy concepts, because there is no clear-cut boundary between *rich* and *not rich*, or *clean* and *not clean*.

b) No, there are some rather straightforward and clear-cut concepts, such as *pope* or *senator*.

5.
a) contradiction: if William is single, he cannot be married
b) paraphrase: if planes are loud, they are also noisy
c) entailment: if James is Mary's husband, Mary must be married
d) paraphrase: if I am exhausted, I am also tired
e) contradiction: if Christina and Mat are workaholics, they cannot be lazy
f) entailment: if my car is red, it cannot be white

6.
a) *The student hits the teacher with the book*

Two interpretations are possible: a student has a book in her or his hands and hits the teacher with it, **or** a student hits a teacher who is carrying a book

b) *A lady watched an actor with opera glasses*

This sentence also allows **two different readings**: a lady watched an actor by using opera glasses, **or** a lady watched an actor who was using opera glasses herself or himself

7. a) presupposition: *Chomsky has written books*
    b) presupposition: *There is a pope*
    c) presupposition: *My colleague sent me an e-mail*
    d) presupposition: *They have closed at least one library already*

8. 1b) contains the presupposition; *realise* implies that Anna was in debt, it is the trigger
    2a) contains the presupposition; *stop* is the trigger, as it implies that the addressee has been running marathons

Chapter 7: Pragmatics

1. a) *I* — person deixis, *like* — points to the present: time deixis (proximal), *this* — place deixis (proximal), *that* — place deixis (distal)
    b) *I* — person deixis, *saw* — points to the past: time deixis (distal), *him* — person deixis, *there* — place deixis (distal)
    c) *I* — person deixis, *will meet* — points to the future: time deixis (distal), *her* — person deixis, *here* — place deixis (proximal)
    d) *I* — person deixis, *will visit* — points to the future: time deixis (distal), *them* — person deixis, *then* — time deixis (distal)

2. a) Frank Rist <u>was</u> (time deixis, distal) in <u>the next room</u> (place deixis, distal). Joseph <u>could</u> (time deixis, distal) even hear <u>that</u> (place deixis, distal, and social deixis) familiar voice, its staccato syllables <u>drawn</u> (time deixis, distal) from deep in the larynx. <u>He</u> (person deixis) <u>could</u> (time deixis, distal) not make out the words.
    b) Joseph is the deictic centre.
    c) The expression *that* indicates distance and is used here to convey Joseph's negative attitude towards Frank Rist and his voice.

3. a) The Maxim of Relation.
    b) The Maxim of Relation.
    c) The Maxim of Quantity.

4. a) She does, because the daughter's "O.K." shows that she has obviously understood her communicative intention.
    b) Her answer violates the Maxim of Relation.

5. a) representative
   b) declaration
   c) directive
   d) commissive
   e) expressive

6. a) imperative
   b) directive
   c) The preparatory condition *H is able to do A* is not fulfilled.
      The cartoon suggests nevertheless that the speaker (i.e. the
      then British Prime Minister Tony Blair) believes that his
      addressee is able to perform the desired action, either
      because of the speaker's authority or because of his super-
      natural powers (the speech act is an allusion to Jesus
      Christ healing a lame man by saying *Take up thy bed and
      walk*).

7. *admitted*   representative
   requested   directive
   forbade   directive
   said   representative

8. a) (1) directive (direct)
      (2) representative (direct)
      (3) directive (indirect)
      (4) representative (direct)
   b) There are two question-answer pairs, each with a question
      by Eddie and an answer by George.
   c) It has features of a dispreferred response. This is indicated
      by dispreference markers such as *well*, pauses and hesita-
      tions.

Chapter 8: Sociolinguistics

1. Weinreich's definition of dialect and language does not hold
   true with reference to BrE, AmE and AusE. The United Kingdom, The United States of America and Australia each have
   their own army and navy, but the corresponding national varieties of English, namely BrE, AmE and AusE, are still said to
   be varieties of English and not independent languages. There

have been proposals to call AmE "The American Language" and AusE "The Australian Language" but this terminology has never become mainstream and there is general agreement among contemporary linguists that we are not concerned with separate languages.

2. This excerpt is obviously written in the **register** of sports reporting, or to be more precise, the reporting of football. To *score*, *first half*, *second half*, *pass* and *68th minute* clearly belong to this kind of register. Registers are functional varieties that depend on the communicative situation rather than on the background of the speaker.

3. a) Among other hints, *fatigued*, *lengthy* and *journey* suggest that the sentence is written in a rather formal style. A less formal alternative would be: *Mum was pretty tired after her long trip.*
   b) The contraction *gotta*, the adjective *beat* and the idiom *hit the hay* are among the expressions that show the utterance to be in a rather informal style. A suggestion for a more formal version would be: *I think I have to go home and go to bed. I am pretty tired.*

4. The following changes would have to be made:
   a) *all **men** are created equal* would have to be replaced by *all **human beings** are created equal*
   b) *no **man** can teach **him**self* would have to be replaced by *nobody can teach **themselves***; *English**men*** should be replaced by *English**people*** or *the English*
   c) *maker* should be changed into *makers* and ***his** horse* into ***their** horse*
   d) ***Miss*** should be replaced by ***Ms*** and *fire**man*** by the gender-neutral form *fire**fighter***
   e) *poet**ess*** should be avoided and replaced by *poet*
   f) the pseudo-generic ***his*** should be avoided by rephrasing the sentence into *Australians love their vegemite sandwiches*

5. a) A non-sexist version of Armstrong's utterance would be: *That's one small step for humankind, [but] one giant leap for humankind.* The sentence does not make sense, as the second part of the utterance contradicts the first part.

b) He probably wanted to say *That's one small step for **a** man, one giant leap for mankind*, which makes perfectly good sense. A non-sexist version of his intended sentence would be the following: *That's one small step for a person/human being, one giant leap for humankind.*

Index

Peter Fenn

A Student's Advanced Grammar of English SAGE

UTB L 8432
2010, XVIII, 581 Seiten, zahlreiche Schemata,
€[D] 39,90/SFr 62,90
ISBN 978-3-8252-8432-9

Whatever kind of high-level language user you are – college or university student, serving language teacher, or advanced school learner – A Student's Advanced Grammar of English (SAGE) offers you support, information, and further training.

SAGE is a reference work as well as a programmed refresher course with exercises on the accompanying website, and a structured teaching aid. It serves as a spot-check in specific cases of uncertainty. But it also answers broader queries and provides comprehensive insights into the major structural areas of English. Its concern is not simply grammar, but above all usage.

SAGE is easy to comprehend and non-specialist in method. All grammatical terminology, whether traditional or innovative, is explained in a simple and straightforward manner. On the other hand, SAGE takes account of current research in language studies. In catering especially for the user with a native German background, SAGE treats many areas of English from a contrastive point of view, highlighting those phenomena which cause typical problems in a German-based learning context.

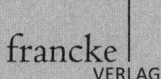
francke
VERLAG

Narr Francke Attempto Verlag GmbH + Co. KG
Postfach 2560 · D-72015 Tübingen · Fax (0 7071) 97 97-11
Internet: www.francke.de · E-Mail: info@francke.de

NEUERSCHEINUNG SEPTEMBER 2011

narr |
VERLAG

francke |
VERLAG

attempto |
VERLAG

Dirk Siepmann / John D. Gallagher
Mike Hannay / J. Lachlan Mackenzie

Writing in English:
A Guide for Advanced Learners

UTB 3124
2., überarbeitete und erweiterte Auflage 2011
X, 469 Seiten, zahlreiche Tabellen
€[D] 24,90 / SFr 35,90
ISBN 978-3-8252-3600-7

This book offers practical advice and guidance to German-speaking undergraduates and academics who aspire to write in English. It also provides valuable assistance to editors, examiners and teachers who conduct English courses for intermediate or advanced students. It consists of four modules and is rounded off with a subject index and a glossary. Making extensive use of authentic texts, the authors adopt a contrastive approach and focus on the major problems encountered by Germans writing in English.

This second edition has been revised, updated and expanded to include, among other things, a new section on coordination and listing as well as new lexico-grammatical material that writers can put to immediate use and benefit.

JETZT BESTELLEN!

Narr Francke Attempto Verlag GmbH+Co. KG · Dischingerweg 5 · D-72070 Tübingen
Tel. +49 (07071) 9797-0 · Fax +49 (07071) 97 97-11 · info@francke.de · **www.francke.de**

Helge Nowak

Literature in Britain and Ireland: A History

UTB M
2010, XII, 628 Seiten, zahlreiche Abbildungen,
€[D] 24,90/SFr 44,00
ISBN 978-3-8252-3148-4

Literature in Britain and Ireland is a survey of literature on the British Isles since the time of the Anglo-Saxons. Despite this deliberately wide angle, the linguistic, regional and ethnic differentiations in each particular period are being emphasized. Because of its combination of traditional and innovative components of English Studies, this history of literature is useful as a study book accompanying courses as well as an incentive for discoveries while reading. The chapters are systematically structured to allow profiles along the history of genres. In addition to poetry, drama, short stories and the novel, different forms of non-fictional prose are being highlighted, too. Innovative tendencies in teaching English literature are taken into account beyond the consideration of popular and contemporary literature.

francke
VERLAG

Narr Francke Attempto Verlag GmbH + Co. KG
Postfach 25 60 · D-72015 Tübingen · Fax (0 7071) 97 97-11
Internet: www.francke.de · E-Mail: info@francke.de